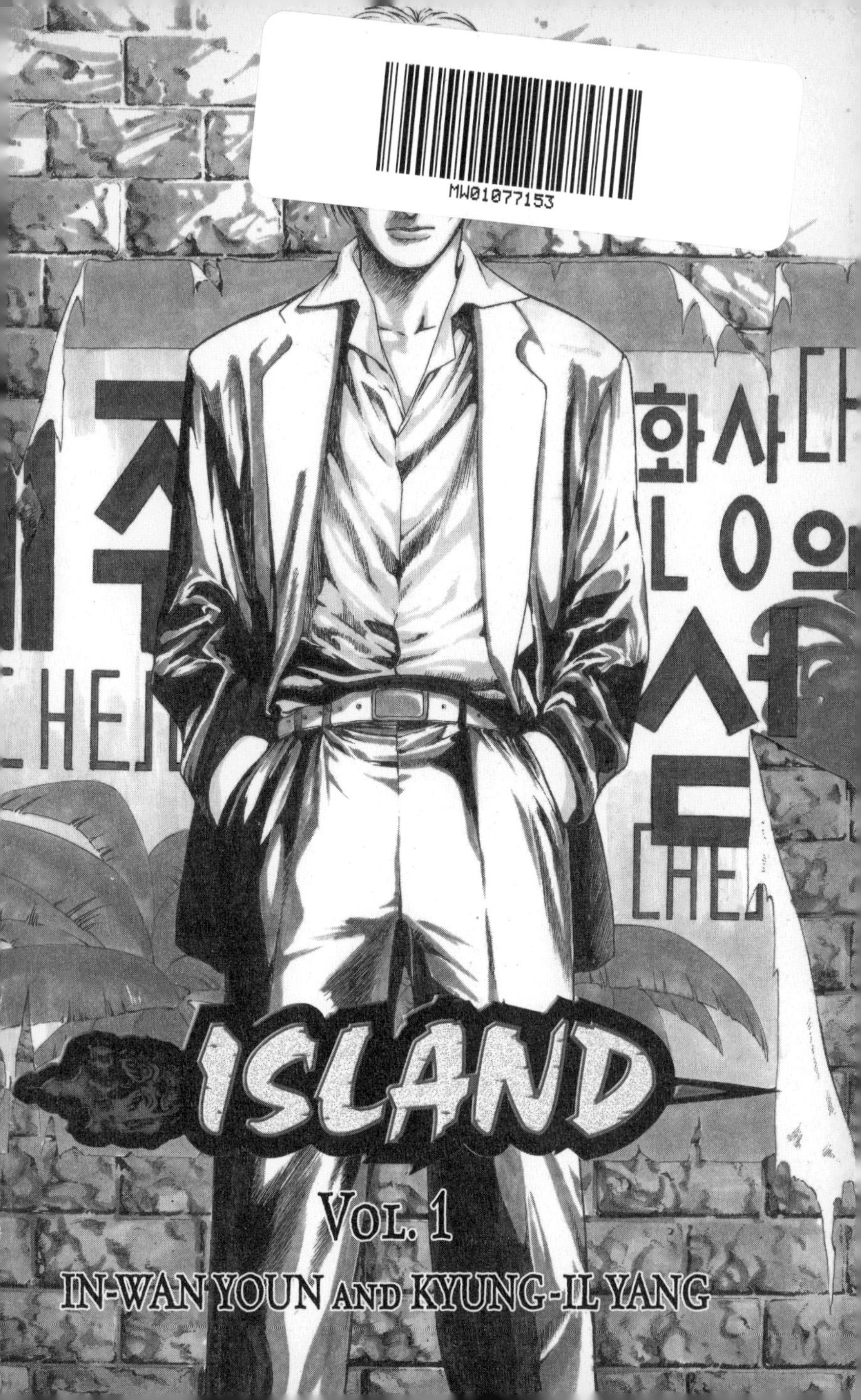
ISLAND
Vol. 1
IN-WAN YOUN AND KYUNG-IL YANG

TOKYOPOP® PRESENTS
ISLAND 1 BY IN-WAN YOUN & KYUNG-IL YANG
TOKYOPOP IS A REGISTERED TRADEMARK
OF MIXX ENTERTAINMENT, INC.

ISBN: 1-931514-33-x
FIRST PRINTING JANUARY 2002

10   9   8   7   6   5   4   3   2

TRANSLATOR - MICKEY HONG. RETOUCH ARTIST - WILBERT LACUNA.
GRAPHIC ASSISTANT - DAO SIRIVISAL. GRAPHIC DESIGNER - AKEMI IMAFUKU.
EDITORS - KATHERINE KIM, MICHAEL SCHUSTER AND ROBERT COYNER.
SENIOR EDITOR - JAKE FORBES. PRODUCTION MANAGER - FRED LUI.

EMAIL: EDITOR@TOKYOPOP.COM
COME VISIT US AT WWW.TOKYOPOP.COM

TOKYOPOP®
LOS ANGELES - TOKYO

ISLAND

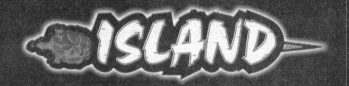

Vol. 1

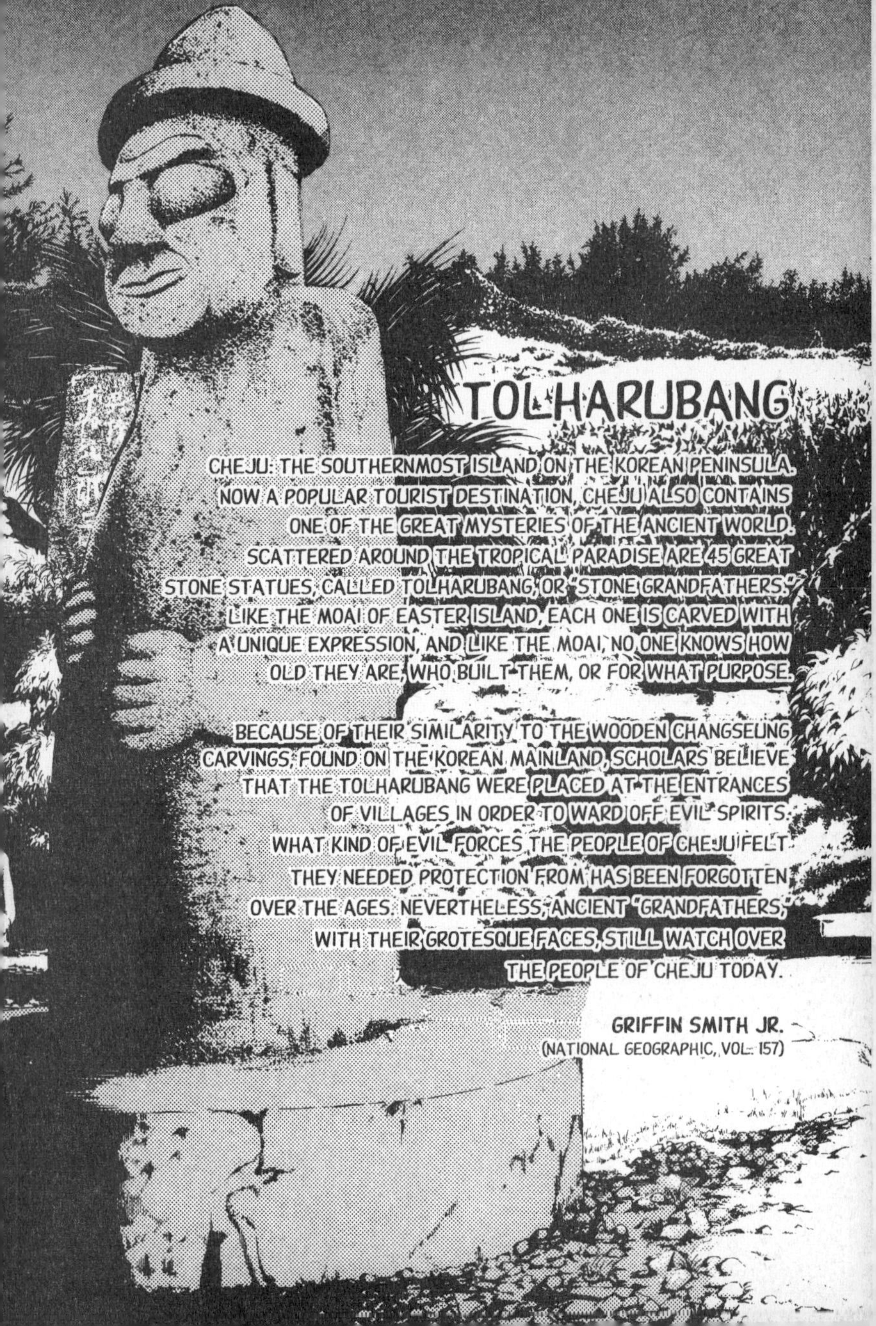

TOLHARUBANG

CHEJU: THE SOUTHERNMOST ISLAND ON THE KOREAN PENINSULA. NOW A POPULAR TOURIST DESTINATION, CHEJU ALSO CONTAINS ONE OF THE GREAT MYSTERIES OF THE ANCIENT WORLD. SCATTERED AROUND THE TROPICAL PARADISE ARE 45 GREAT STONE STATUES, CALLED TOLHARUBANG, OR "STONE GRANDFATHERS." LIKE THE MOAI OF EASTER ISLAND, EACH ONE IS CARVED WITH A UNIQUE EXPRESSION, AND LIKE THE MOAI, NO ONE KNOWS HOW OLD THEY ARE, WHO BUILT THEM, OR FOR WHAT PURPOSE.

BECAUSE OF THEIR SIMILARITY TO THE WOODEN CHANGSEUNG CARVINGS, FOUND ON THE KOREAN MAINLAND, SCHOLARS BELIEVE THAT THE TOLHARUBANG WERE PLACED AT THE ENTRANCES OF VILLAGES IN ORDER TO WARD OFF EVIL SPIRITS. WHAT KIND OF EVIL FORCES THE PEOPLE OF CHEJU FELT THEY NEEDED PROTECTION FROM HAS BEEN FORGOTTEN OVER THE AGES. NEVERTHELESS, ANCIENT "GRANDFATHERS," WITH THEIR GROTESQUE FACES, STILL WATCH OVER THE PEOPLE OF CHEJU TODAY.

GRIFFIN SMITH JR.
(NATIONAL GEOGRAPHIC, VOL. 157)

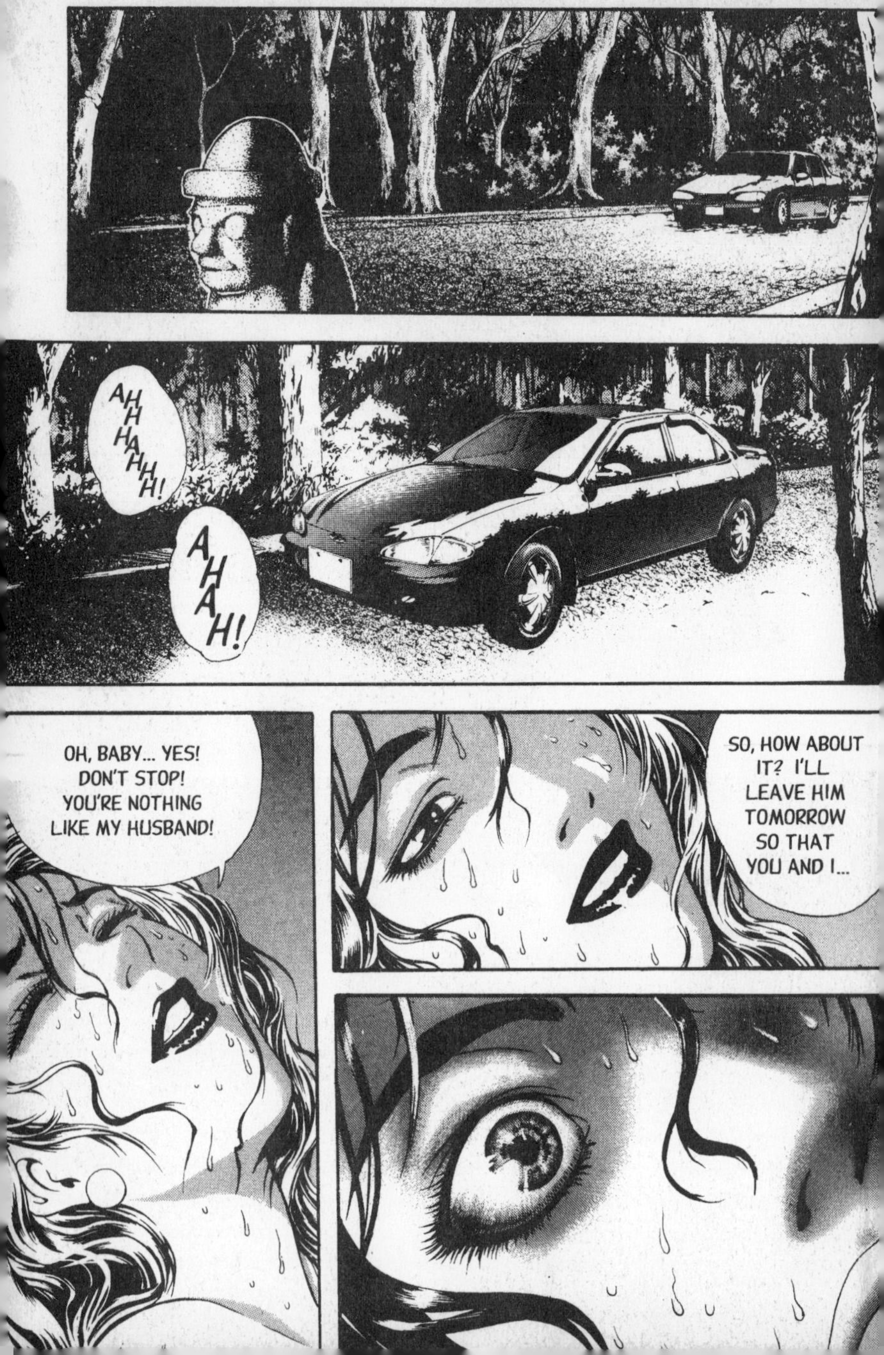
AHHHAHHH!
AHAH!
OH, BABY... YES! DON'T STOP! YOU'RE NOTHING LIKE MY HUSBAND!
SO, HOW ABOUT IT? I'LL LEAVE HIM TOMORROW SO THAT YOU AND I...

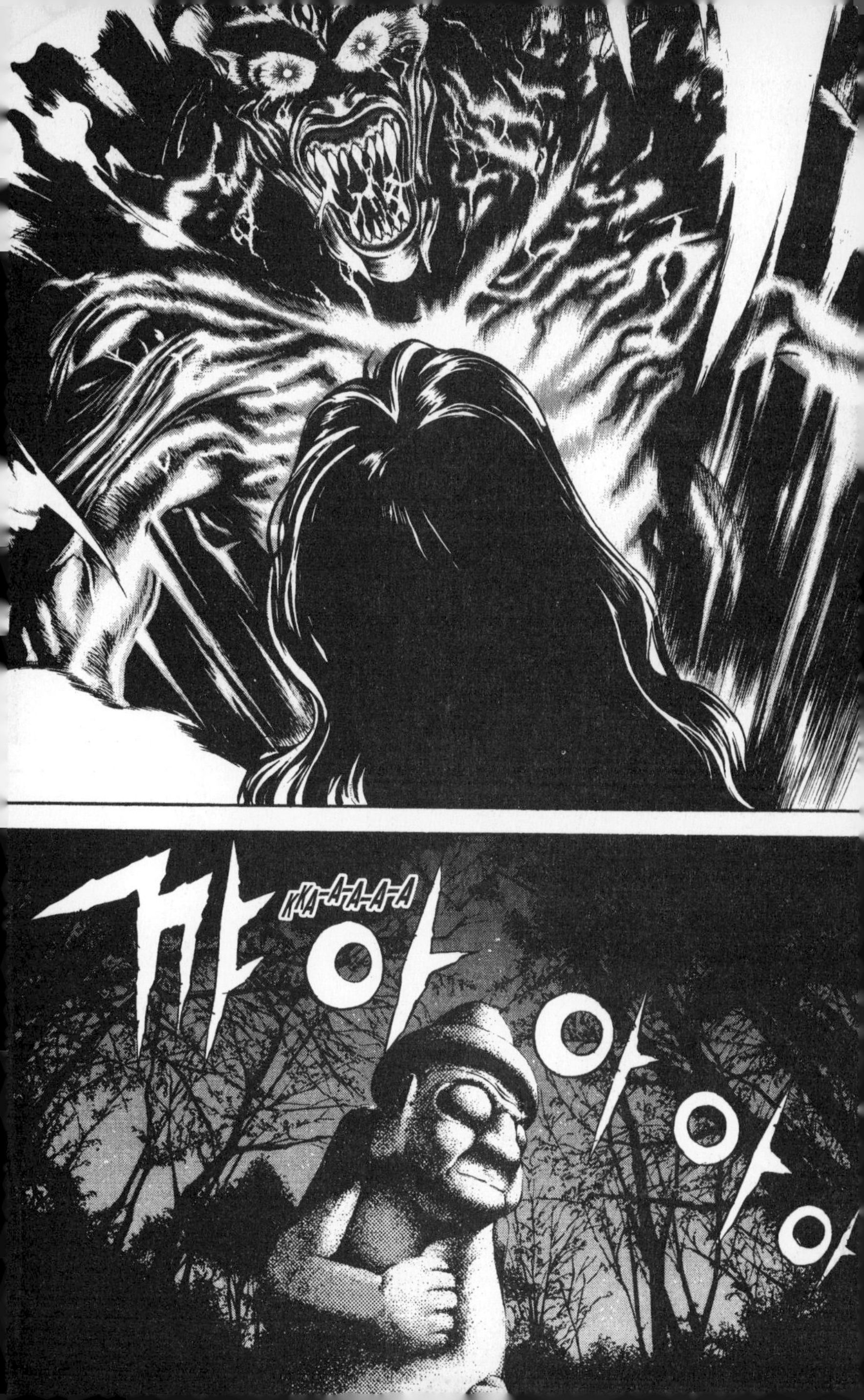
까아아아아
KKA-A-A-A-A

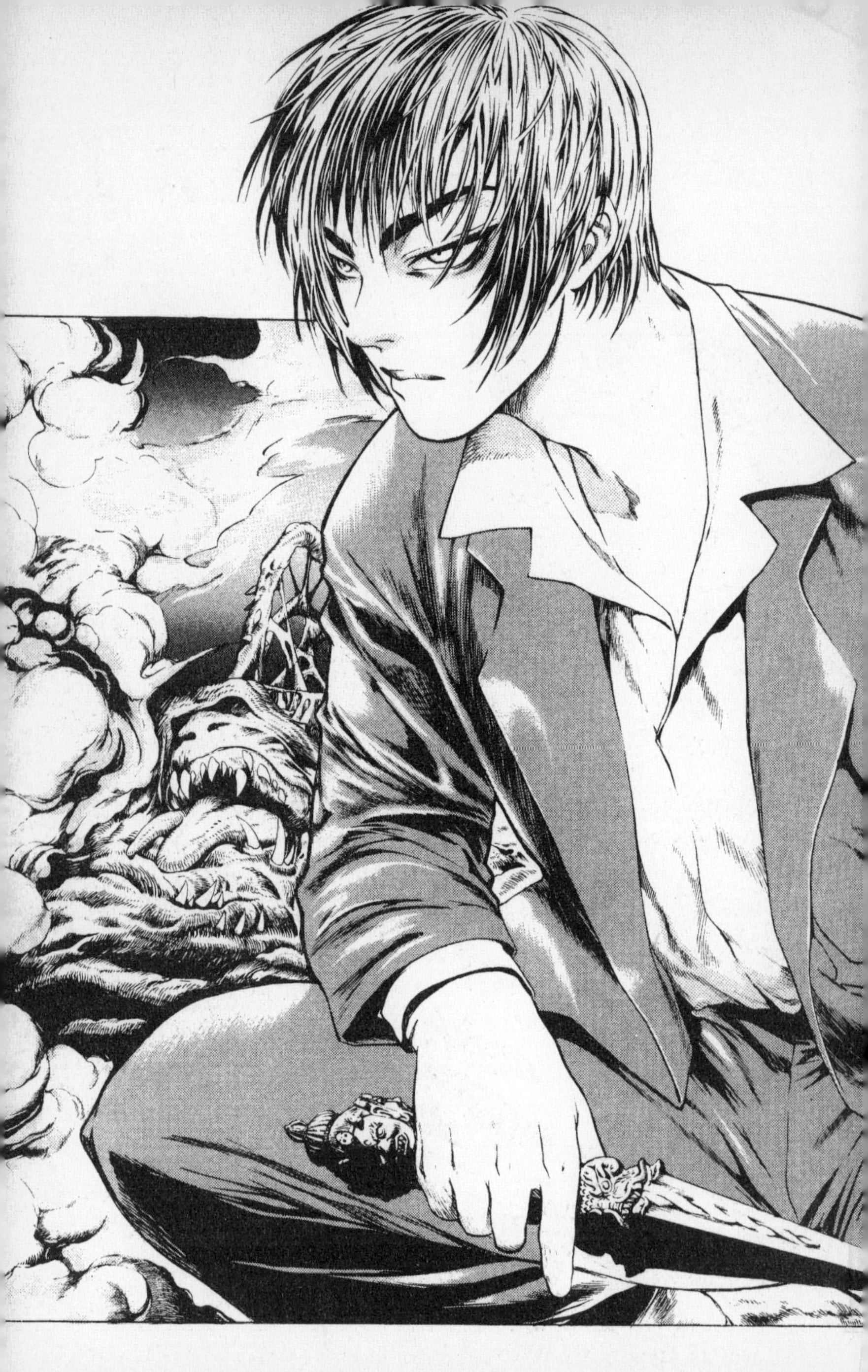

CHAPTER 1
THE MYSTERY MAN

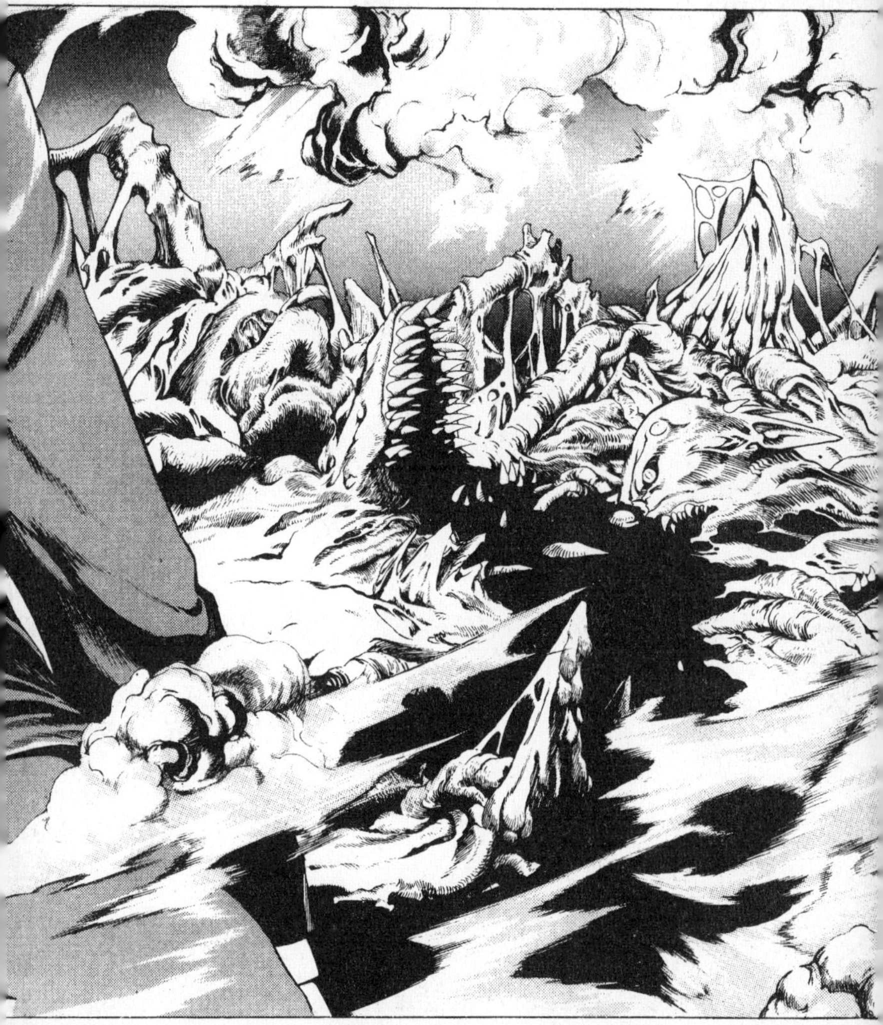

Written by: IN-WAN YOUN Illustrated by: KYUNG-IL YANG

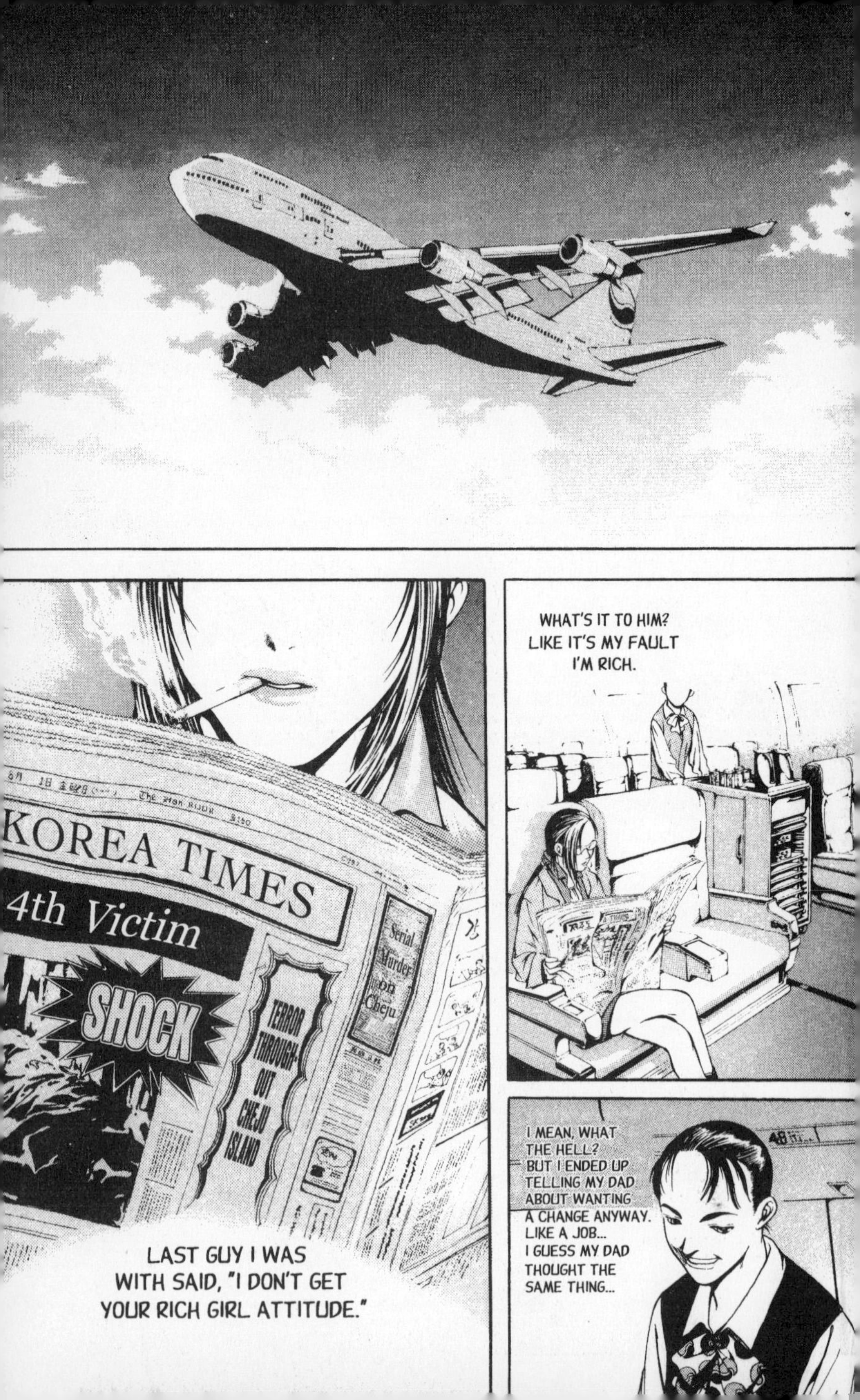
KOREA TIMES
4th Victim
SHOCK
Serial Murder on Cheju
TERROR THROUGH-OUT CHEJU ISLAND
LAST GUY I WAS WITH SAID, "I DON'T GET YOUR RICH GIRL ATTITUDE."
WHAT'S IT TO HIM? LIKE IT'S MY FAULT I'M RICH.
I MEAN, WHAT THE HELL? BUT I ENDED UP TELLING MY DAD ABOUT WANTING A CHANGE ANYWAY. LIKE A JOB... I GUESS MY DAD THOUGHT THE SAME THING...

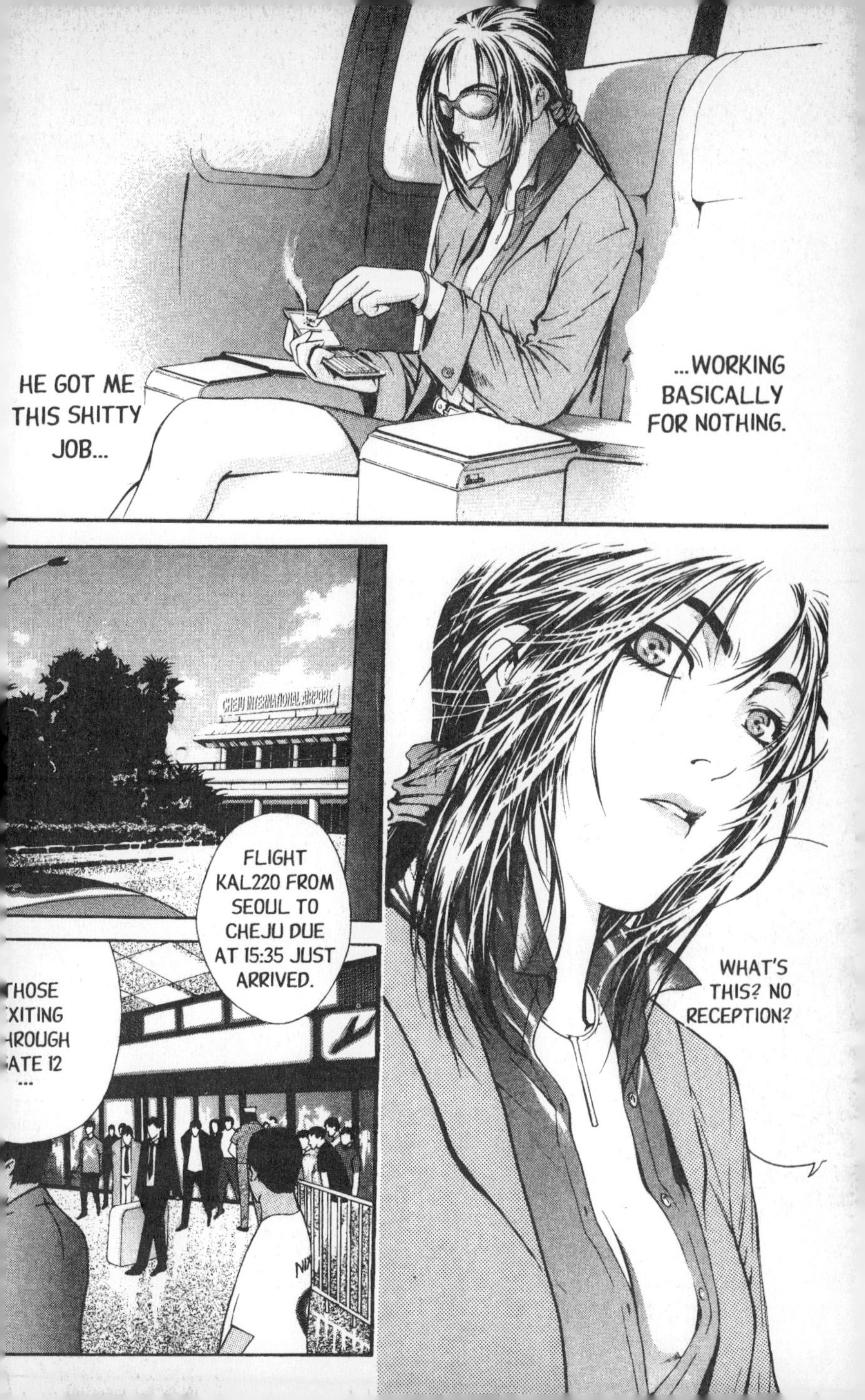
HE GOT ME THIS SHITTY JOB...
...WORKING BASICALLY FOR NOTHING.
CHEJU INTERNATIONAL AIRPORT
FLIGHT KAL220 FROM SEOUL TO CHEJU DUE AT 15:35 JUST ARRIVED.
THOSE EXITING THROUGH GATE 12 ...
WHAT'S THIS? NO RECEPTION?

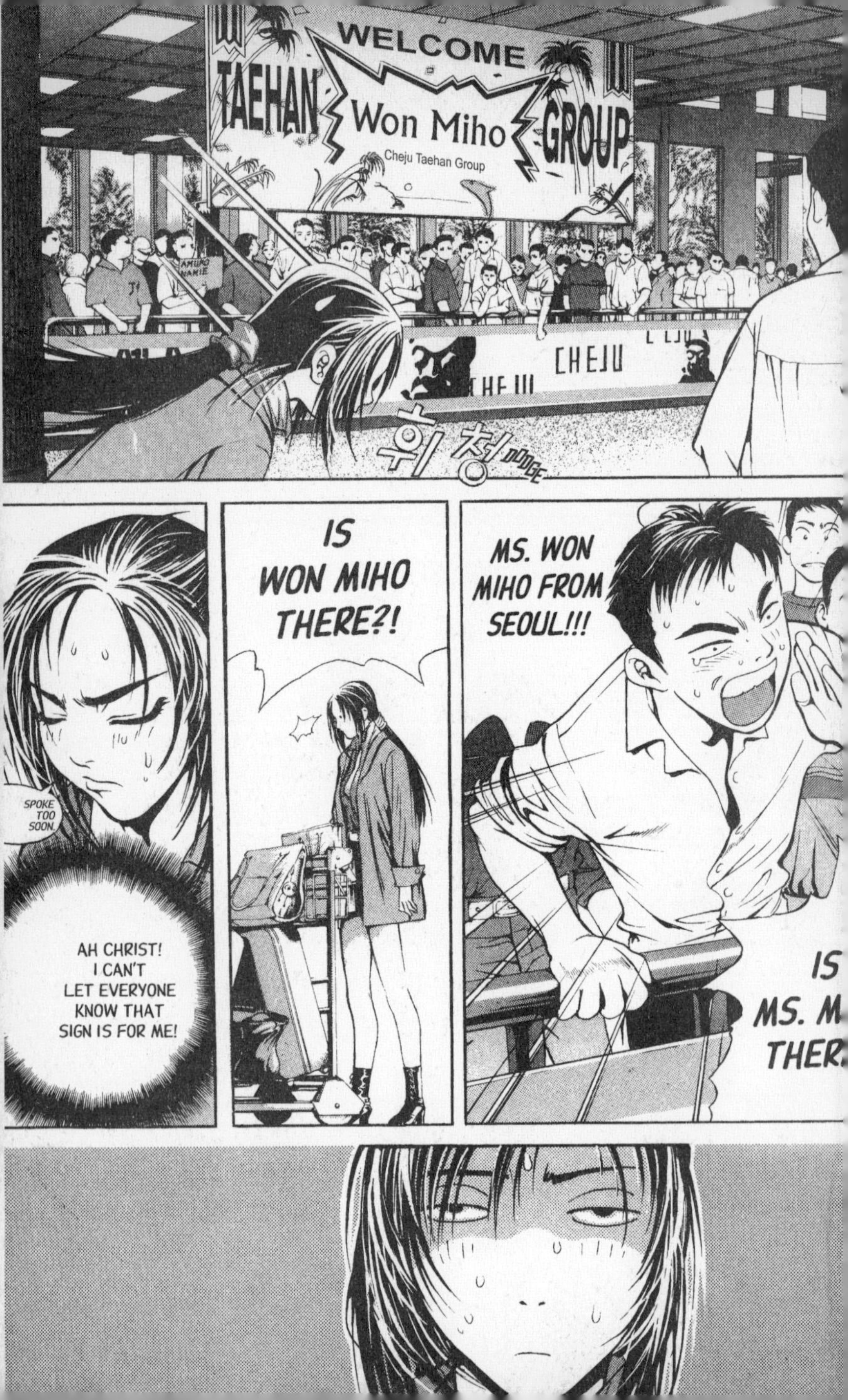

WELCOME
TAEHAN
Won Miho
GROUP
Cheju Taehan Group
CHEJU
휘청
DODGE
SPOKE TOO SOON.
AH CHRIST! I CAN'T LET EVERYONE KNOW THAT SIGN IS FOR ME!
IS WON MIHO THERE?!
MS. WON MIHO FROM SEOUL!!!
IS MS. M THER

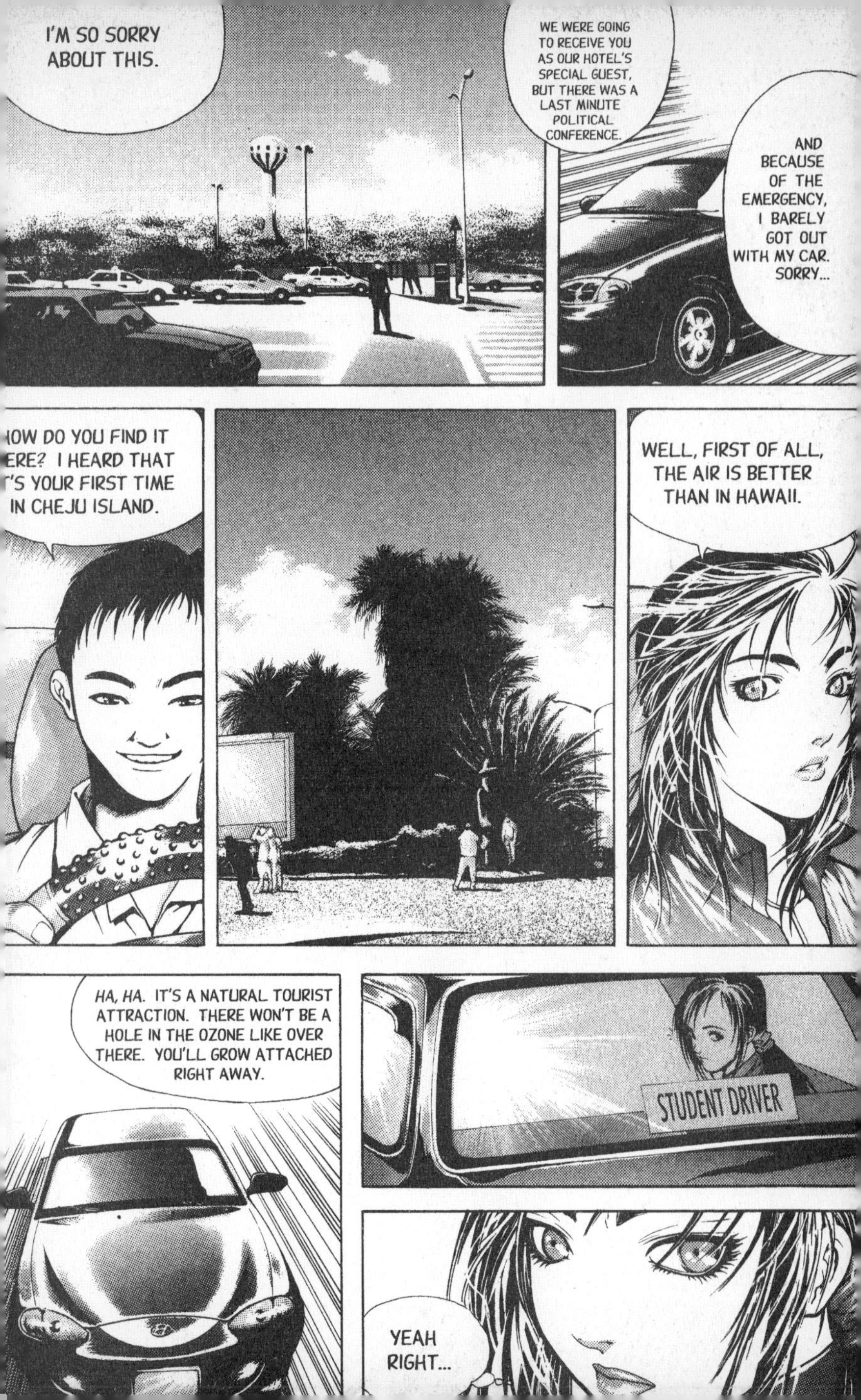
I'M SO SORRY ABOUT THIS.
WE WERE GOING TO RECEIVE YOU AS OUR HOTEL'S SPECIAL GUEST, BUT THERE WAS A LAST MINUTE POLITICAL CONFERENCE.
AND BECAUSE OF THE EMERGENCY, I BARELY GOT OUT WITH MY CAR. SORRY...
HOW DO YOU FIND IT HERE? I HEARD THAT IT'S YOUR FIRST TIME IN CHEJU ISLAND.
WELL, FIRST OF ALL, THE AIR IS BETTER THAN IN HAWAII.
HA, HA. IT'S A NATURAL TOURIST ATTRACTION. THERE WON'T BE A HOLE IN THE OZONE LIKE OVER THERE. YOU'LL GROW ATTACHED RIGHT AWAY.
STUDENT DRIVER
YEAH RIGHT...

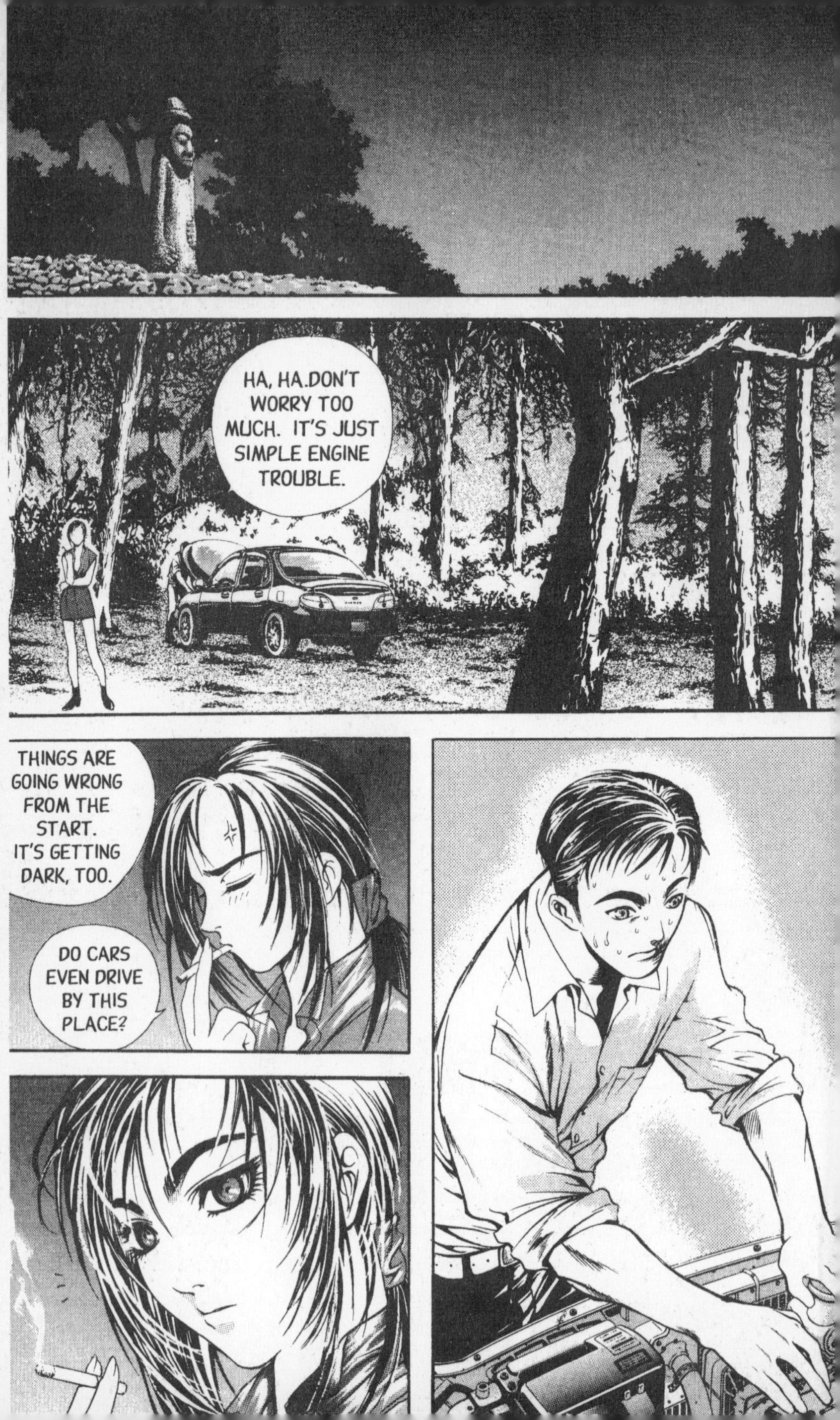
HA, HA.DON'T WORRY TOO MUCH. IT'S JUST SIMPLE ENGINE TROUBLE.
THINGS ARE GOING WRONG FROM THE START. IT'S GETTING DARK, TOO.
DO CARS EVEN DRIVE BY THIS PLACE?

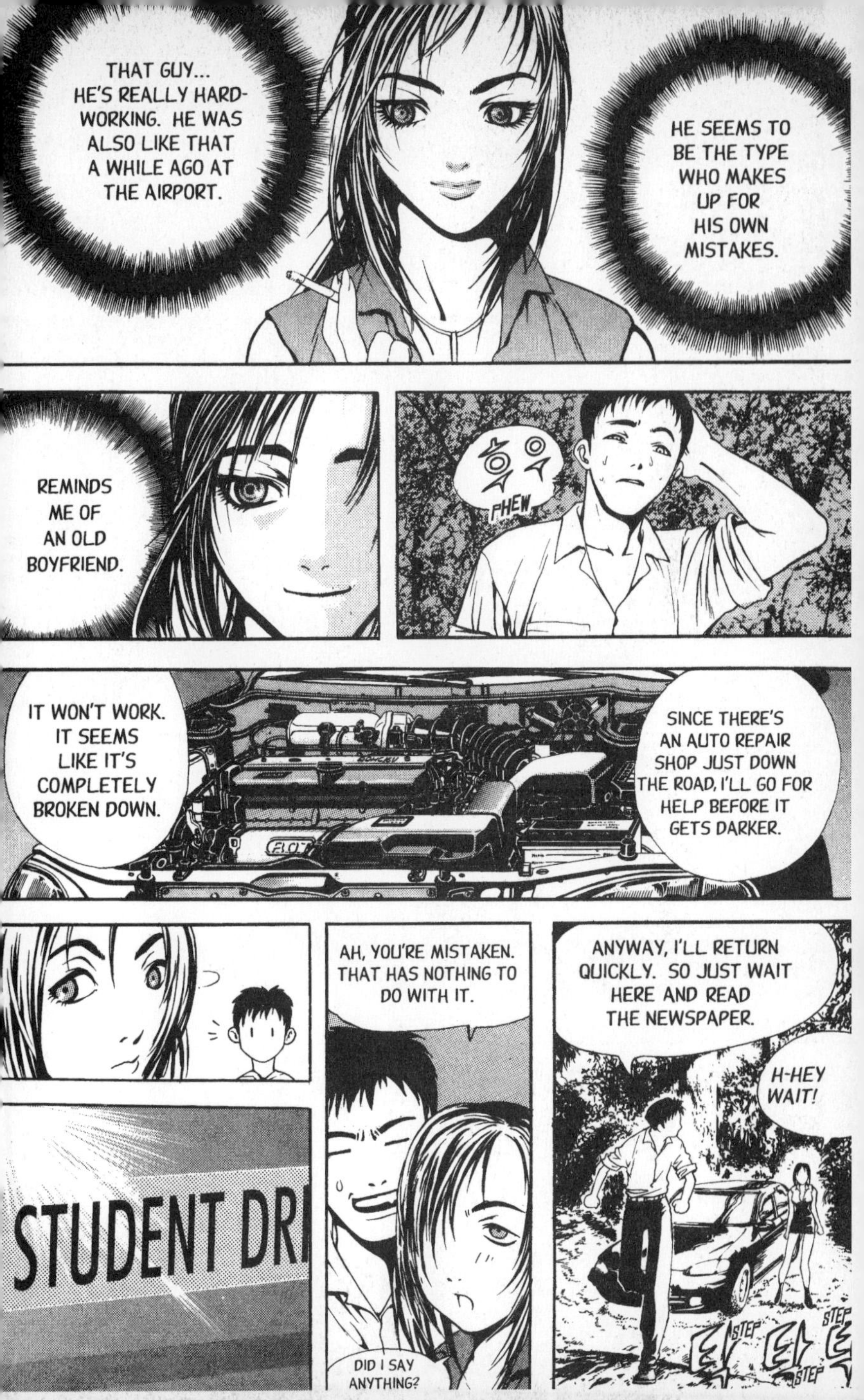
THAT GUY... HE'S REALLY HARD-WORKING. HE WAS ALSO LIKE THAT A WHILE AGO AT THE AIRPORT.
HE SEEMS TO BE THE TYPE WHO MAKES UP FOR HIS OWN MISTAKES.
REMINDS ME OF AN OLD BOYFRIEND.
PHEW
IT WON'T WORK. IT SEEMS LIKE IT'S COMPLETELY BROKEN DOWN.
SINCE THERE'S AN AUTO REPAIR SHOP JUST DOWN THE ROAD, I'LL GO FOR HELP BEFORE IT GETS DARKER.
STUDENT DR
AH, YOU'RE MISTAKEN. THAT HAS NOTHING TO DO WITH IT.
DID I SAY ANYTHING?
ANYWAY, I'LL RETURN QUICKLY. SO JUST WAIT HERE AND READ THE NEWSPAPER.
H-HEY WAIT!
STEP
STEP
STEP

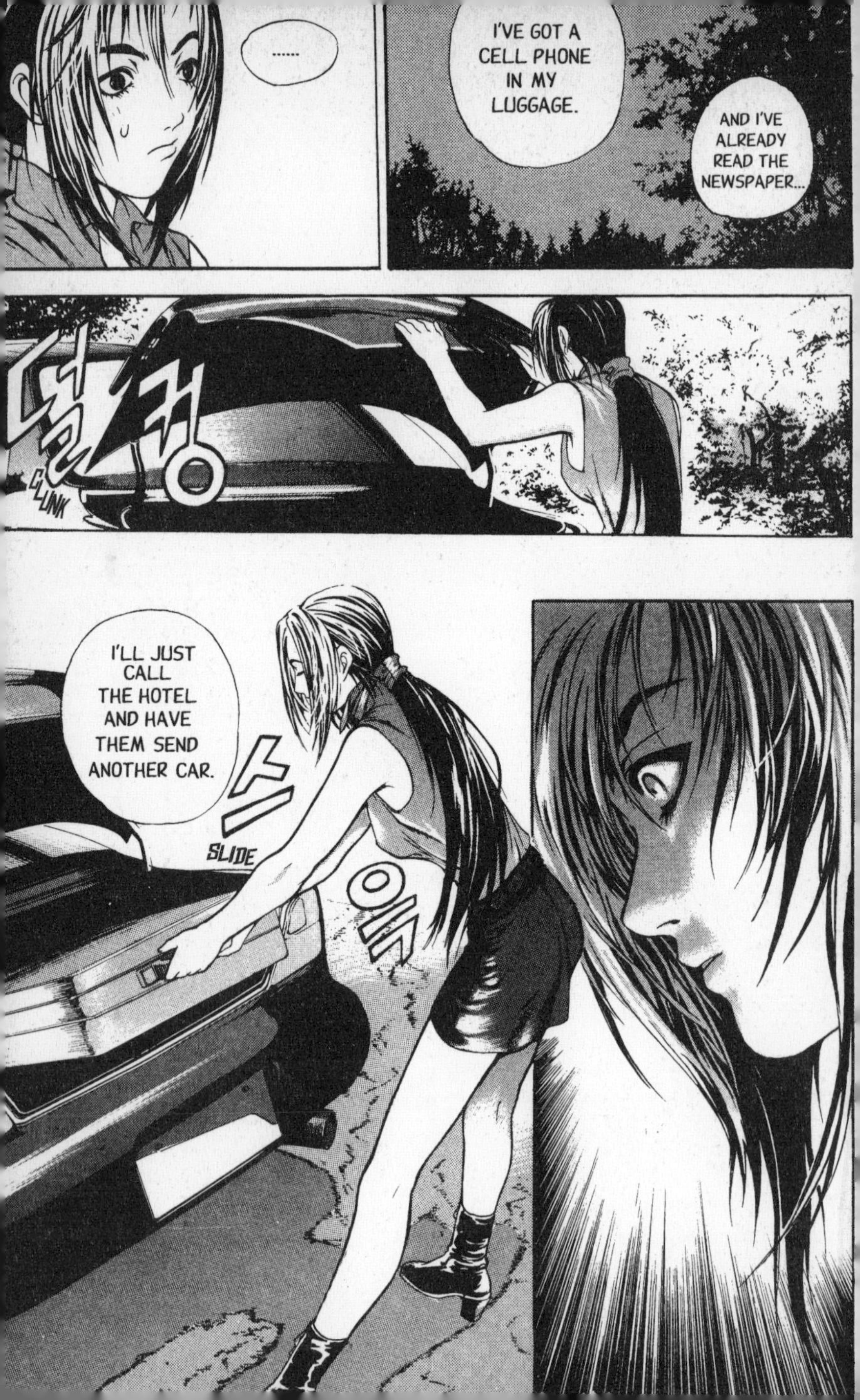
......
I'VE GOT A CELL PHONE IN MY LUGGAGE.
AND I'VE ALREADY READ THE NEWSPAPER...
덜컹
CLUNK
I'LL JUST CALL THE HOTEL AND HAVE THEM SEND ANOTHER CAR.
SLIDE

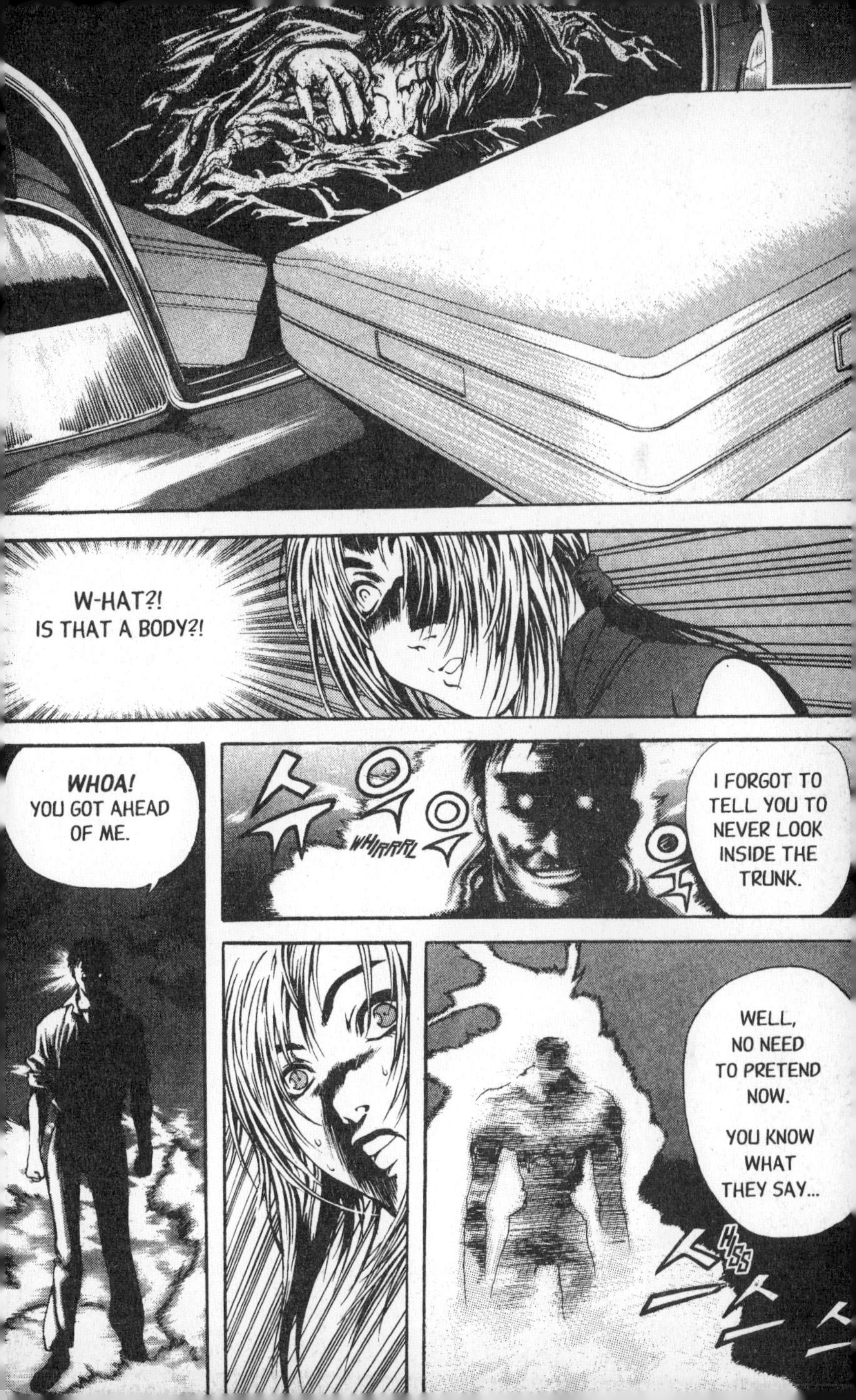
W-HAT?! IS THAT A BODY?!
WHOA! YOU GOT AHEAD OF ME.
WHIRRRL
I FORGOT TO TELL YOU TO NEVER LOOK INSIDE THE TRUNK.
WELL, NO NEED TO PRETEND NOW.
YOU KNOW WHAT THEY SAY...
HISS

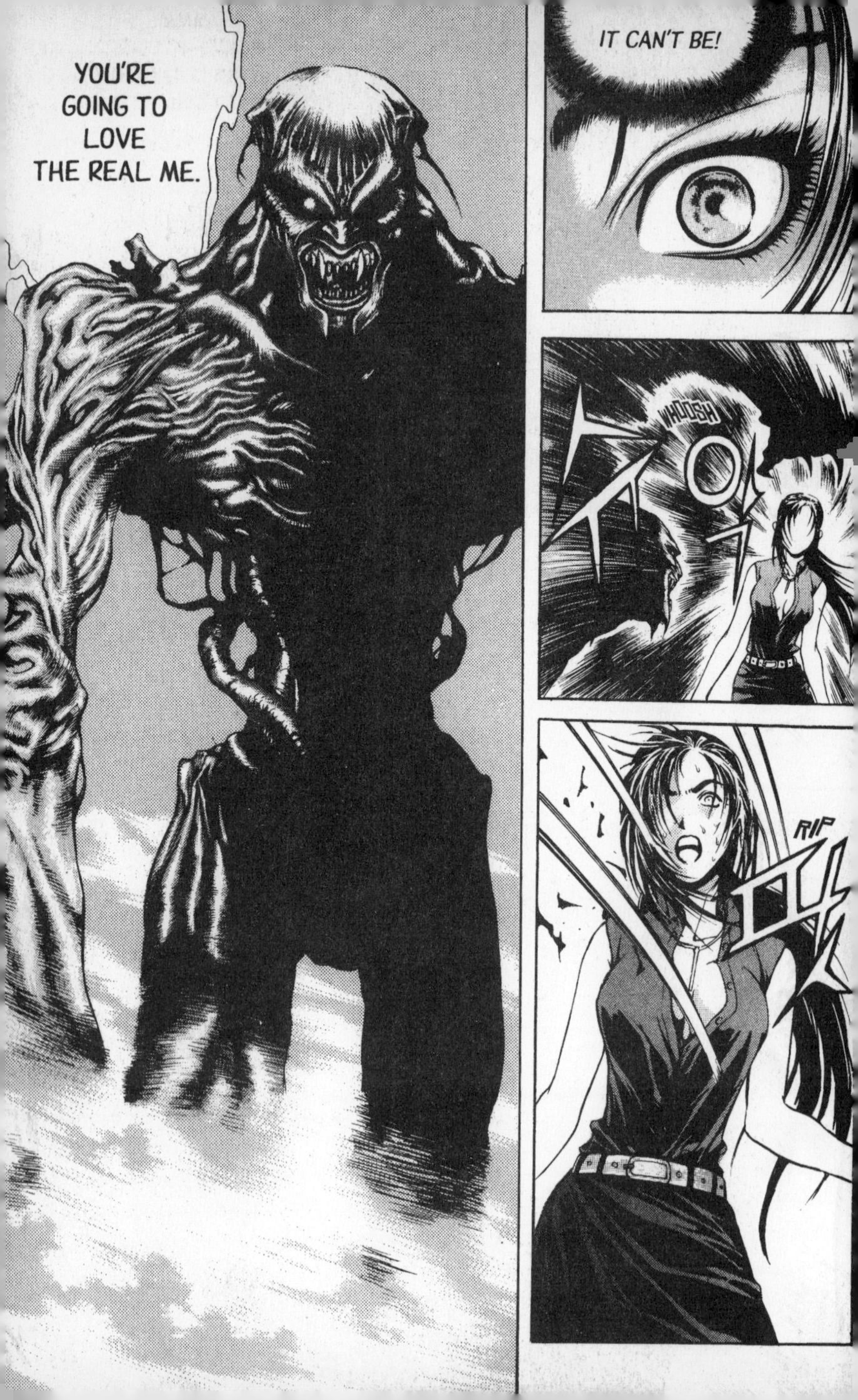
YOU'RE GOING TO LOVE THE REAL ME.
IT CAN'T BE!
WHOOSH
RIP

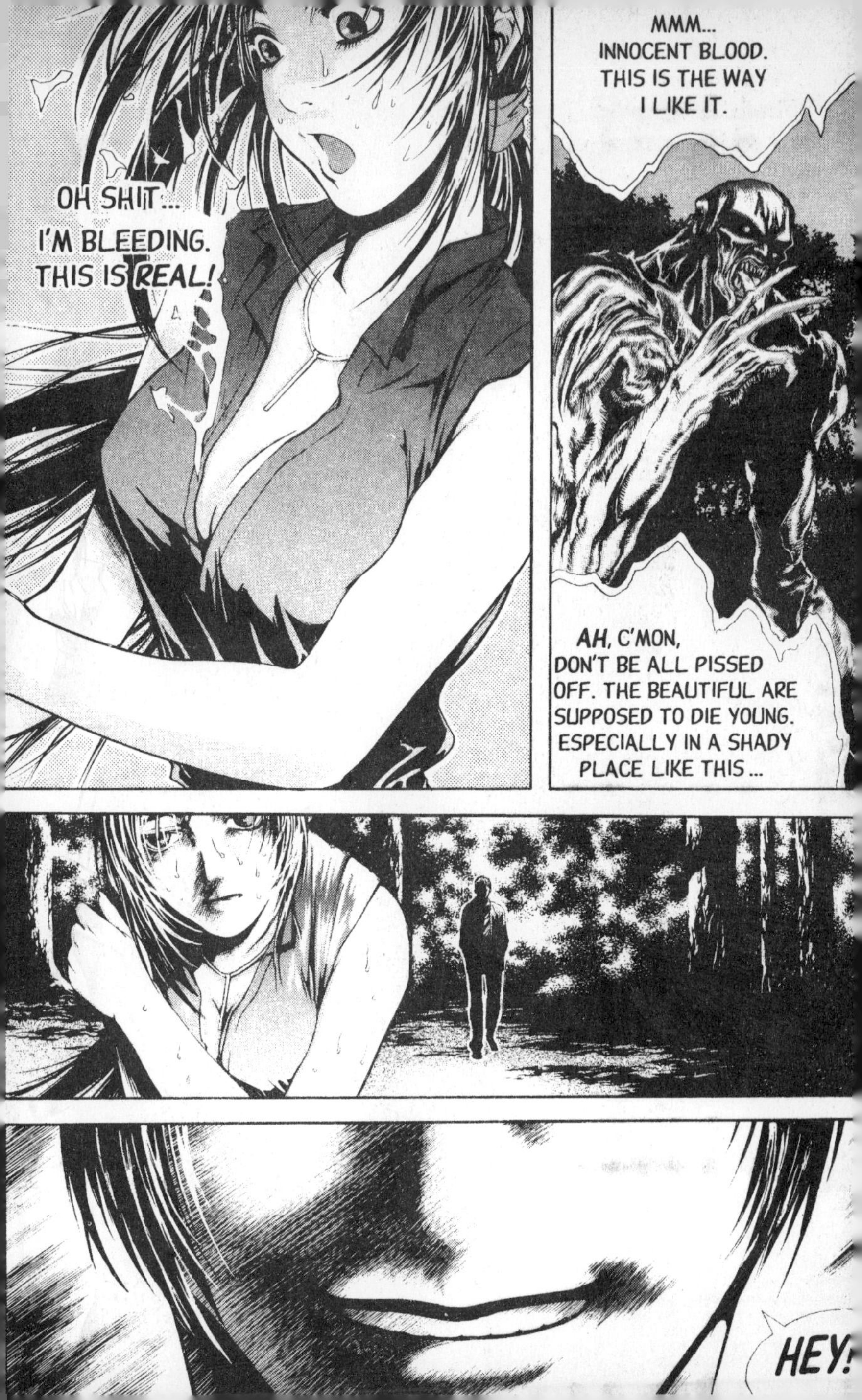
OH SHIT...
I'M BLEEDING. THIS IS REAL!
MMM... INNOCENT BLOOD. THIS IS THE WAY I LIKE IT.
AH, C'MON, DON'T BE ALL PISSED OFF. THE BEAUTIFUL ARE SUPPOSED TO DIE YOUNG. ESPECIALLY IN A SHADY PLACE LIKE THIS...
HEY!

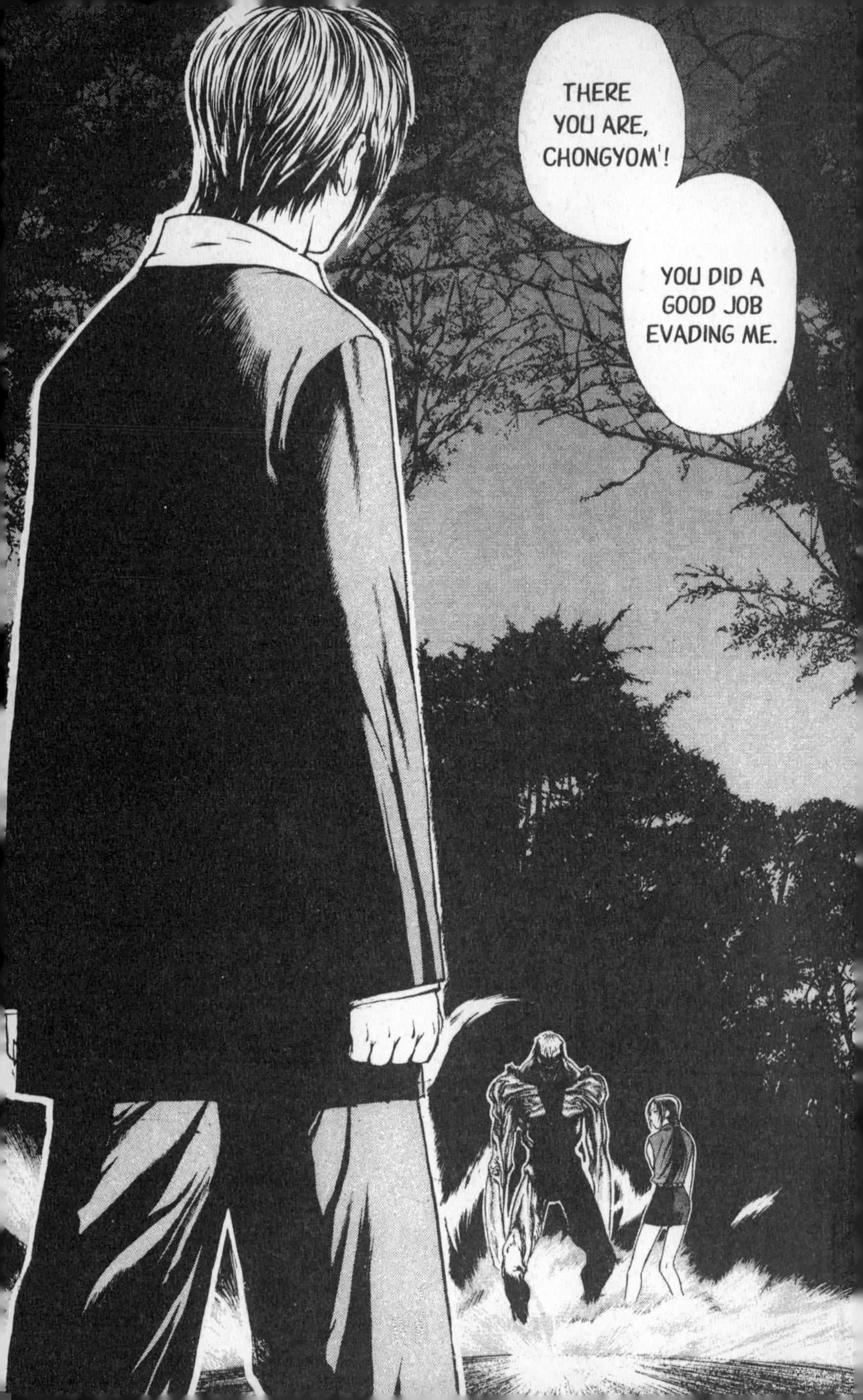
THERE YOU ARE, CHONGYOM'!
YOU DID A GOOD JOB EVADING ME.

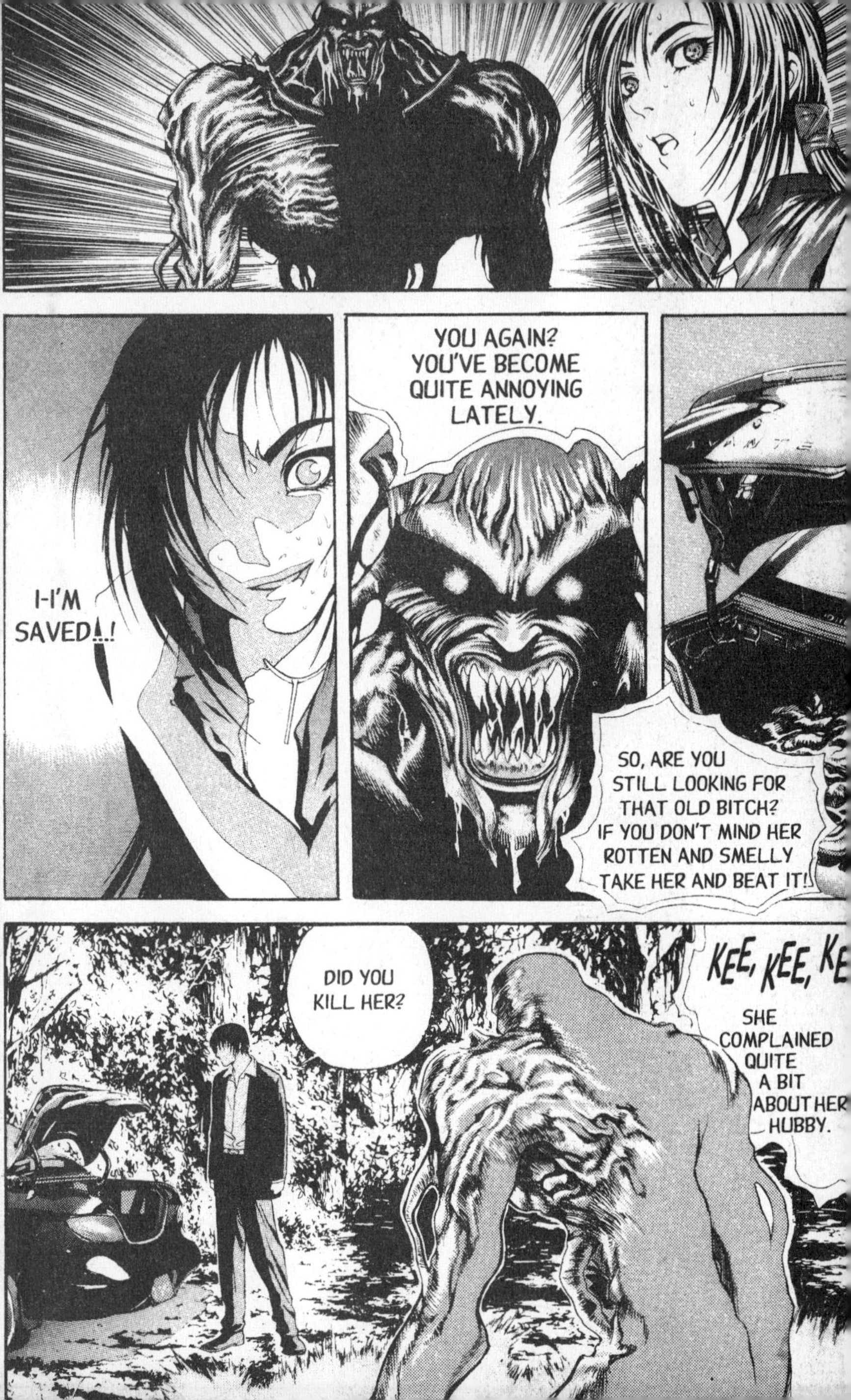
I-I'M SAVED...!
YOU AGAIN? YOU'VE BECOME QUITE ANNOYING LATELY.
SO, ARE YOU STILL LOOKING FOR THAT OLD BITCH? IF YOU DON'T MIND HER ROTTEN AND SMELLY TAKE HER AND BEAT IT!
DID YOU KILL HER?
KEE, KEE, KE
SHE COMPLAINED QUITE A BIT ABOUT HER HUBBY.

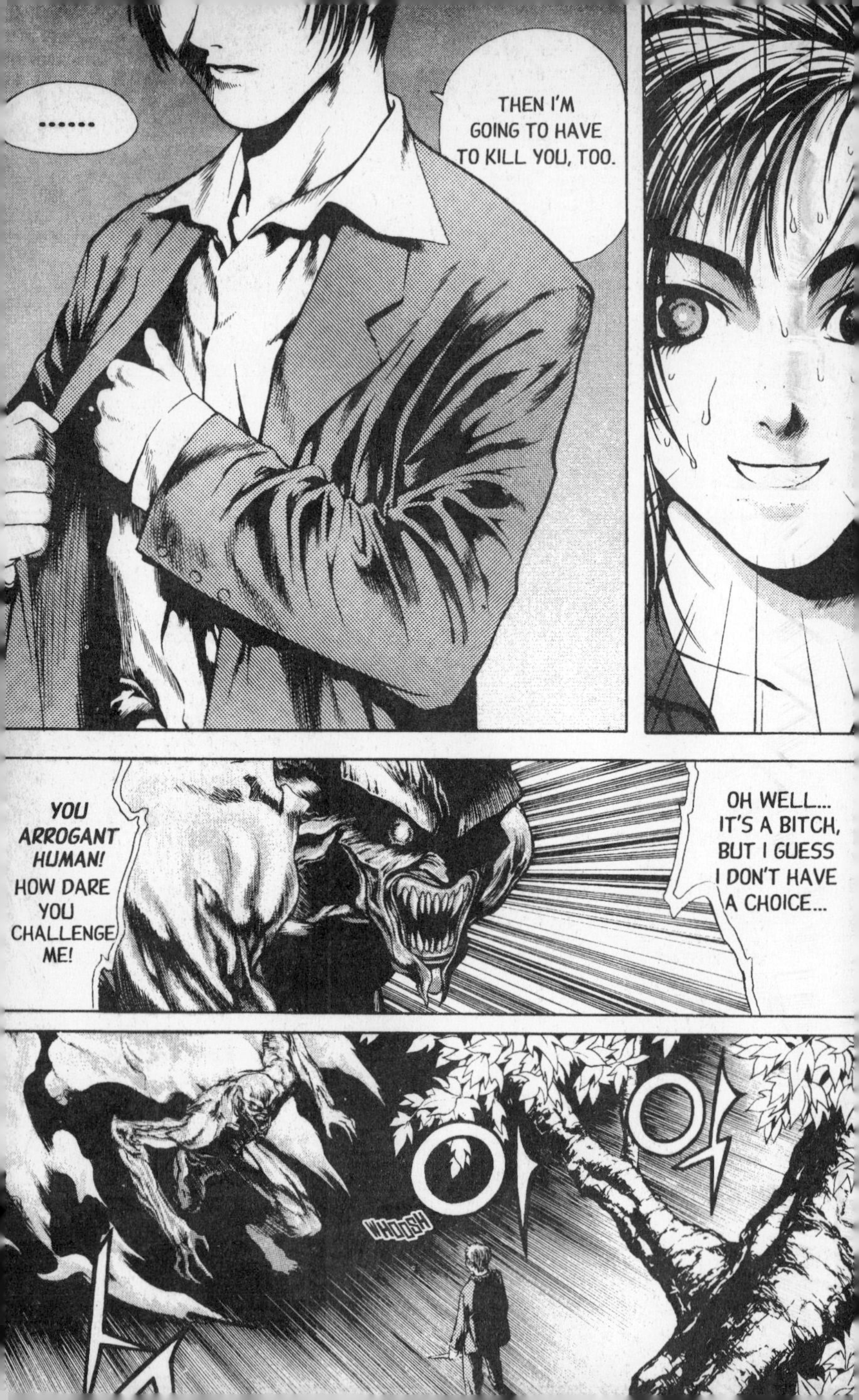
......
THEN I'M GOING TO HAVE TO KILL YOU, TOO.
YOU ARROGANT HUMAN! HOW DARE YOU CHALLENGE ME!
OH WELL... IT'S A BITCH, BUT I GUESS I DON'T HAVE A CHOICE...
WHOOSH

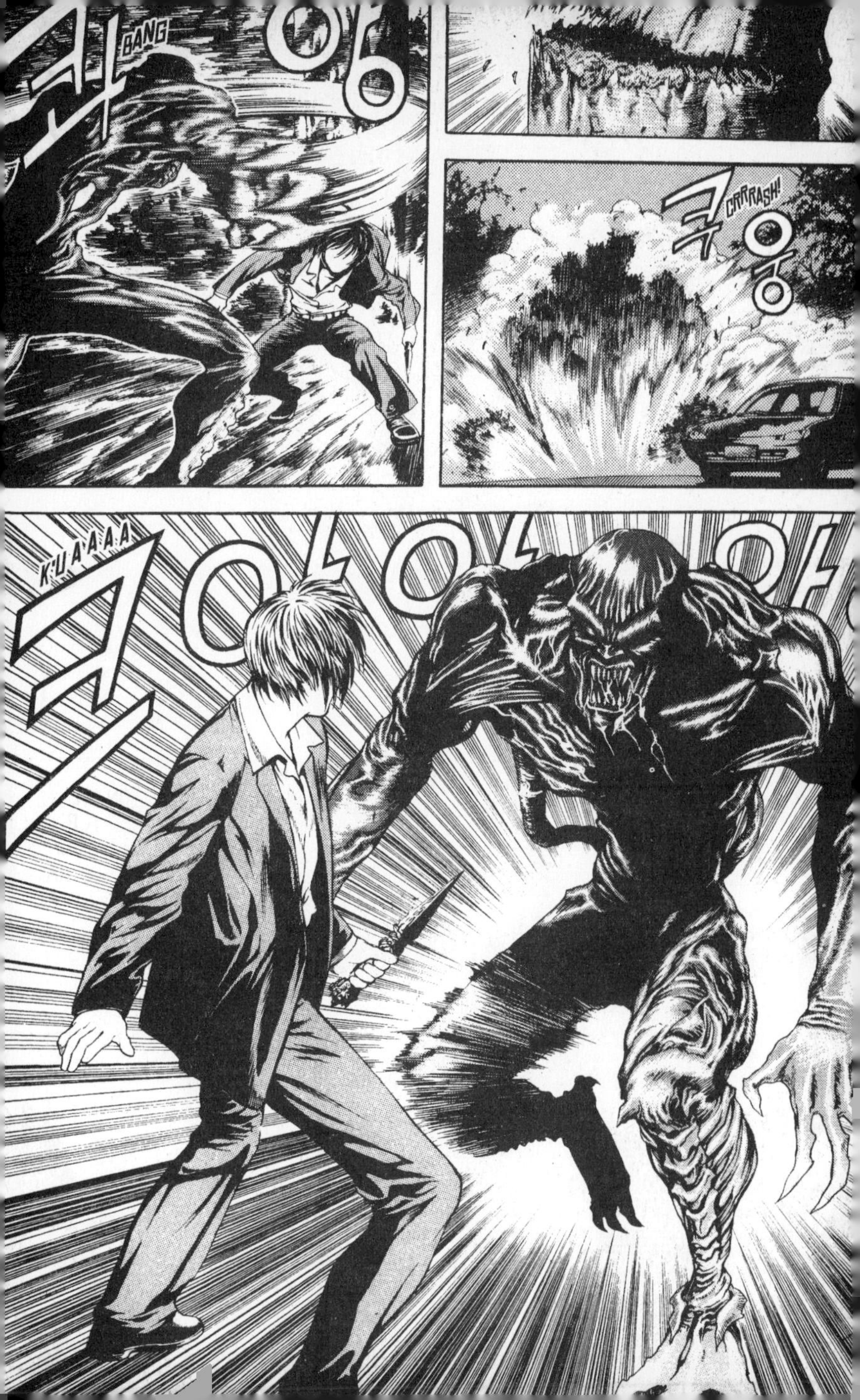
BANG
CRRRASH!
K'UAAAA

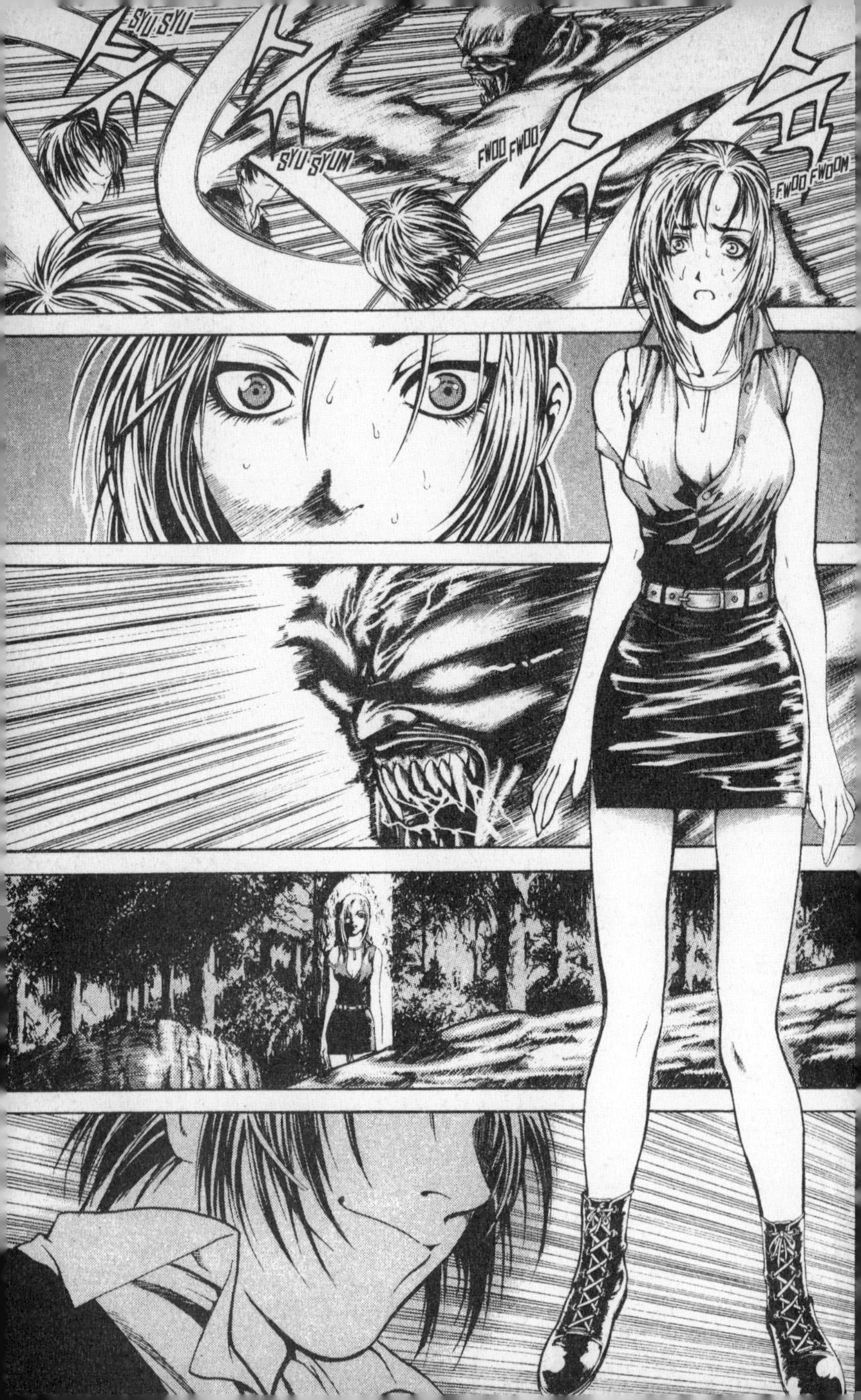
SYU SYU
SYU SYUM
FWOO FWOO
FWOO FWOOM

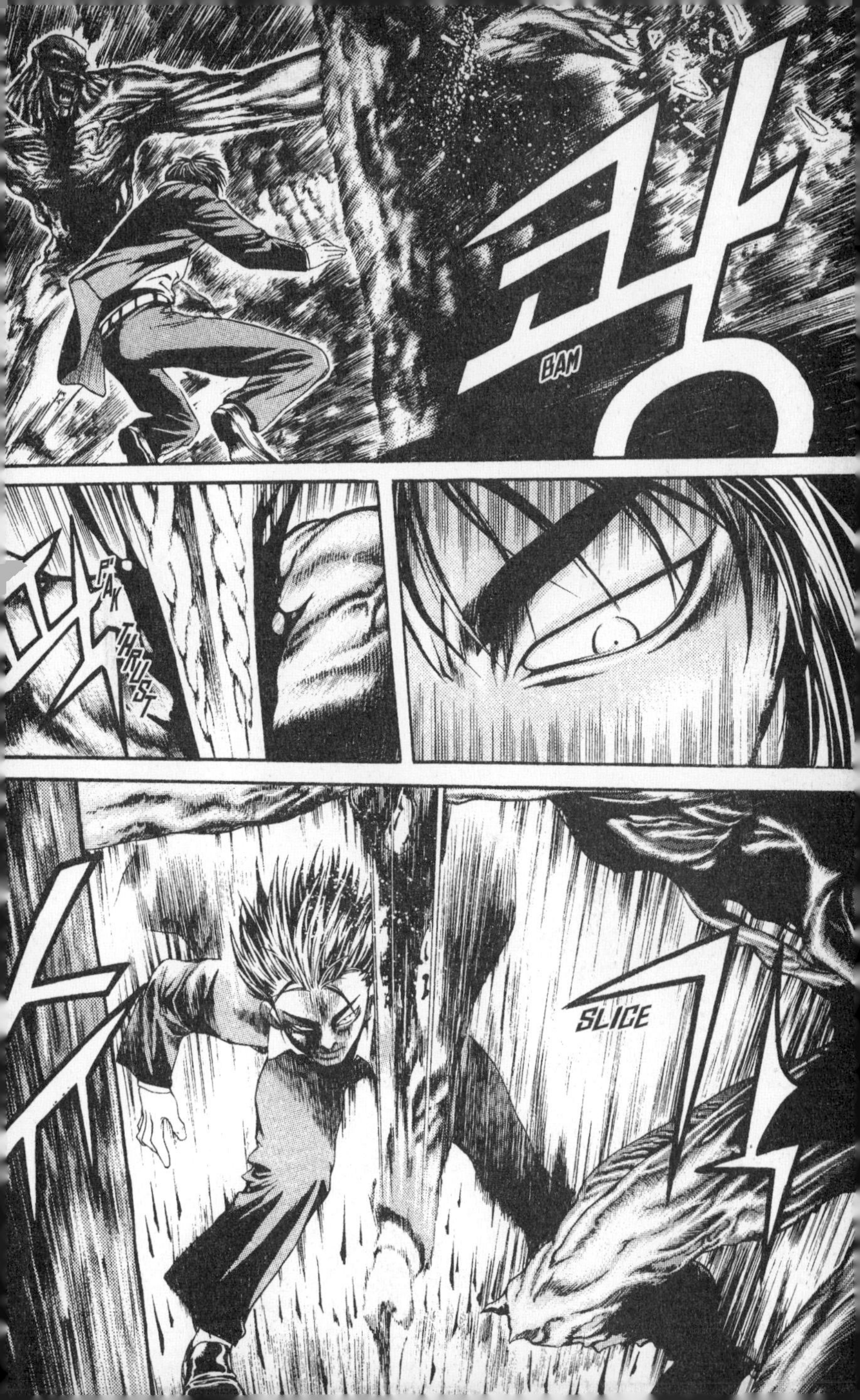
BAM
PIAK
THRUST
SLICE

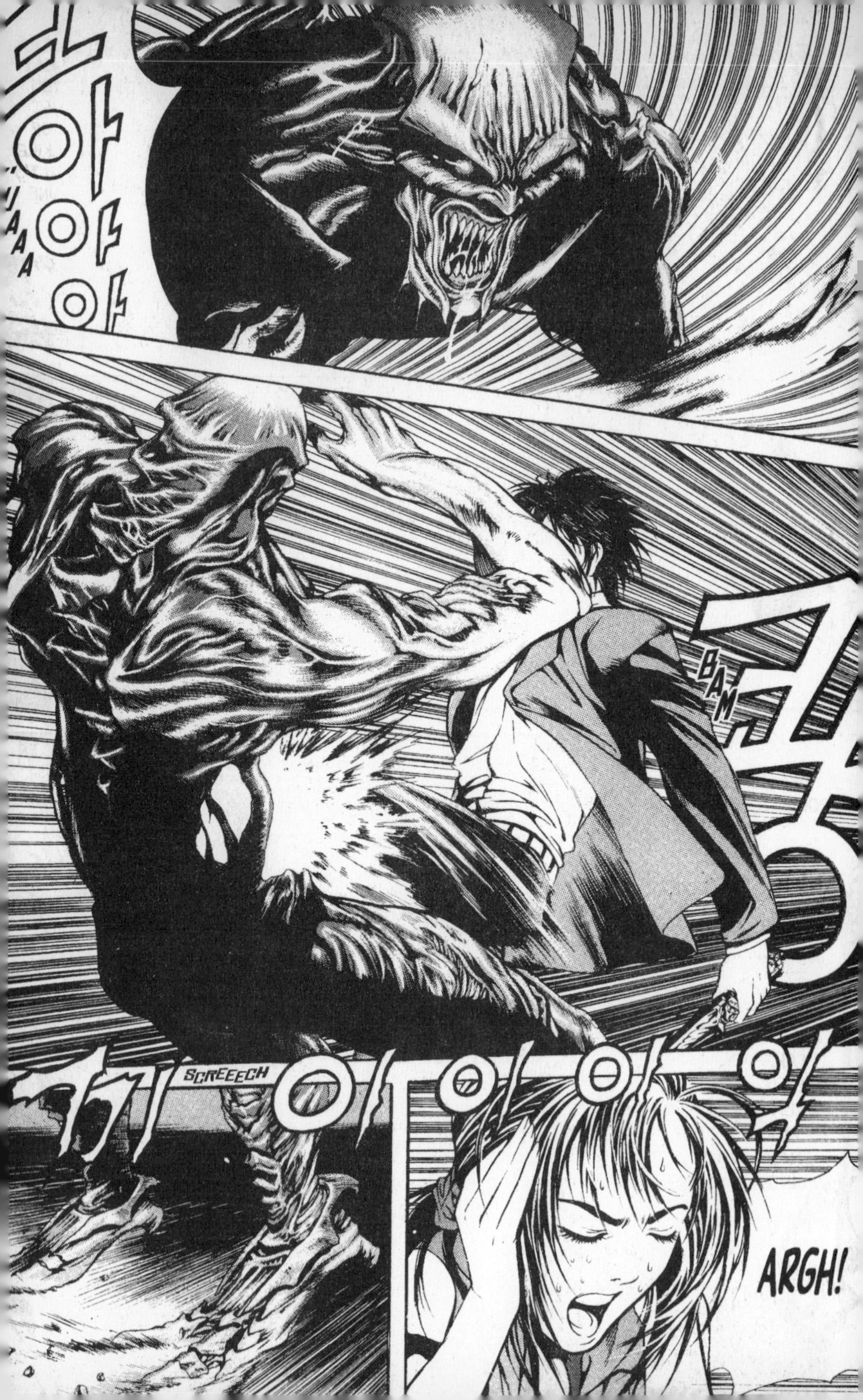
BAM
SCREEECH
ARGH!

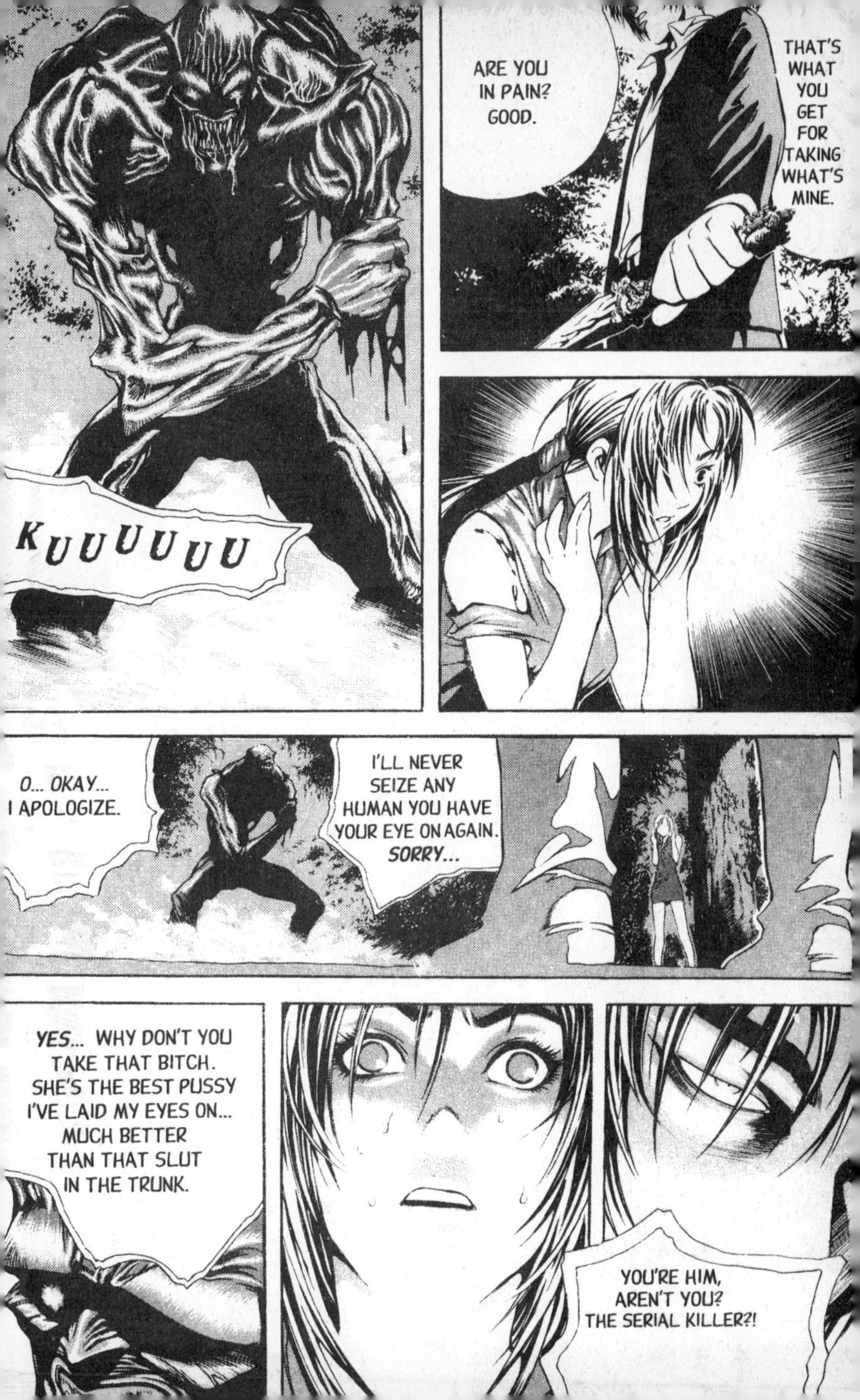
KUUUUUUU
ARE YOU IN PAIN? GOOD.
THAT'S WHAT YOU GET FOR TAKING WHAT'S MINE.
O... OKAY... I APOLOGIZE.
I'LL NEVER SEIZE ANY HUMAN YOU HAVE YOUR EYE ON AGAIN. SORRY...
YES... WHY DON'T YOU TAKE THAT BITCH. SHE'S THE BEST PUSSY I'VE LAID MY EYES ON... MUCH BETTER THAN THAT SLUT IN THE TRUNK.
YOU'RE HIM, AREN'T YOU? THE SERIAL KILLER?!

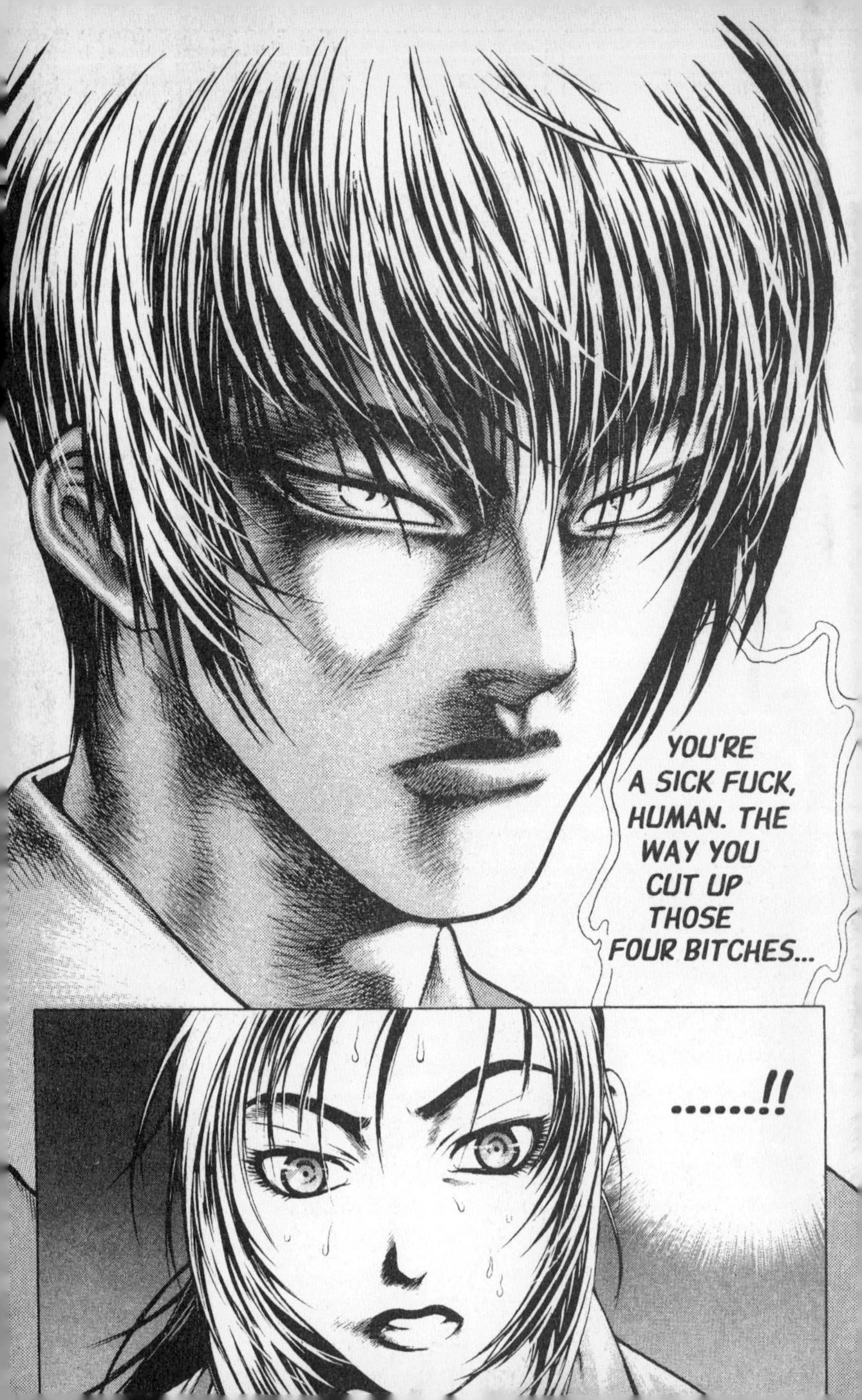
YOU'RE A SICK FUCK, HUMAN. THE WAY YOU CUT UP THOSE FOUR BITCHES...
.......!!

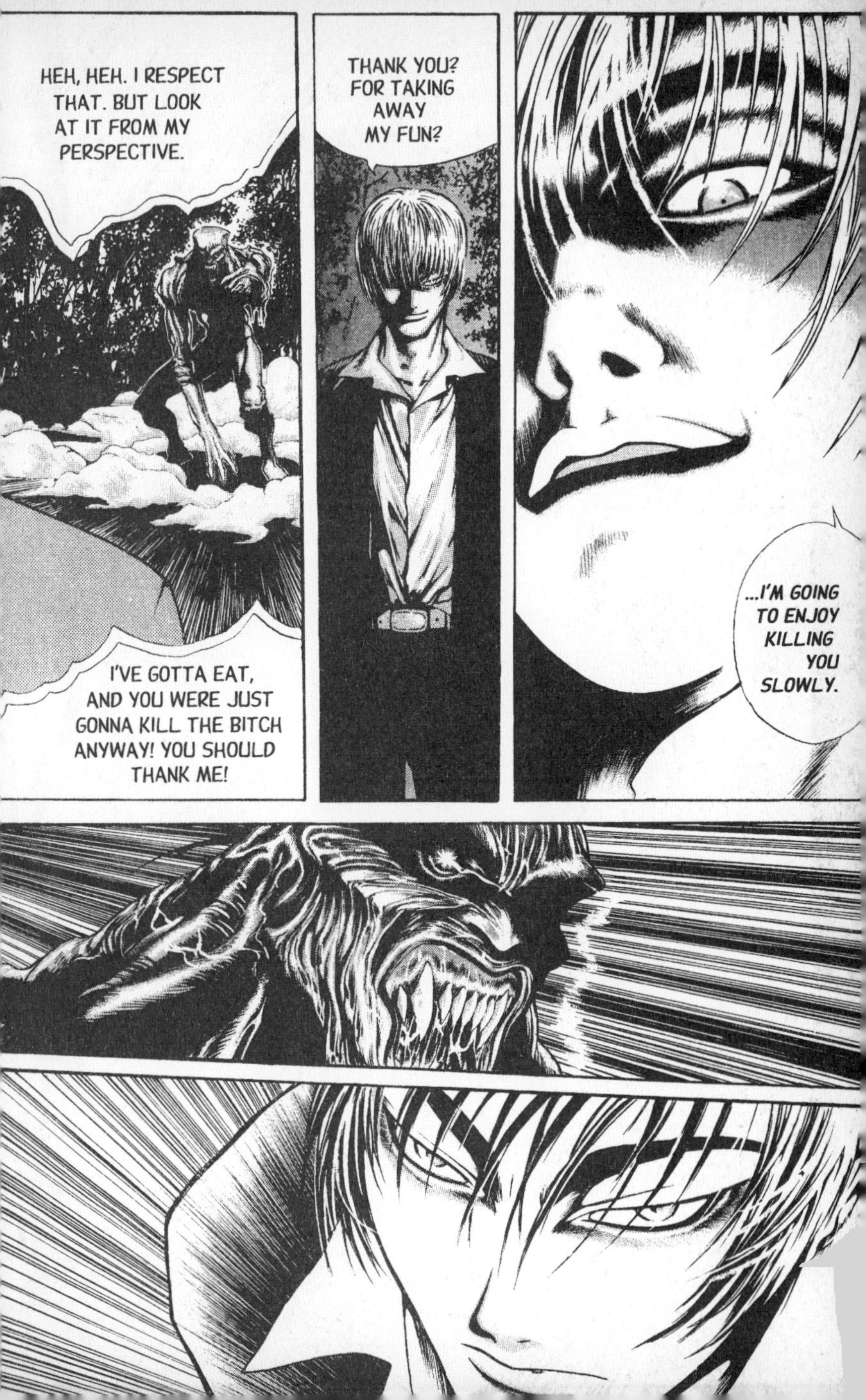
HEH, HEH. I RESPECT THAT. BUT LOOK AT IT FROM MY PERSPECTIVE.
I'VE GOTTA EAT, AND YOU WERE JUST GONNA KILL THE BITCH ANYWAY! YOU SHOULD THANK ME!
THANK YOU? FOR TAKING AWAY MY FUN?
...I'M GOING TO ENJOY KILLING YOU SLOWLY.

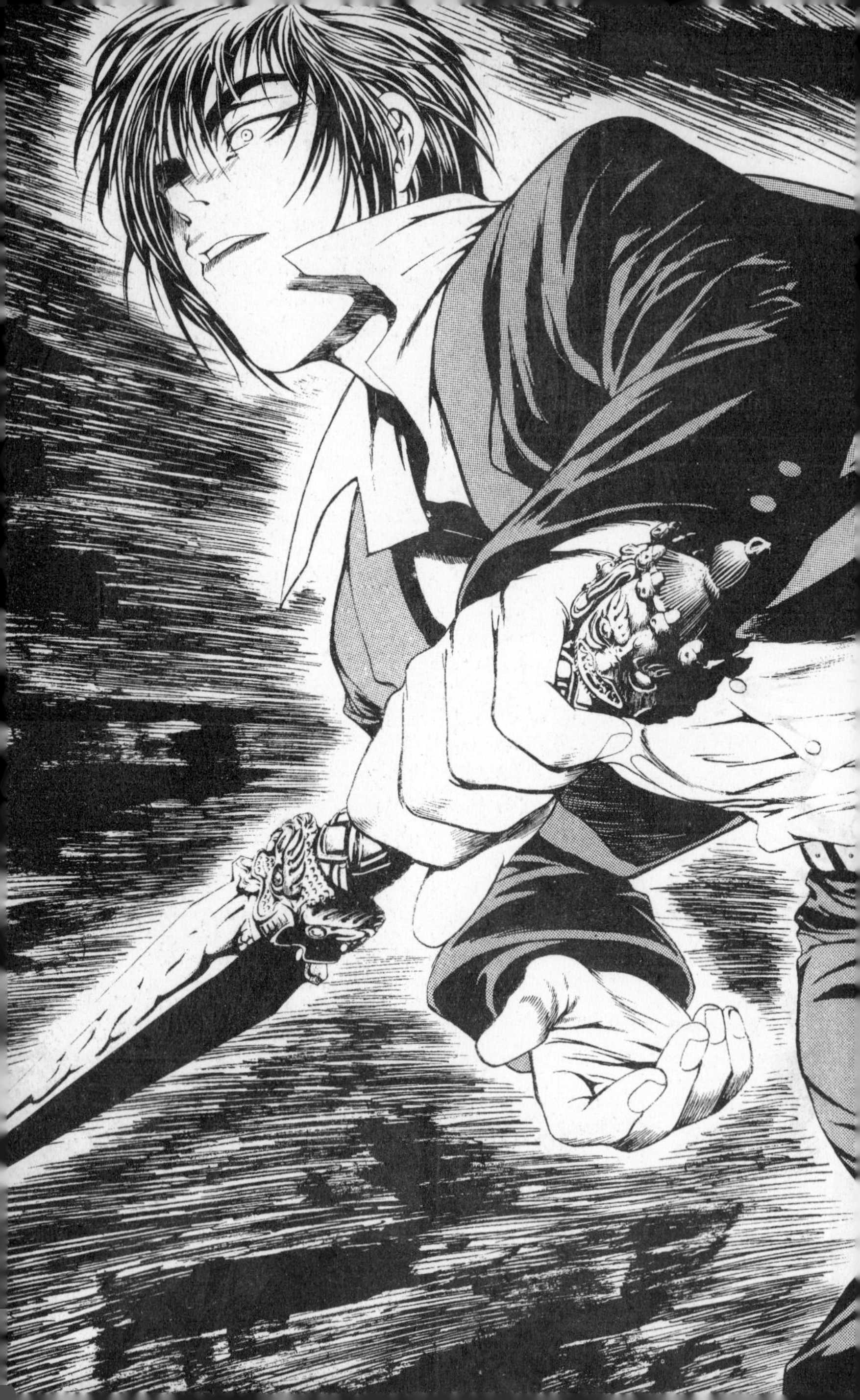

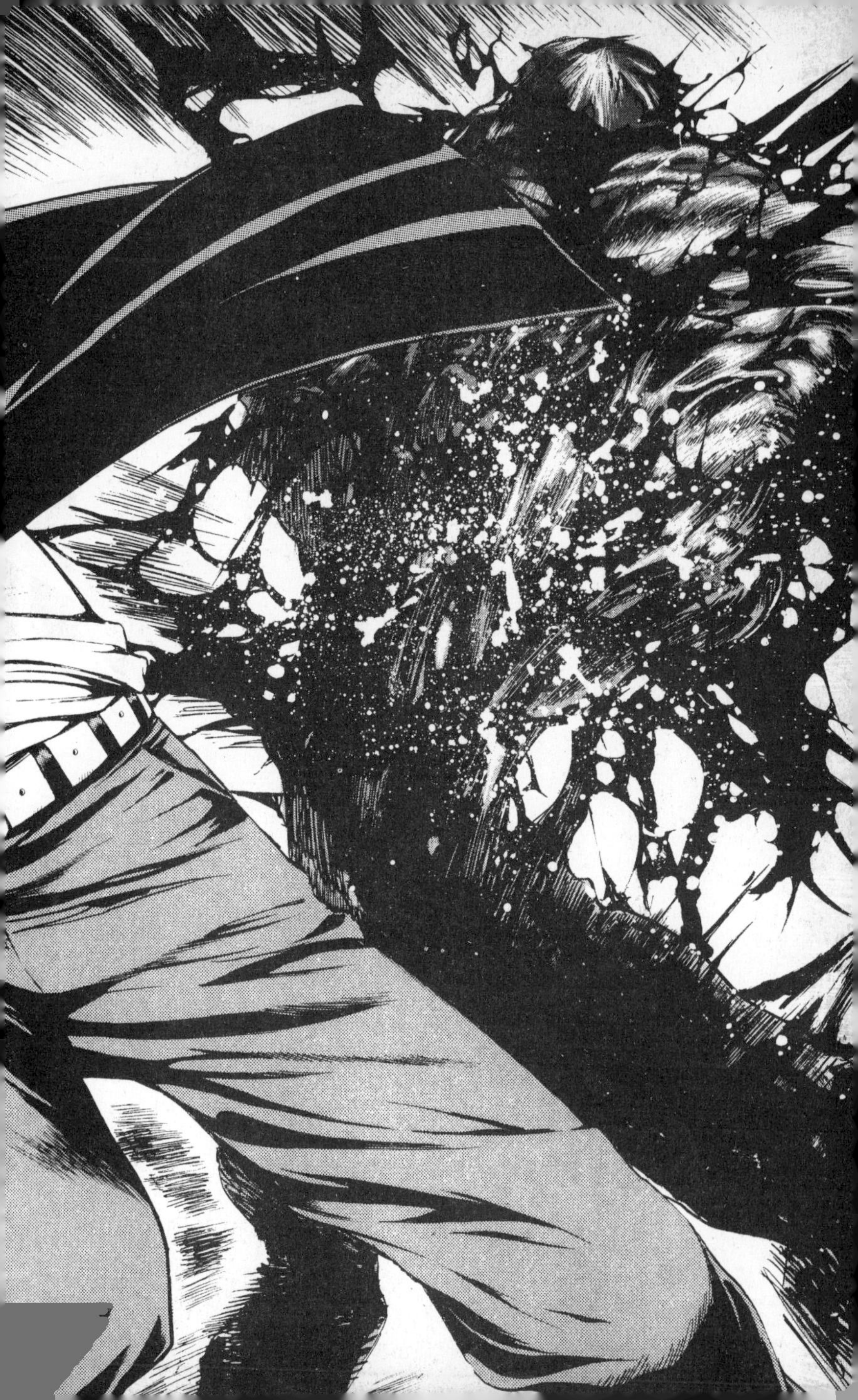

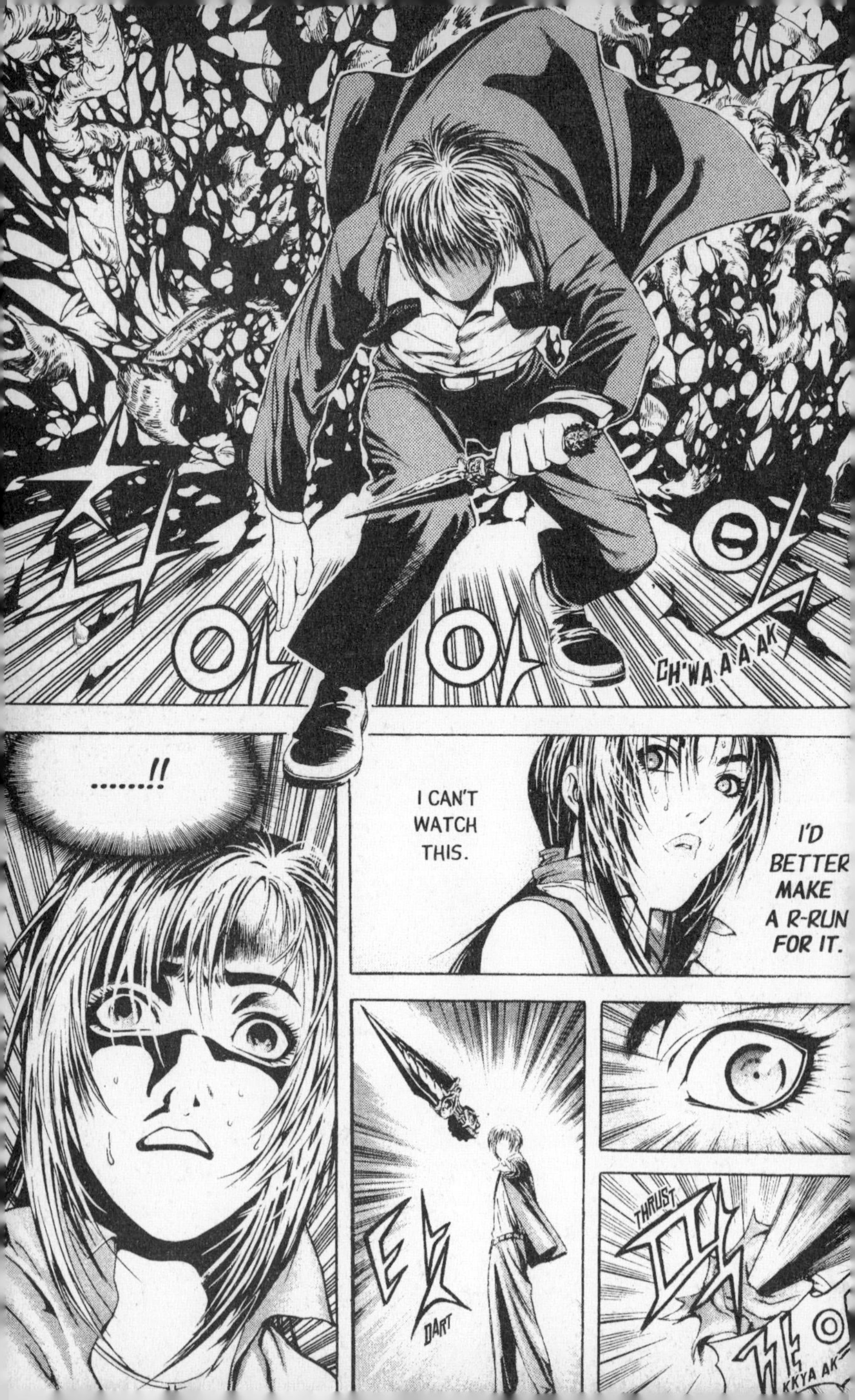

CH'WA A A AK
......!!
I CAN'T WATCH THIS.
I'D BETTER MAKE A R-RUN FOR IT.
DART
THRUST
KKYA AK

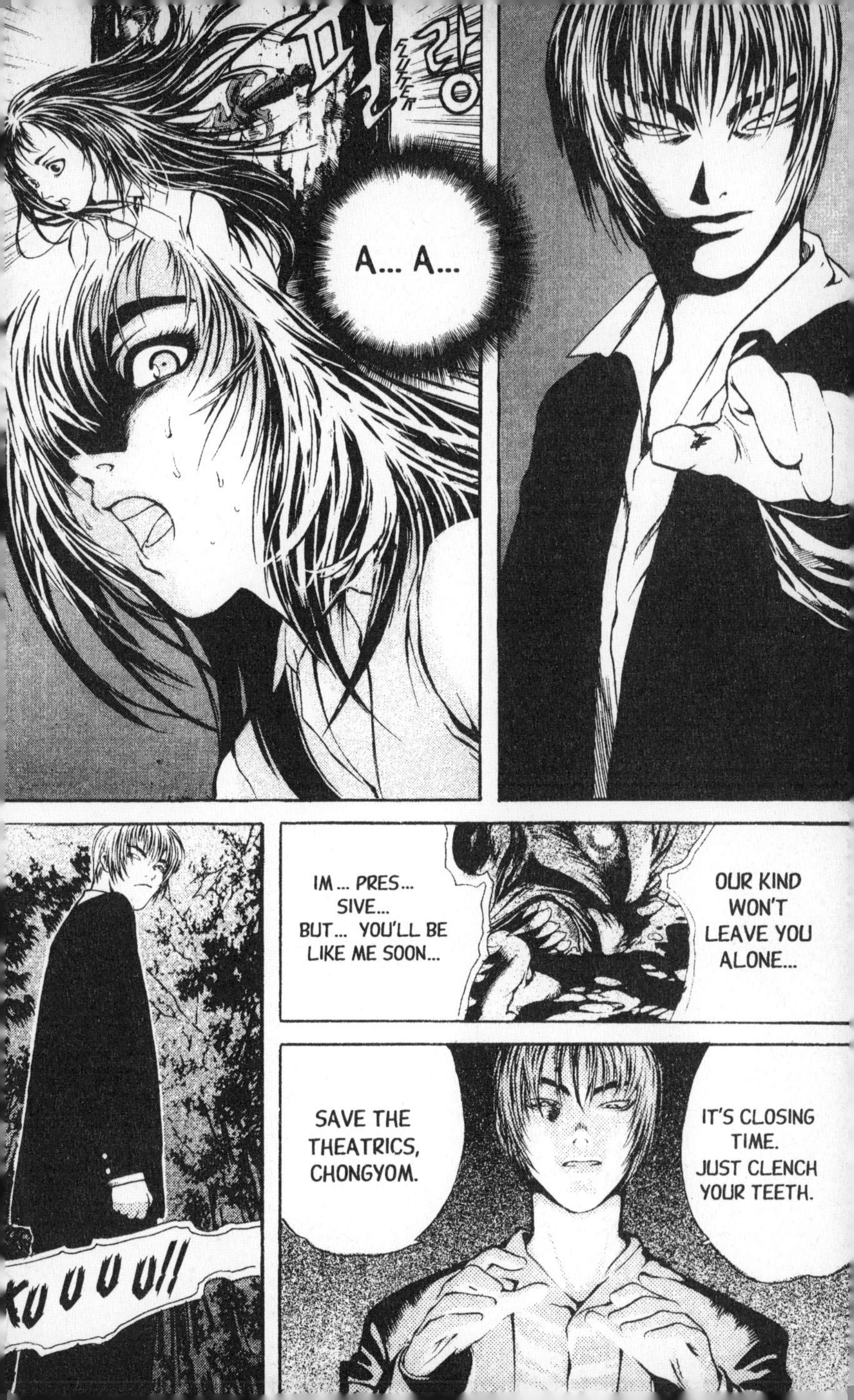
FLUTTER
A... A...
KUUUU!!
IM... PRES... SIVE... BUT... YOU'LL BE LIKE ME SOON...
OUR KIND WON'T LEAVE YOU ALONE...
SAVE THE THEATRICS, CHONGYOM.
IT'S CLOSING TIME. JUST CLENCH YOUR TEETH.

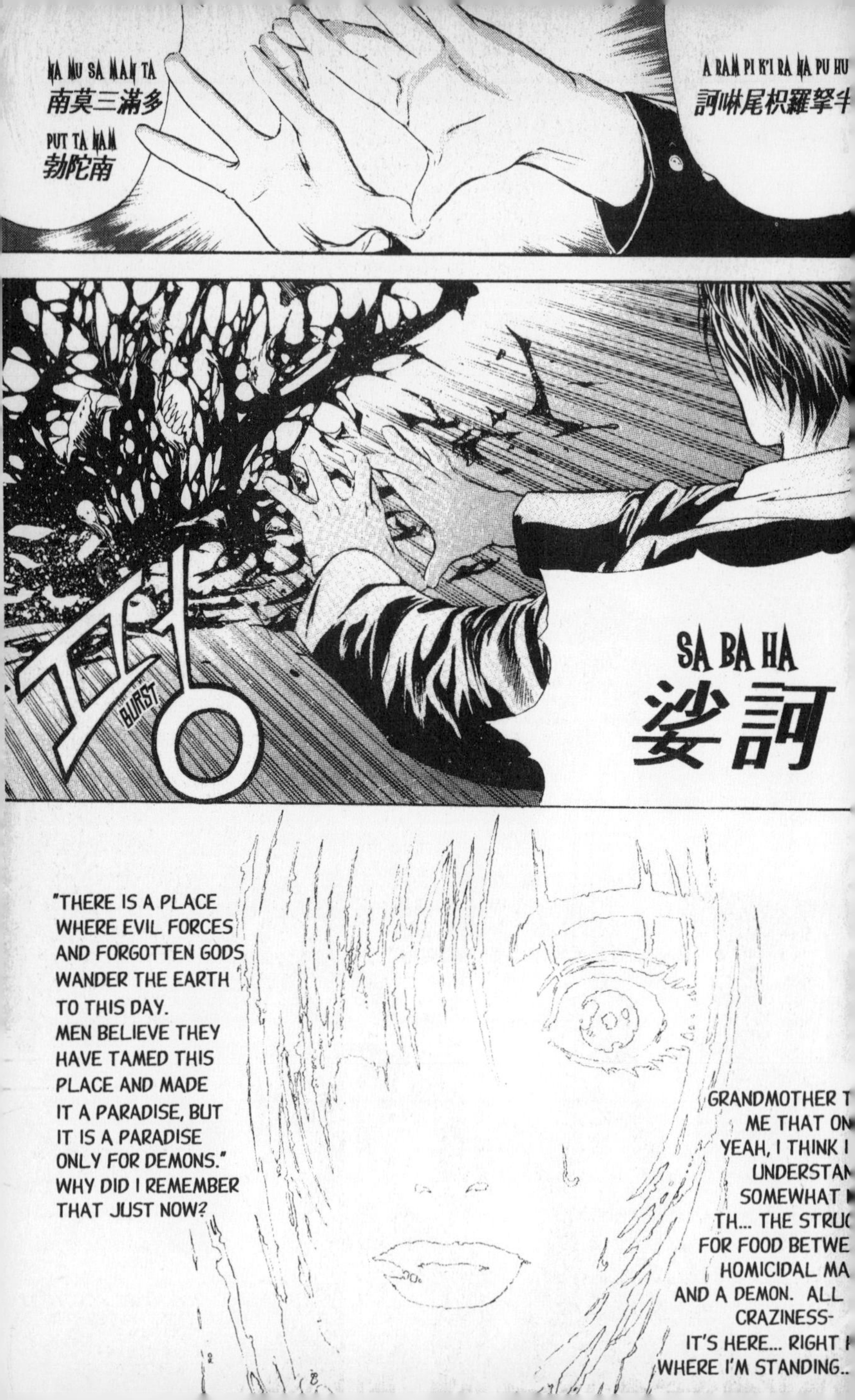
NA MU SA MAN TA
南莫三満多
PUT TA NAM
勃陀南
A RAM PI K'I RA HA PU HU
訶啉尾枳羅拏斗
BURST
SA BA HA
娑訶
"THERE IS A PLACE WHERE EVIL FORCES AND FORGOTTEN GODS WANDER THE EARTH TO THIS DAY. MEN BELIEVE THEY HAVE TAMED THIS PLACE AND MADE IT A PARADISE, BUT IT IS A PARADISE ONLY FOR DEMONS." WHY DID I REMEMBER THAT JUST NOW?
GRANDMOTHER T ME THAT ON YEAH, I THINK I UNDERSTAN SOMEWHAT TH... THE STRUG FOR FOOD BETWE HOMICIDAL MA AND A DEMON. ALL CRAZINESS- IT'S HERE... RIGHT WHERE I'M STANDING..

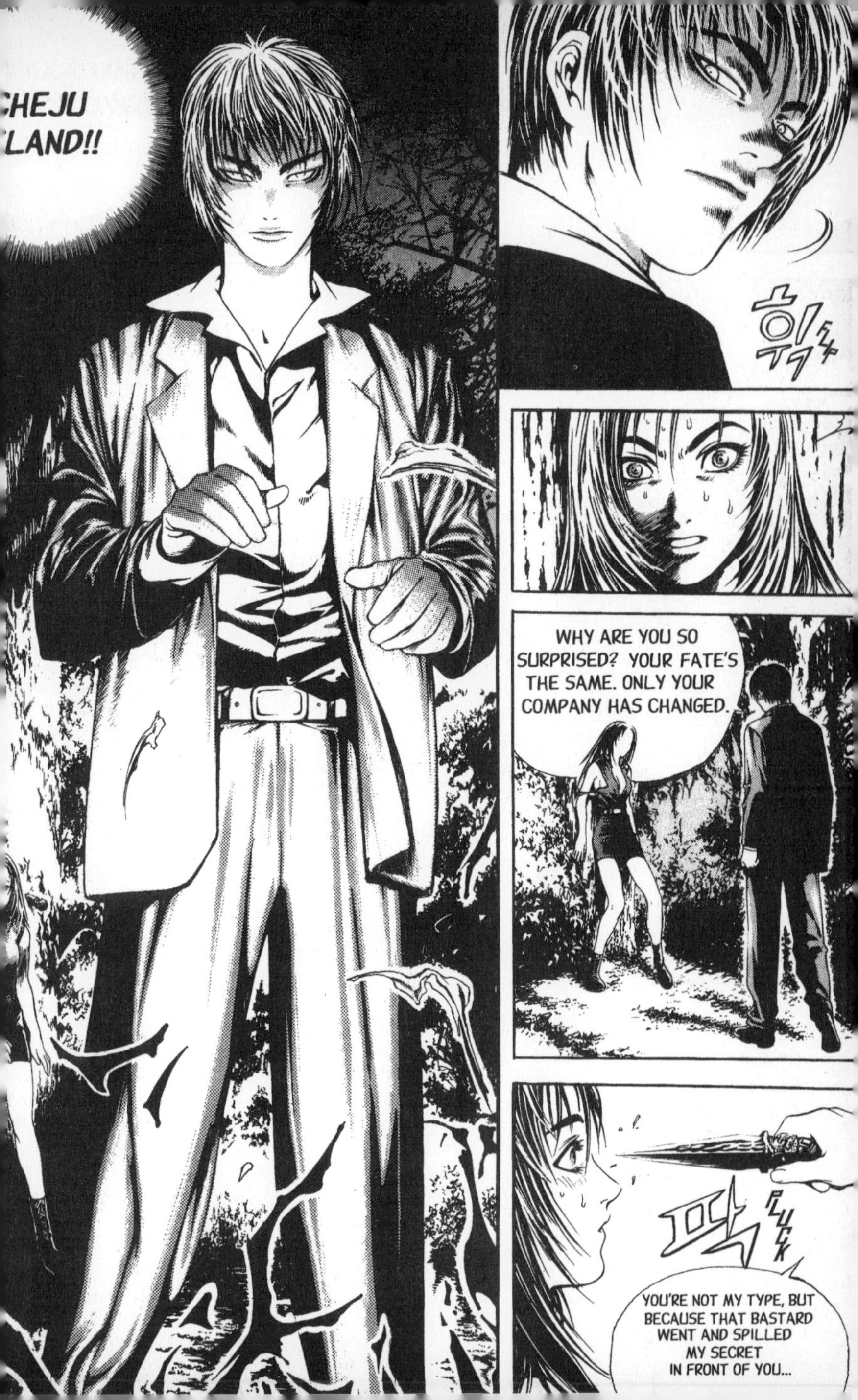
HEJU
LAND!!
WHY ARE YOU SO SURPRISED? YOUR FATE'S THE SAME. ONLY YOUR COMPANY HAS CHANGED.
PLUCK
YOU'RE NOT MY TYPE, BUT BECAUSE THAT BASTARD WENT AND SPILLED MY SECRET IN FRONT OF YOU...

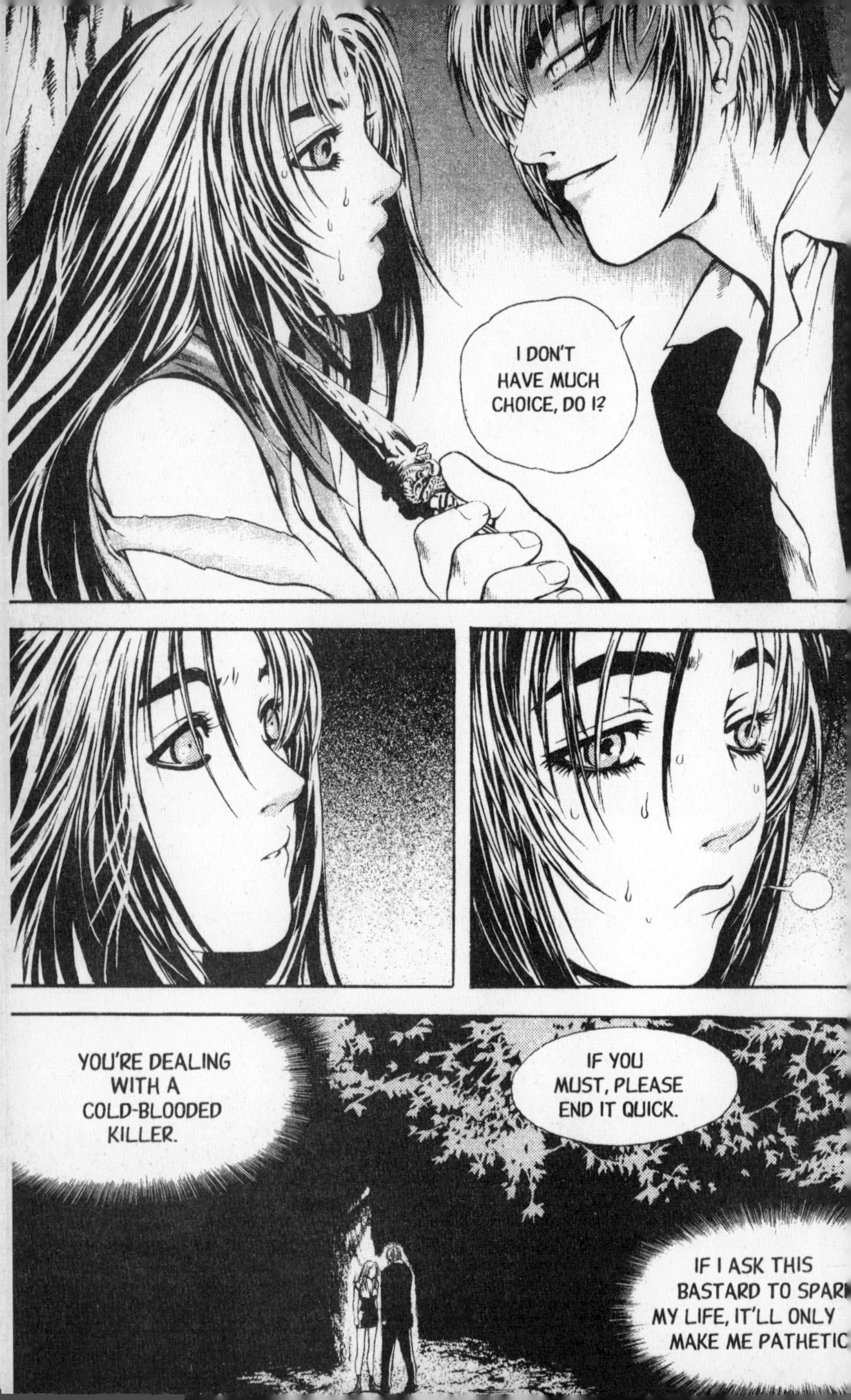
I DON'T HAVE MUCH CHOICE, DO I?
YOU'RE DEALING WITH A COLD-BLOODED KILLER.
IF YOU MUST, PLEASE END IT QUICK.
IF I ASK THIS BASTARD TO SPARE MY LIFE, IT'LL ONLY MAKE ME PATHETIC.

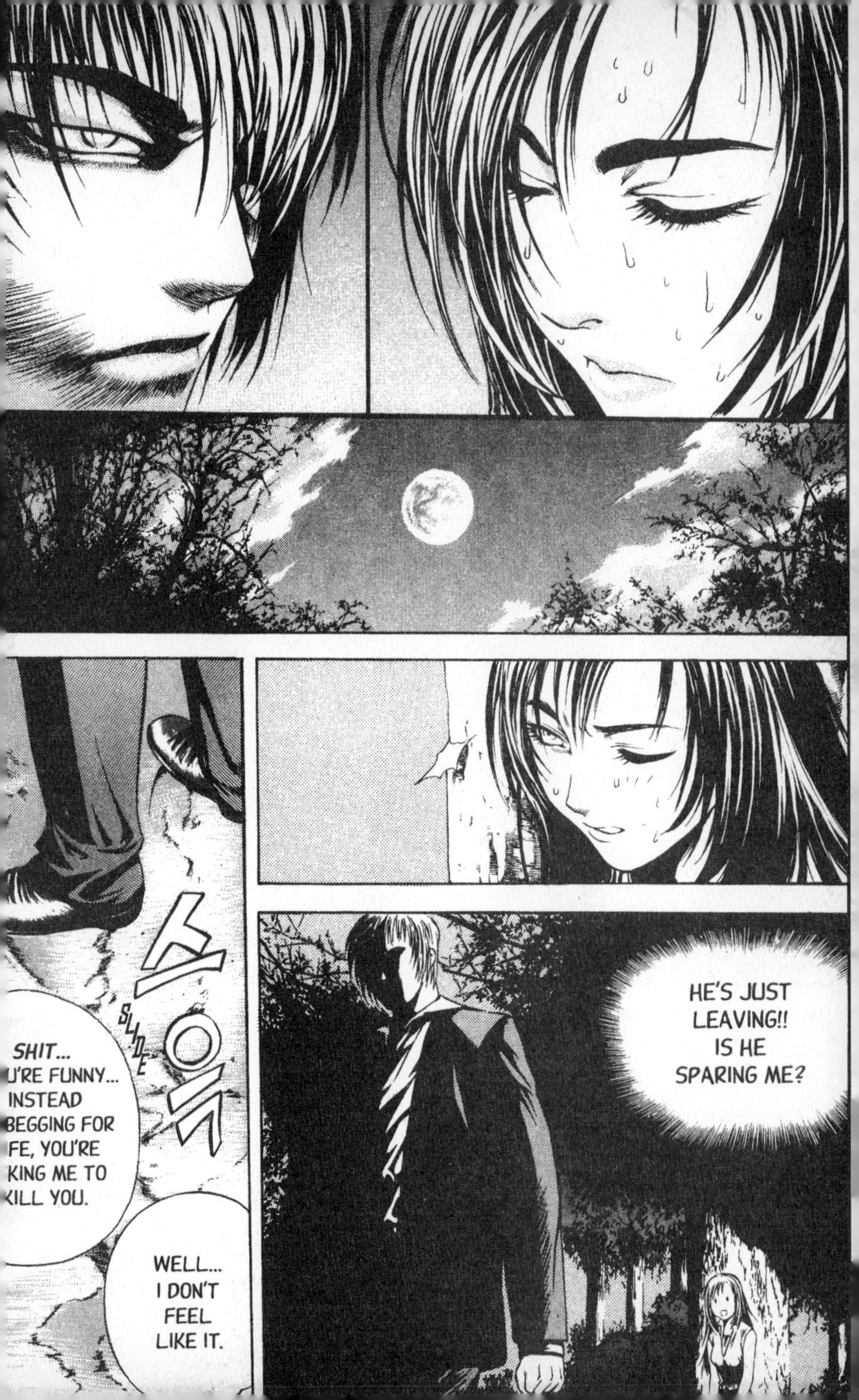

SHIT...
U'RE FUNNY...
INSTEAD
BEGGING FOR
FE, YOU'RE
KING ME TO
KILL YOU.
SLIDE
WELL...
I DON'T
FEEL
LIKE IT.
HE'S JUST
LEAVING!!
IS HE
SPARING ME?

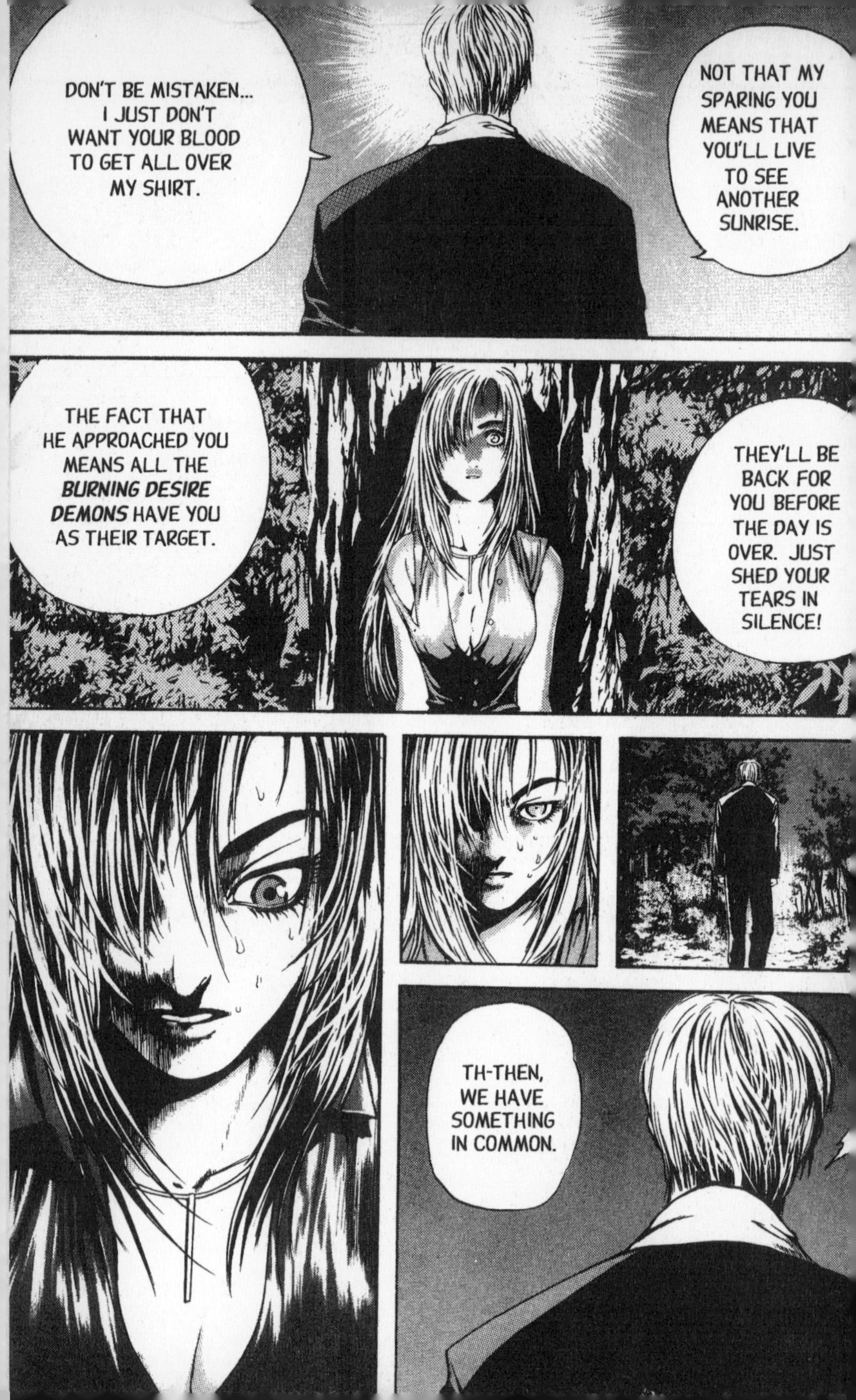
DON'T BE MISTAKEN... I JUST DON'T WANT YOUR BLOOD TO GET ALL OVER MY SHIRT.
NOT THAT MY SPARING YOU MEANS THAT YOU'LL LIVE TO SEE ANOTHER SUNRISE.
THE FACT THAT HE APPROACHED YOU MEANS ALL THE *BURNING DESIRE DEMONS* HAVE YOU AS THEIR TARGET.
THEY'LL BE BACK FOR YOU BEFORE THE DAY IS OVER. JUST SHED YOUR TEARS IN SILENCE!
TH-THEN, WE HAVE SOMETHING IN COMMON.

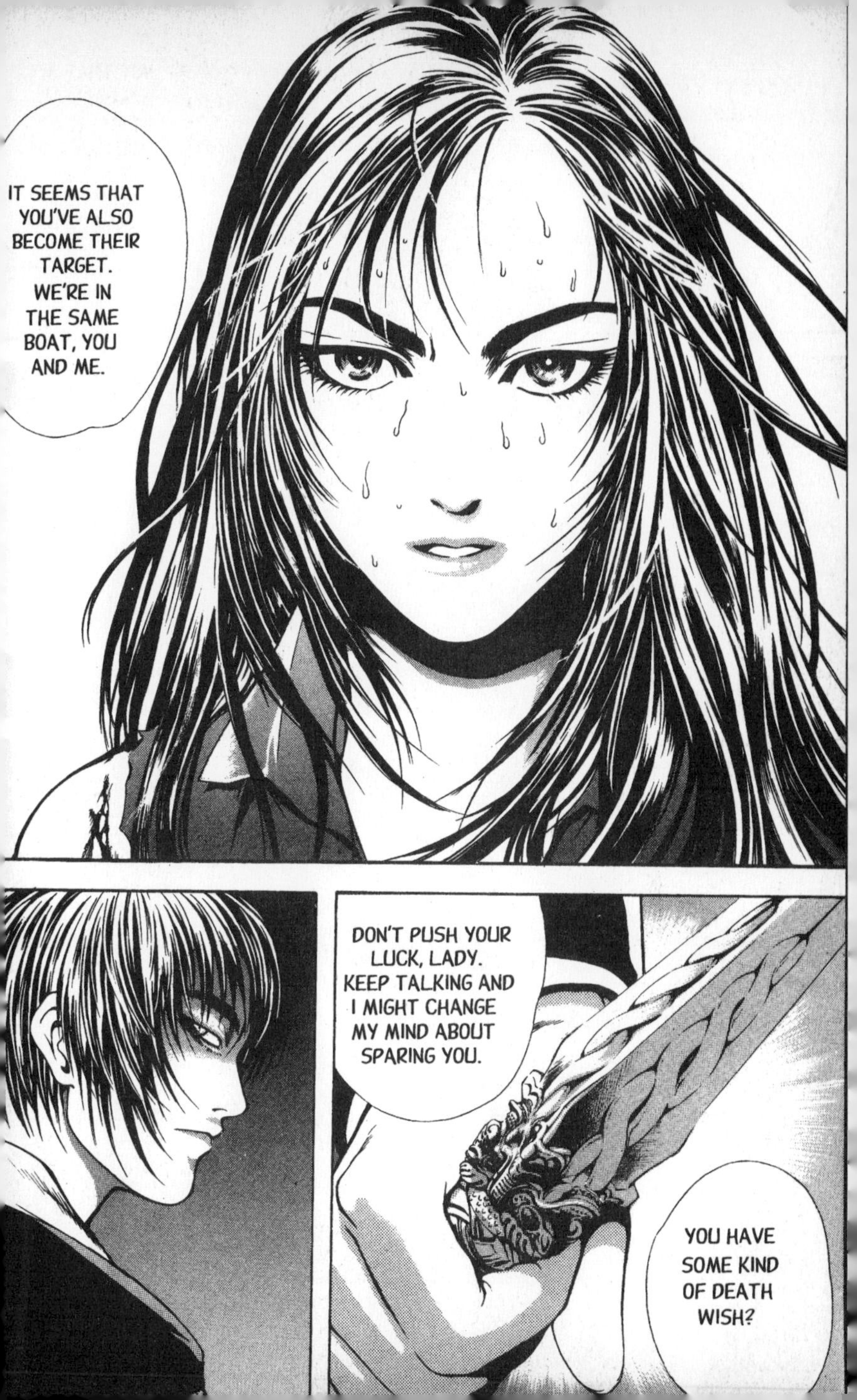
IT SEEMS THAT YOU'VE ALSO BECOME THEIR TARGET. WE'RE IN THE SAME BOAT, YOU AND ME.
DON'T PUSH YOUR LUCK, LADY. KEEP TALKING AND I MIGHT CHANGE MY MIND ABOUT SPARING YOU.
YOU HAVE SOME KIND OF DEATH WISH?

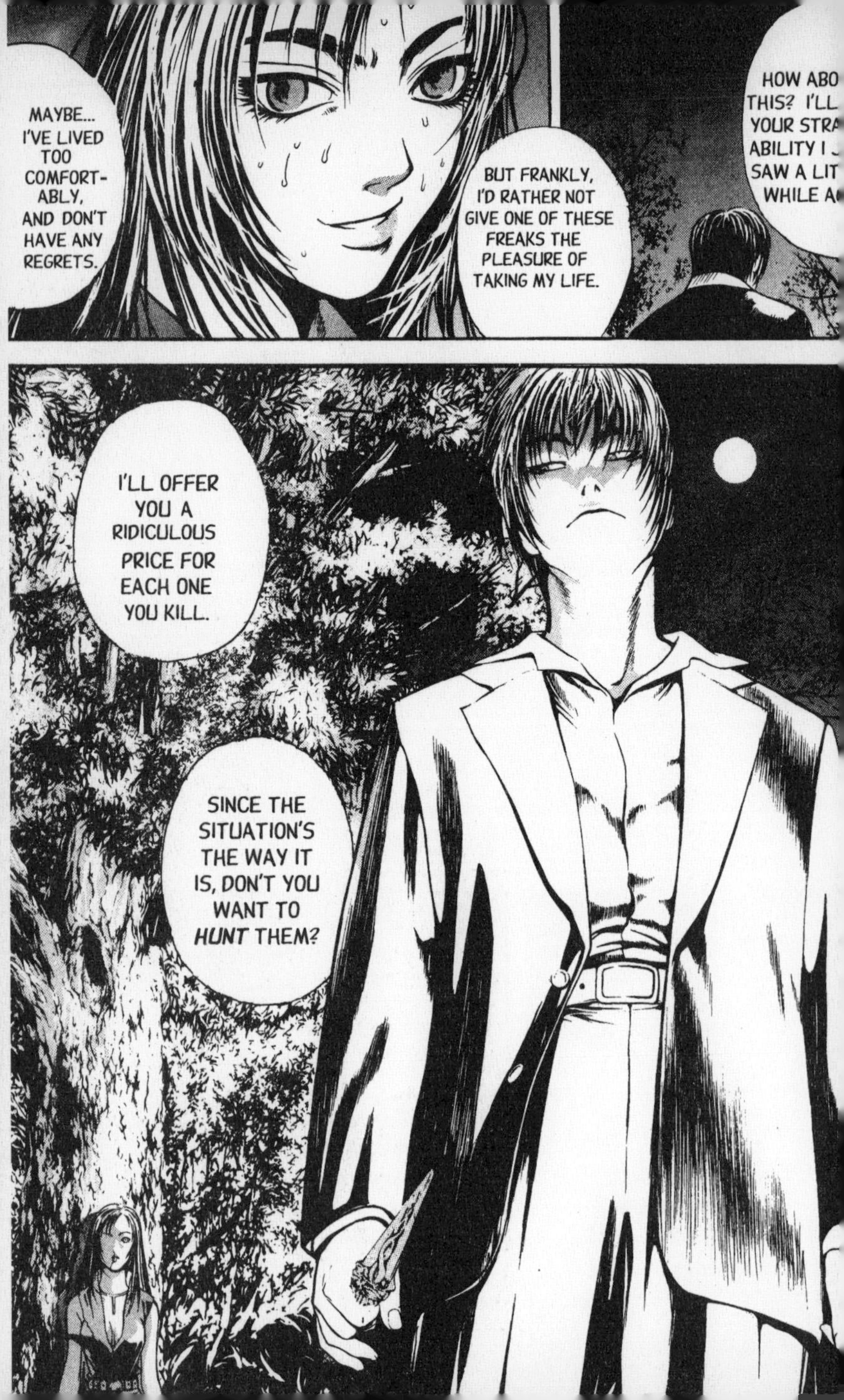
MAYBE... I'VE LIVED TOO COMFORT-ABLY, AND DON'T HAVE ANY REGRETS.
BUT FRANKLY, I'D RATHER NOT GIVE ONE OF THESE FREAKS THE PLEASURE OF TAKING MY LIFE.
HOW ABO THIS? I'LL YOUR STRA ABILITY I SAW A LIT WHILE A
I'LL OFFER YOU A RIDICULOUS PRICE FOR EACH ONE YOU KILL.
SINCE THE SITUATION'S THE WAY IT IS, DON'T YOU WANT TO *HUNT* THEM?

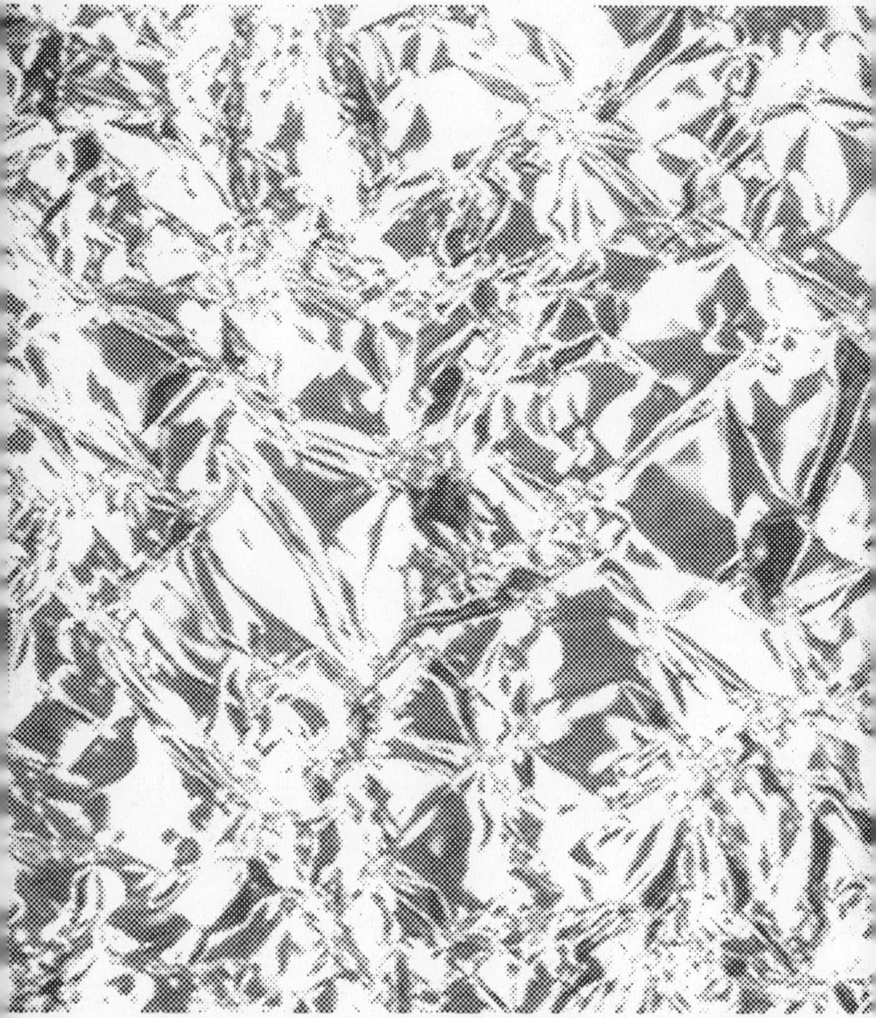

CHAPTER 2
THE PURITY OF 18

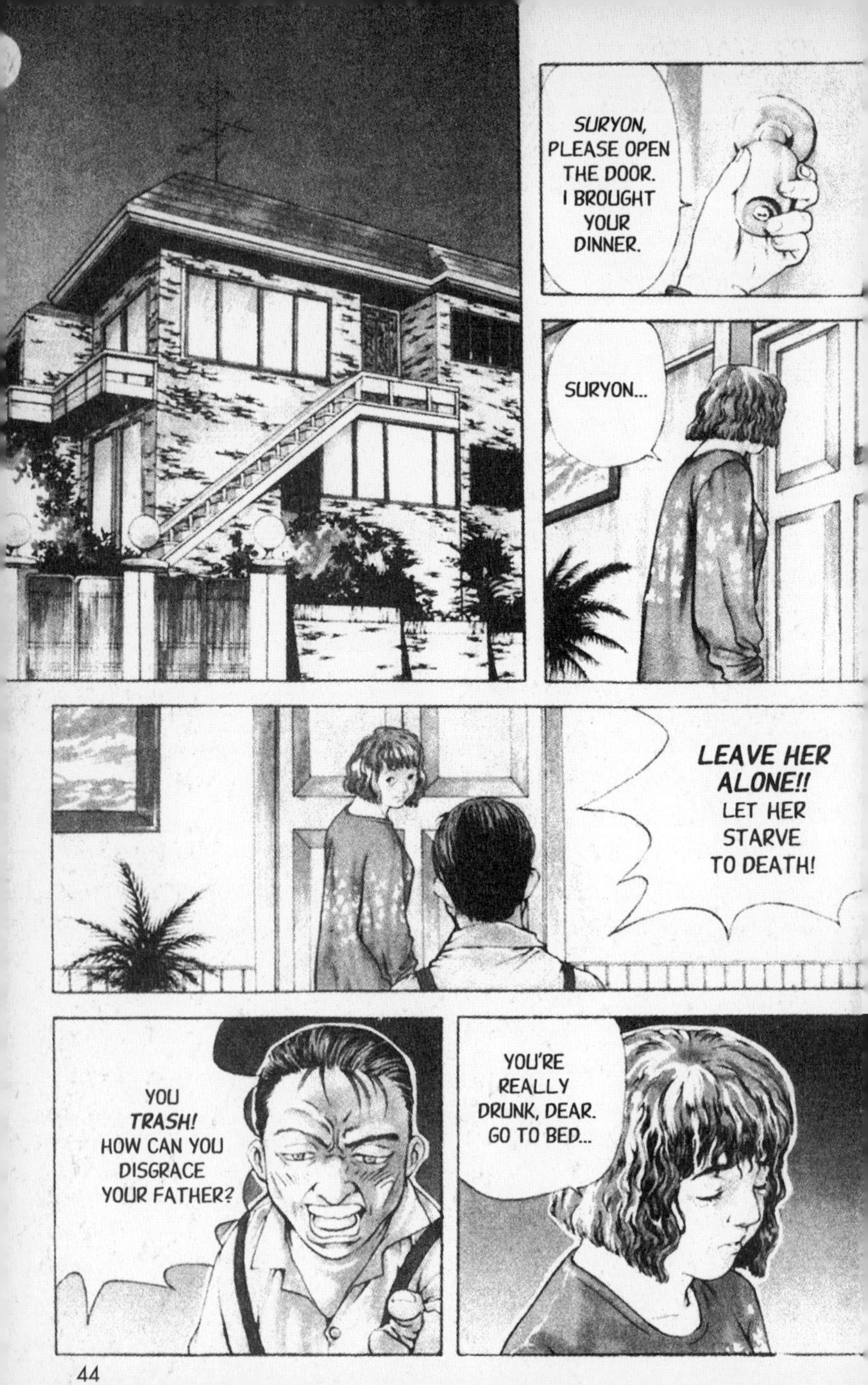
SURYON, PLEASE OPEN THE DOOR. I BROUGHT YOUR DINNER.
SURYON...
LEAVE HER ALONE!! LET HER STARVE TO DEATH!
YOU TRASH! HOW CAN YOU DISGRACE YOUR FATHER?
YOU'RE REALLY DRUNK, DEAR. GO TO BED...

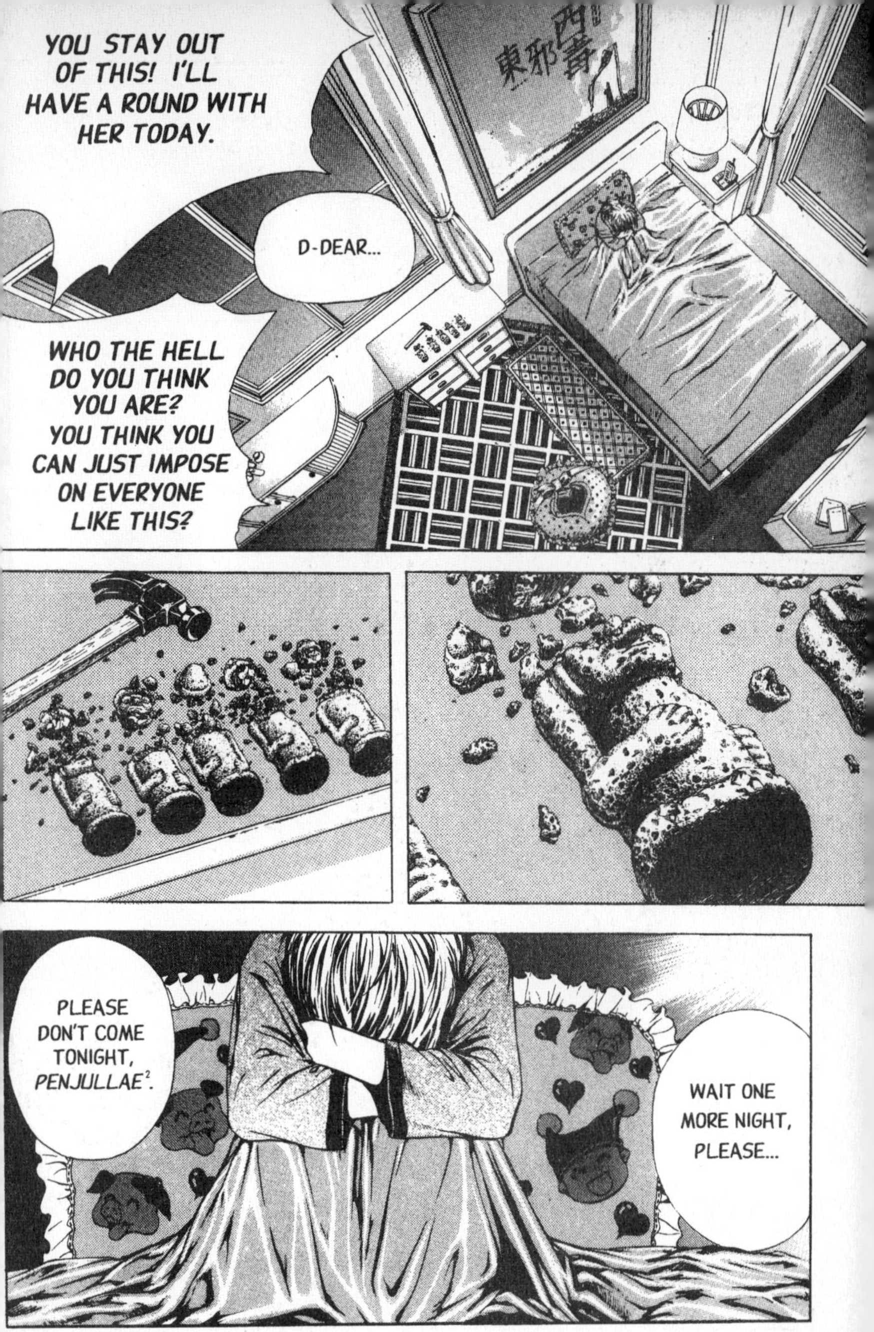

YOU STAY OUT OF THIS! I'LL HAVE A ROUND WITH HER TODAY.
D-DEAR...
WHO THE HELL DO YOU THINK YOU ARE? YOU THINK YOU CAN JUST IMPOSE ON EVERYONE LIKE THIS?
PLEASE DON'T COME TONIGHT, PENJULLAE[2].
WAIT ONE MORE NIGHT, PLEASE...

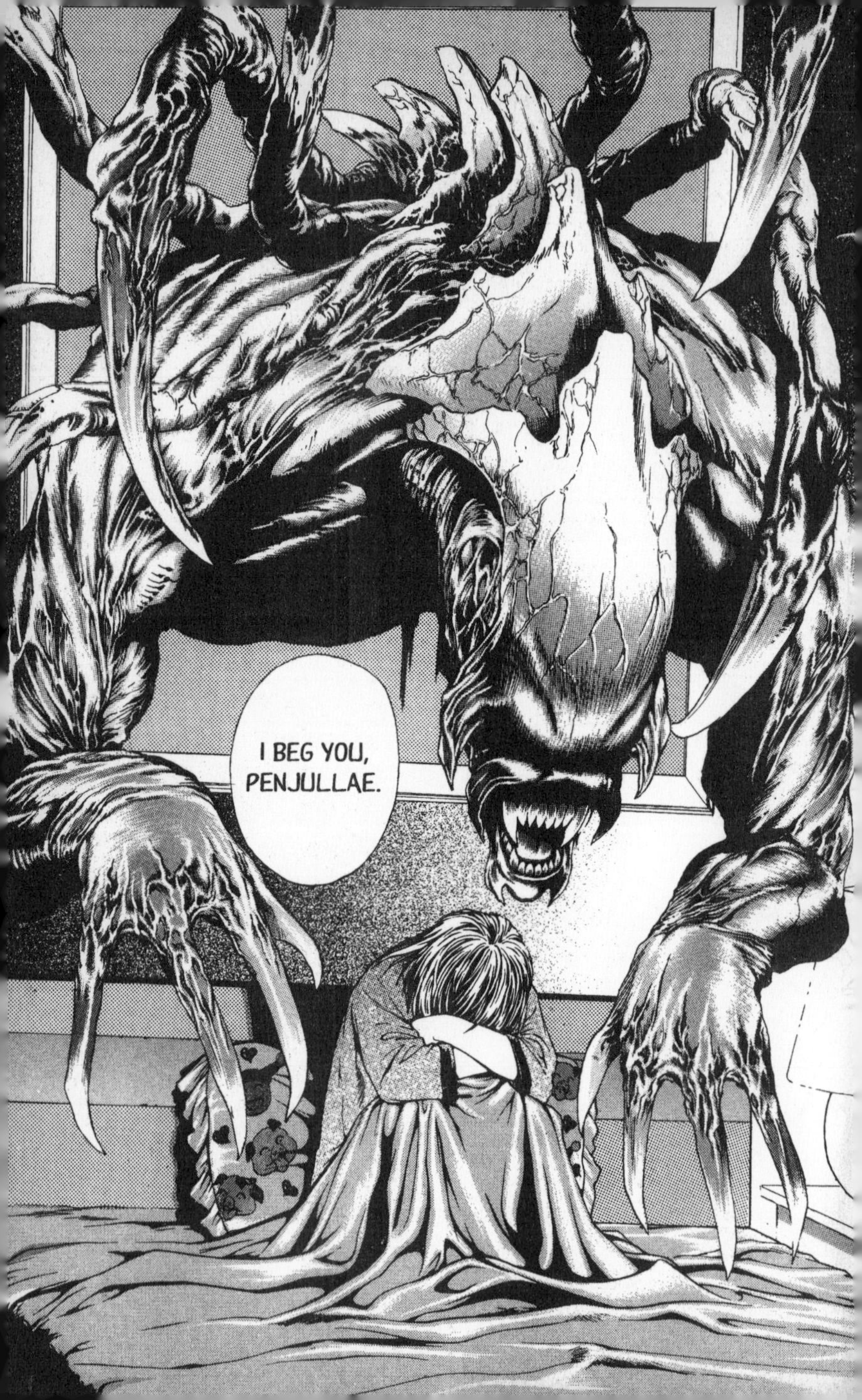
I BEG YOU, PENJULLAE.

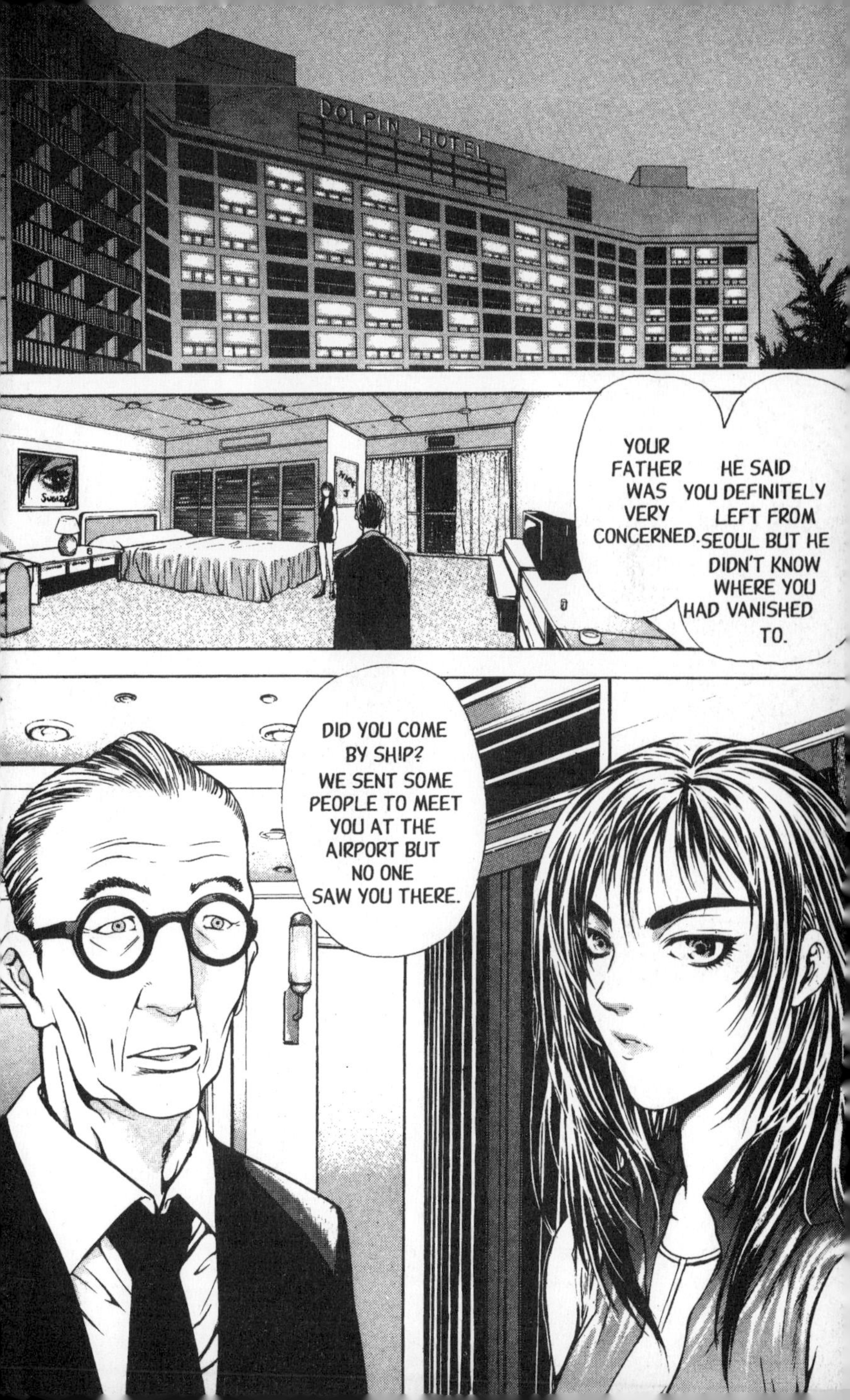
DOLPIN HOTEL
YOUR FATHER WAS VERY CONCERNED.
HE SAID YOU DEFINITELY LEFT FROM SEOUL BUT HE DIDN'T KNOW WHERE YOU HAD VANISHED TO.
DID YOU COME BY SHIP? WE SENT SOME PEOPLE TO MEET YOU AT THE AIRPORT BUT NO ONE SAW YOU THERE.

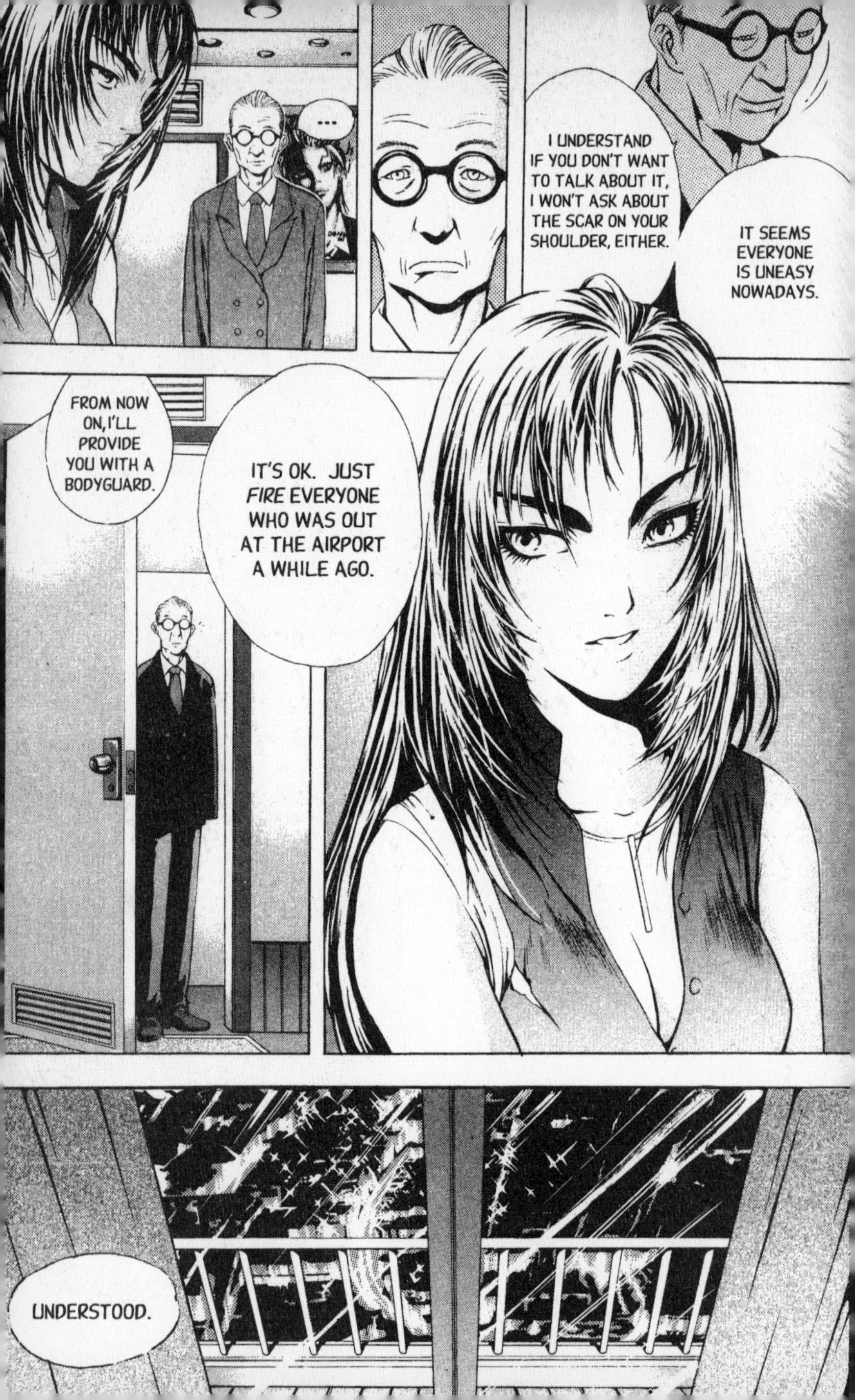
...
I UNDERSTAND IF YOU DON'T WANT TO TALK ABOUT IT, I WON'T ASK ABOUT THE SCAR ON YOUR SHOULDER, EITHER.
IT SEEMS EVERYONE IS UNEASY NOWADAYS.
FROM NOW ON, I'LL PROVIDE YOU WITH A BODYGUARD.
IT'S OK. JUST *FIRE* EVERYONE WHO WAS OUT AT THE AIRPORT A WHILE AGO.
UNDERSTOOD.

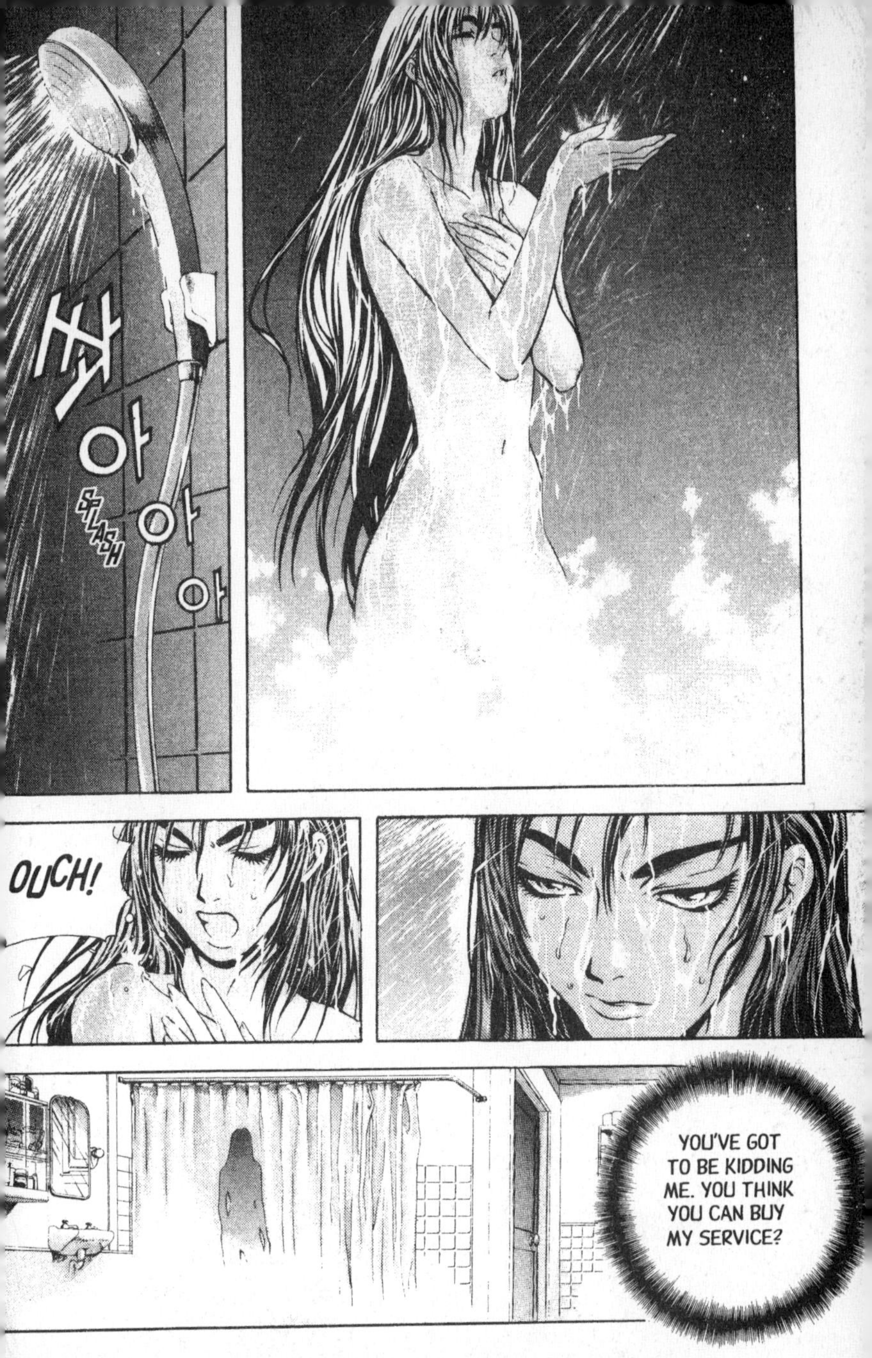
쏴아아아
SPLASH
OUCH!
YOU'VE GOT TO BE KIDDING ME. YOU THINK YOU CAN BUY MY SERVICE?

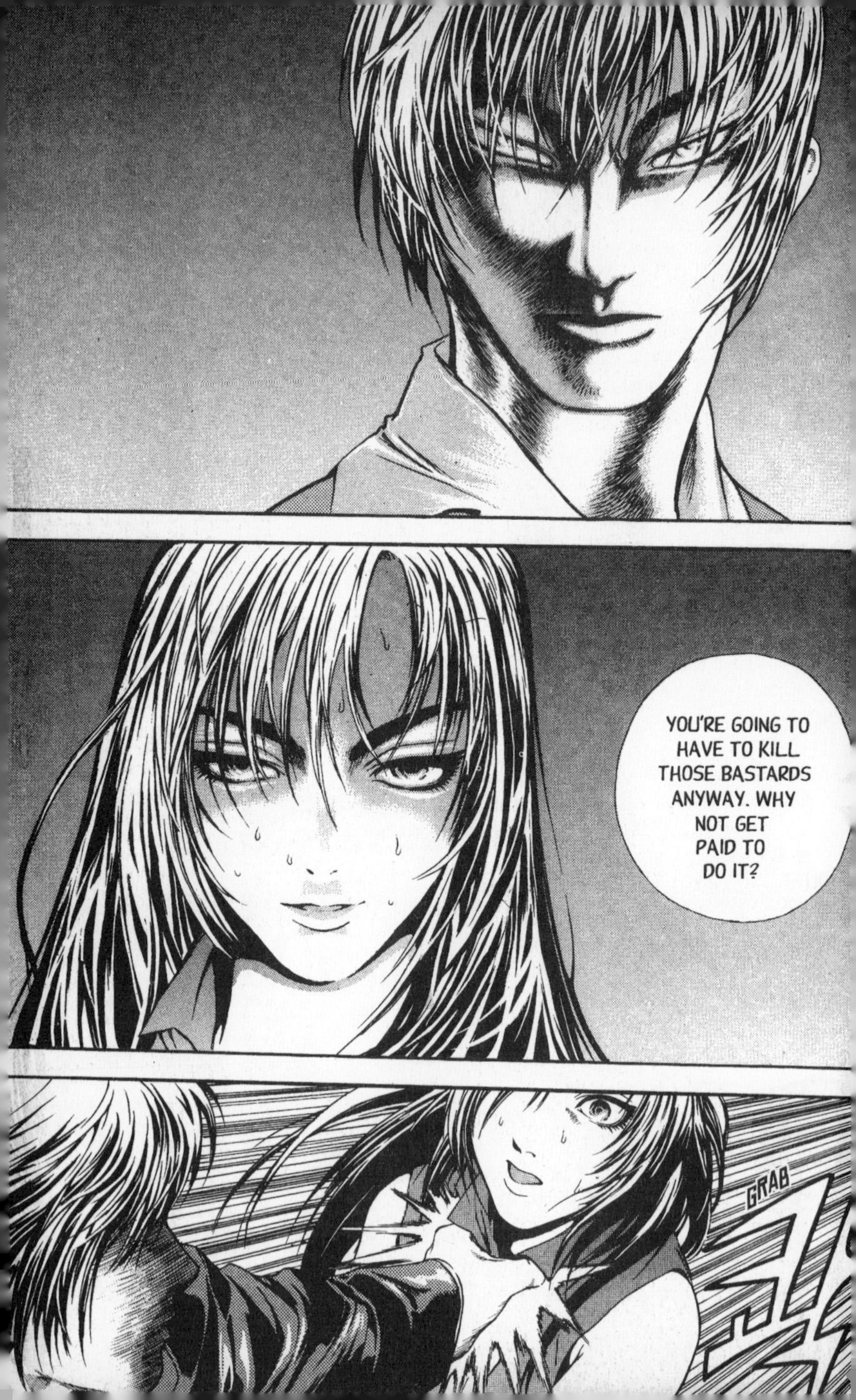
YOU'RE GOING TO HAVE TO KILL THOSE BASTARDS ANYWAY. WHY NOT GET PAID TO DO IT?
GRAB

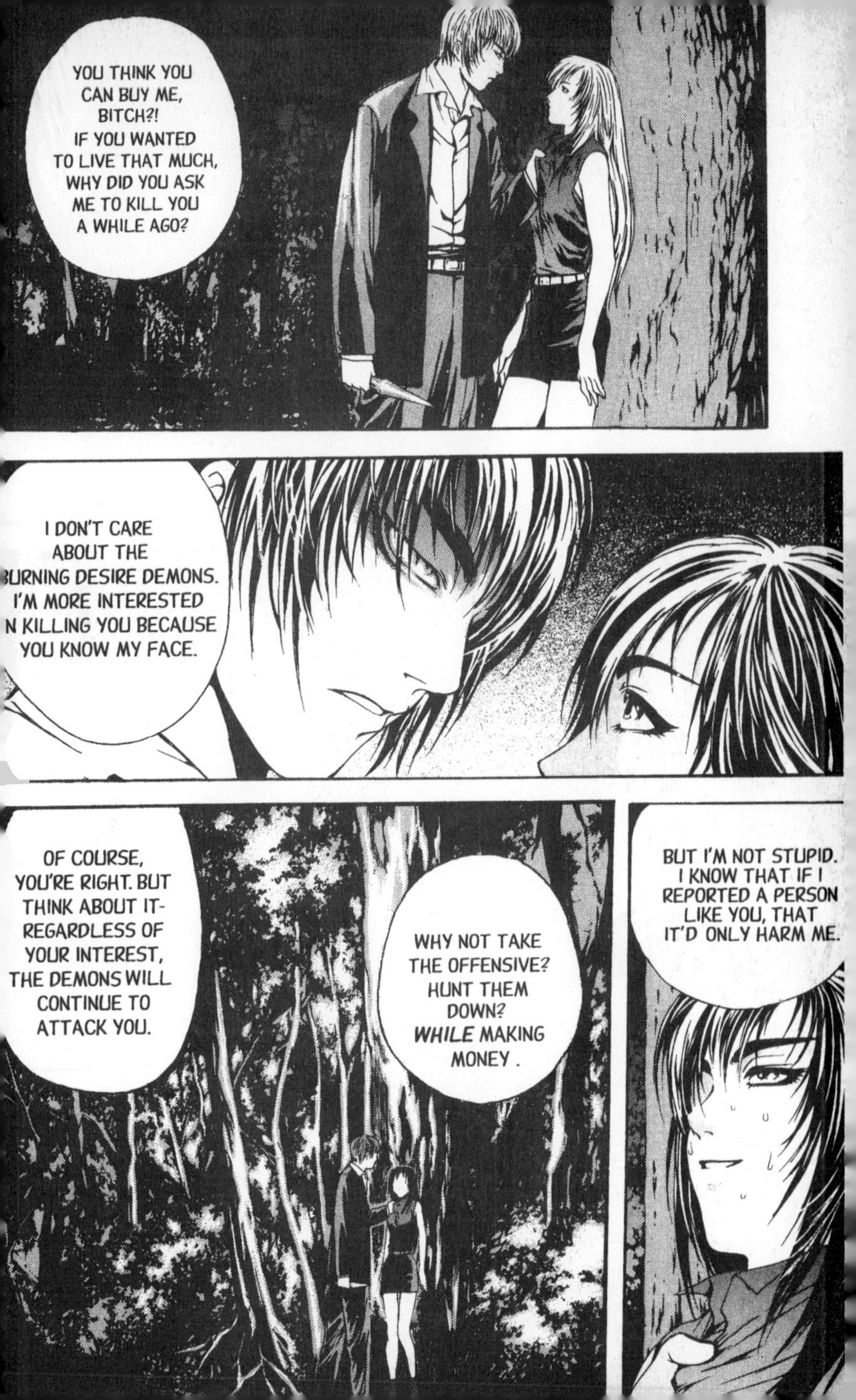
YOU THINK YOU CAN BUY ME, BITCH?! IF YOU WANTED TO LIVE THAT MUCH, WHY DID YOU ASK ME TO KILL YOU A WHILE AGO?
I DON'T CARE ABOUT THE BURNING DESIRE DEMONS. I'M MORE INTERESTED IN KILLING YOU BECAUSE YOU KNOW MY FACE.
OF COURSE, YOU'RE RIGHT. BUT THINK ABOUT IT- REGARDLESS OF YOUR INTEREST, THE DEMONS WILL CONTINUE TO ATTACK YOU.
WHY NOT TAKE THE OFFENSIVE? HUNT THEM DOWN? *WHILE* MAKING MONEY .
BUT I'M NOT STUPID. I KNOW THAT IF I REPORTED A PERSON LIKE YOU, THAT IT'D ONLY HARM ME.

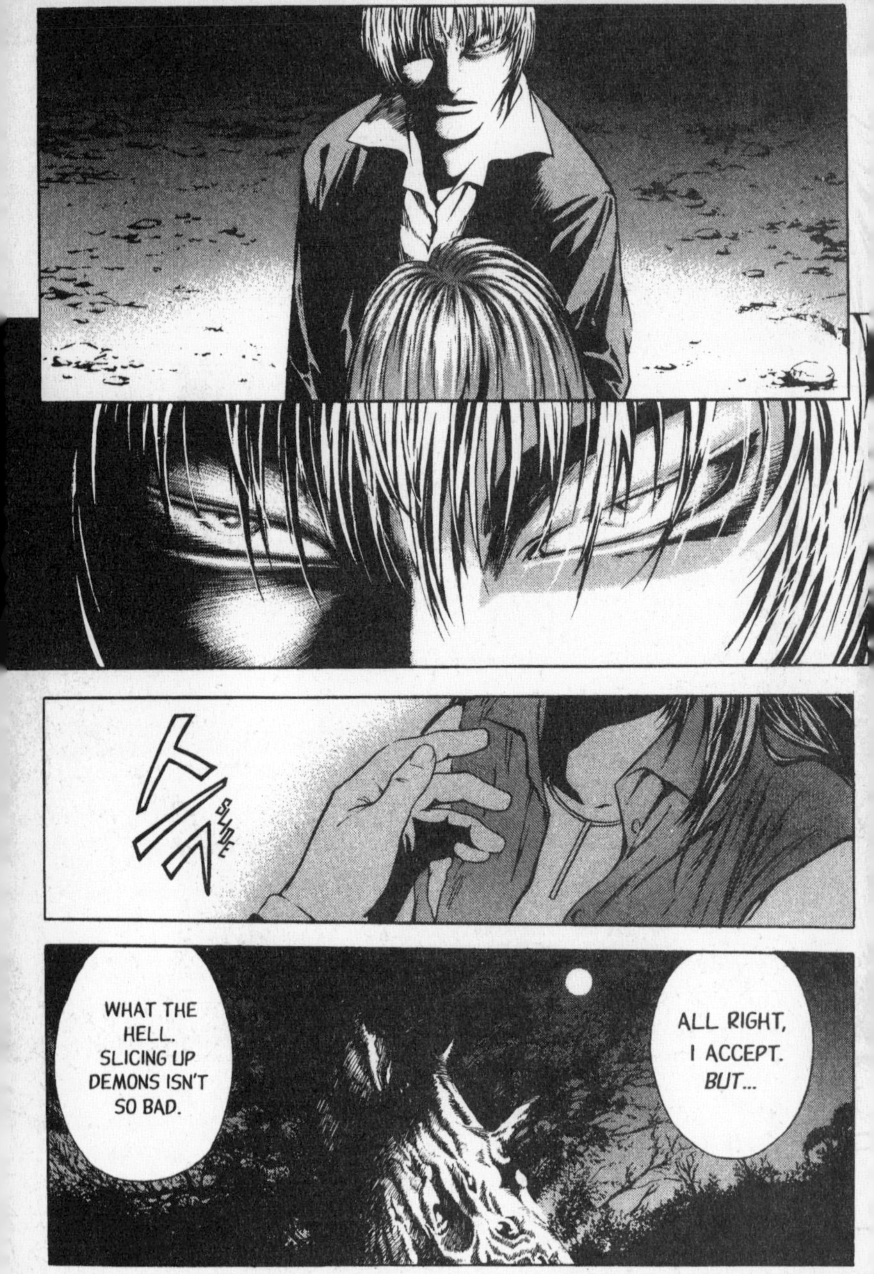
SLIDE
WHAT THE HELL. SLICING UP DEMONS ISN'T SO BAD.
ALL RIGHT, I ACCEPT. *BUT...*

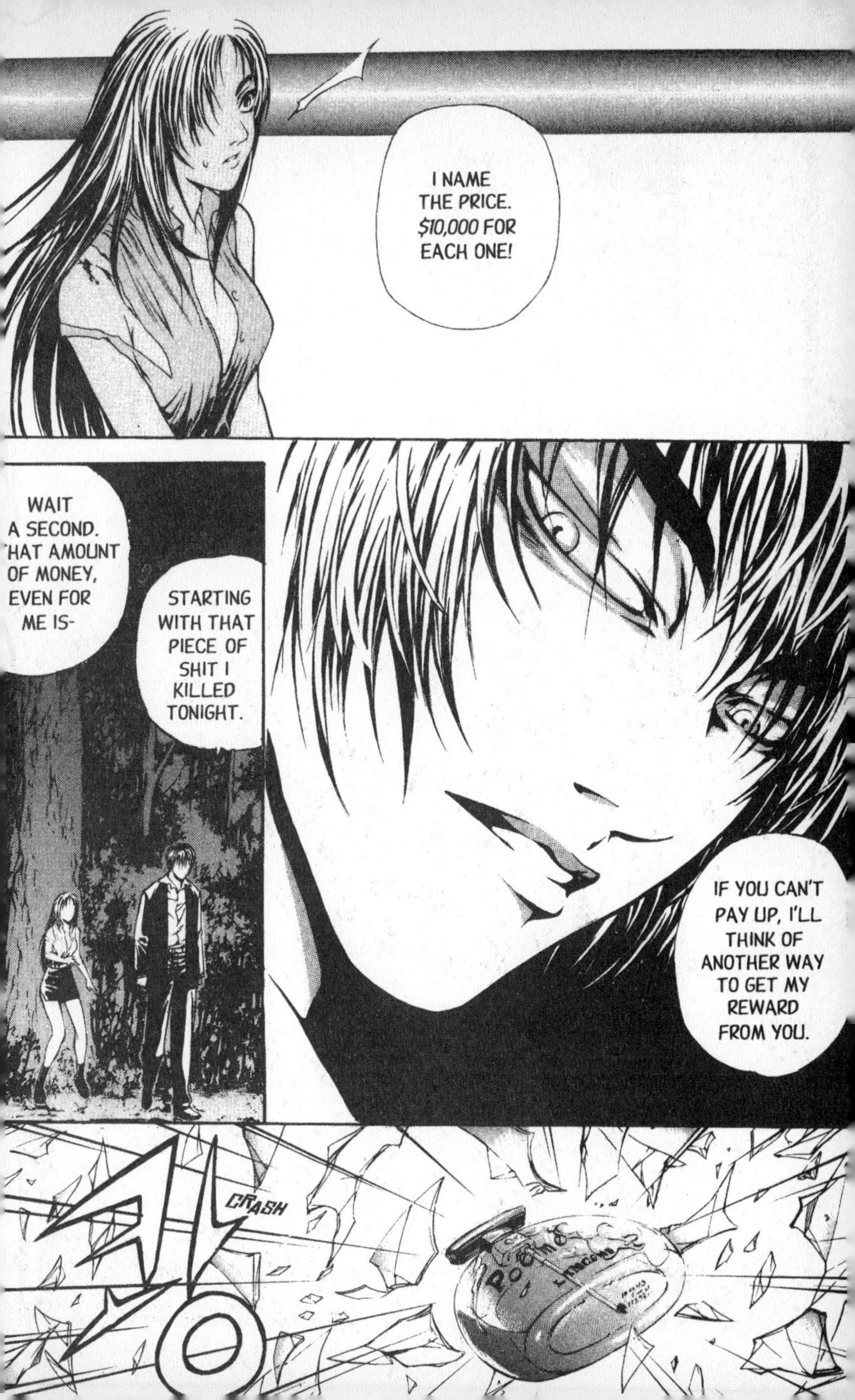
I NAME THE PRICE. $10,000 FOR EACH ONE!
WAIT A SECOND. HAT AMOUNT OF MONEY, EVEN FOR ME IS-
STARTING WITH THAT PIECE OF SHIT I KILLED TONIGHT.
IF YOU CAN'T PAY UP, I'LL THINK OF ANOTHER WAY TO GET MY REWARD FROM YOU.
CRASH

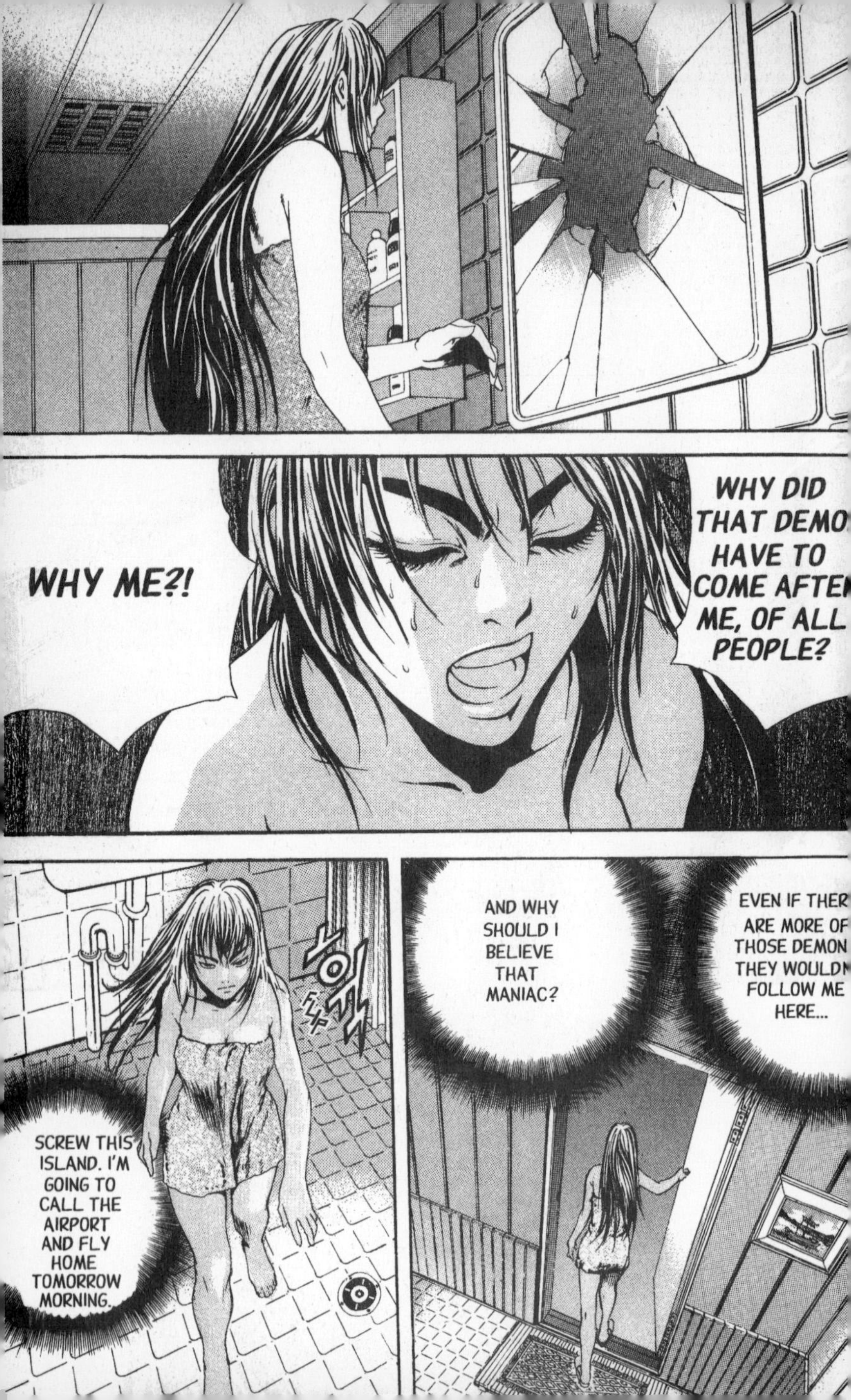
WHY ME?!
WHY DID THAT DEMO HAVE TO COME AFTE ME, OF ALL PEOPLE?
FLIP
SCREW THIS ISLAND. I'M GOING TO CALL THE AIRPORT AND FLY HOME TOMORROW MORNING.
AND WHY SHOULD I BELIEVE THAT MANIAC?
EVEN IF THER ARE MORE OF THOSE DEMON THEY WOULD FOLLOW ME HERE...

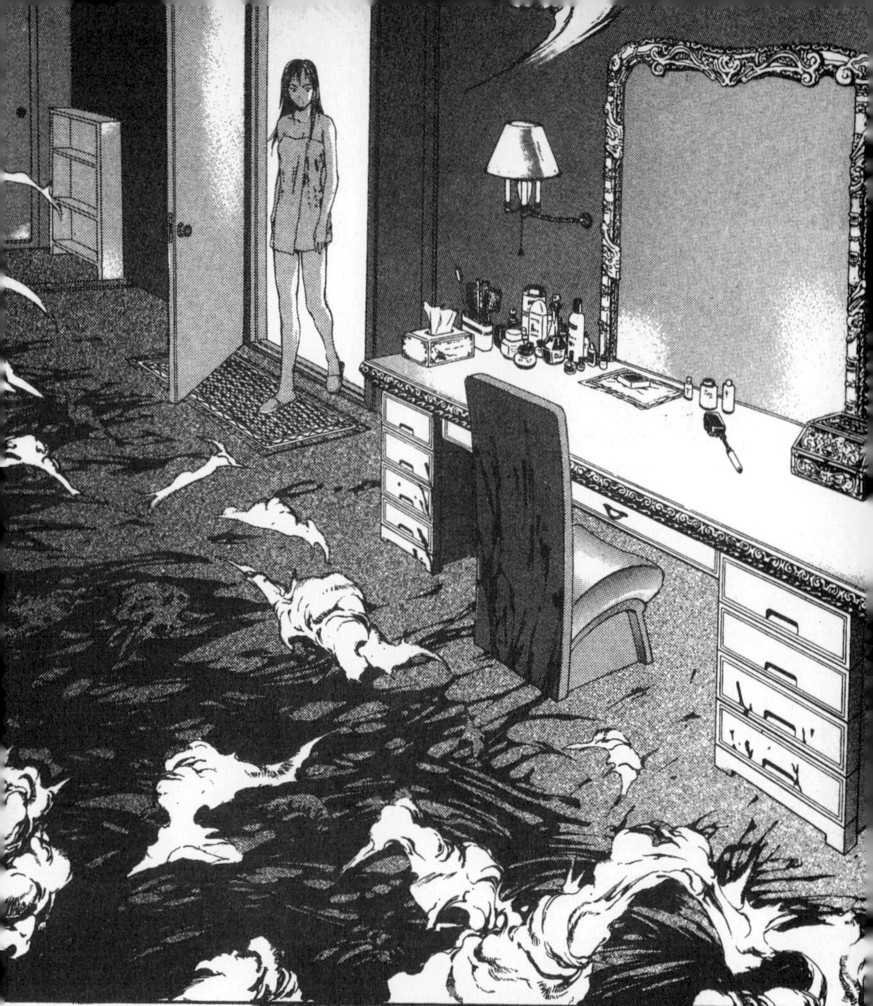
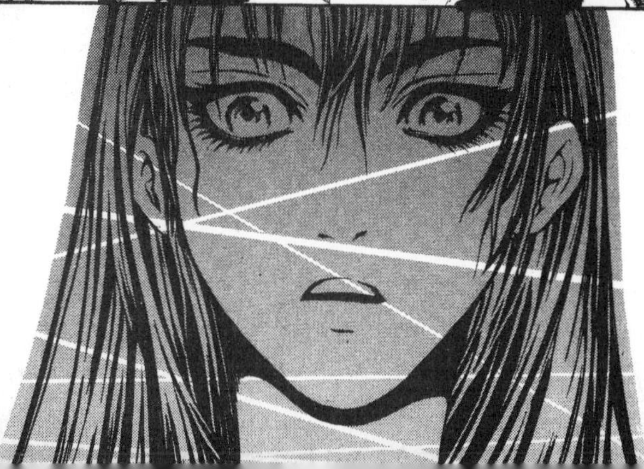

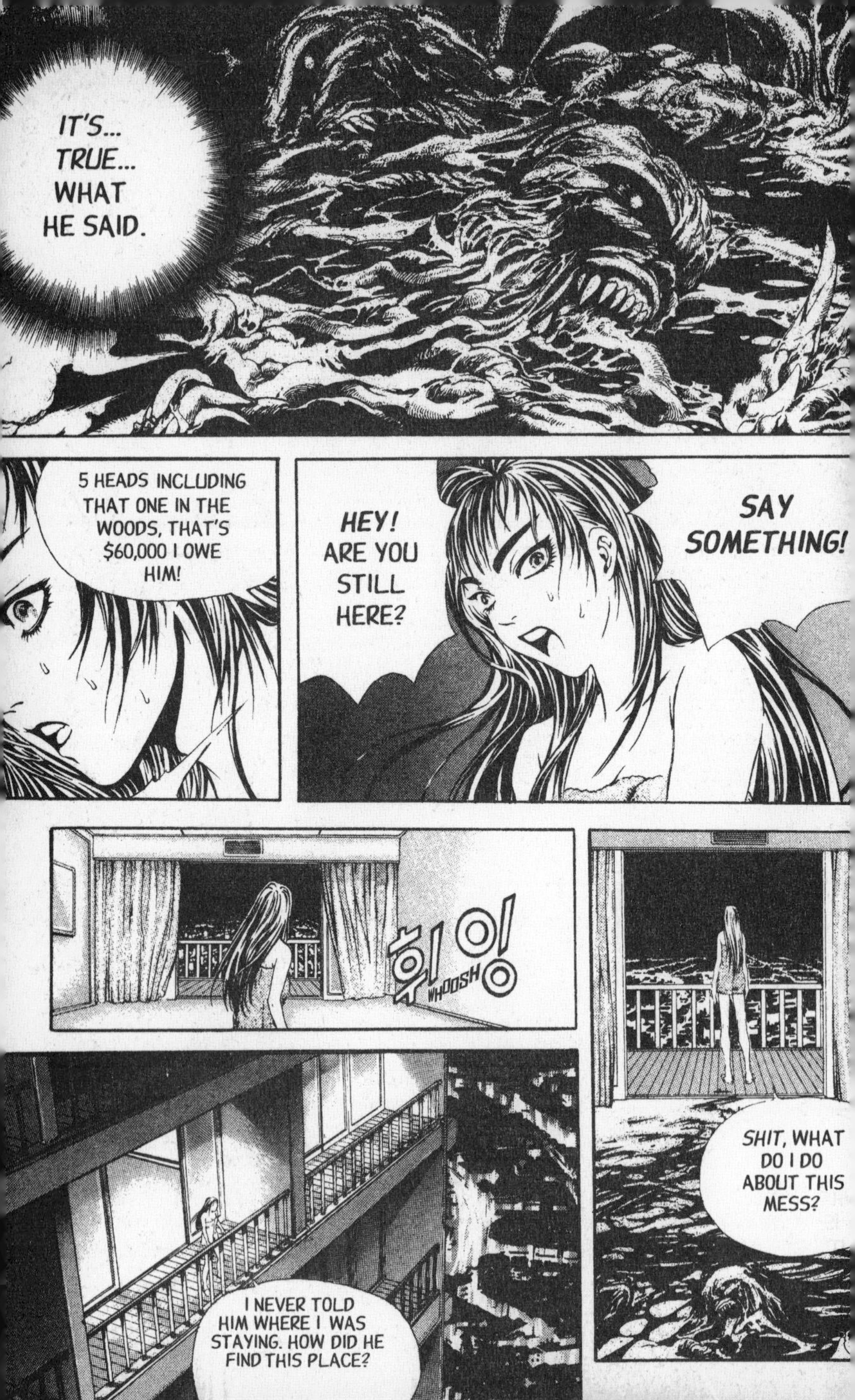
IT'S... TRUE... WHAT HE SAID.
5 HEADS INCLUDING THAT ONE IN THE WOODS, THAT'S $60,000 I OWE HIM!
HEY! ARE YOU STILL HERE?
SAY SOMETHING!
휘잉
WHOOSH
I NEVER TOLD HIM WHERE I WAS STAYING. HOW DID HE FIND THIS PLACE?
SHIT, WHAT DO I DO ABOUT THIS MESS?

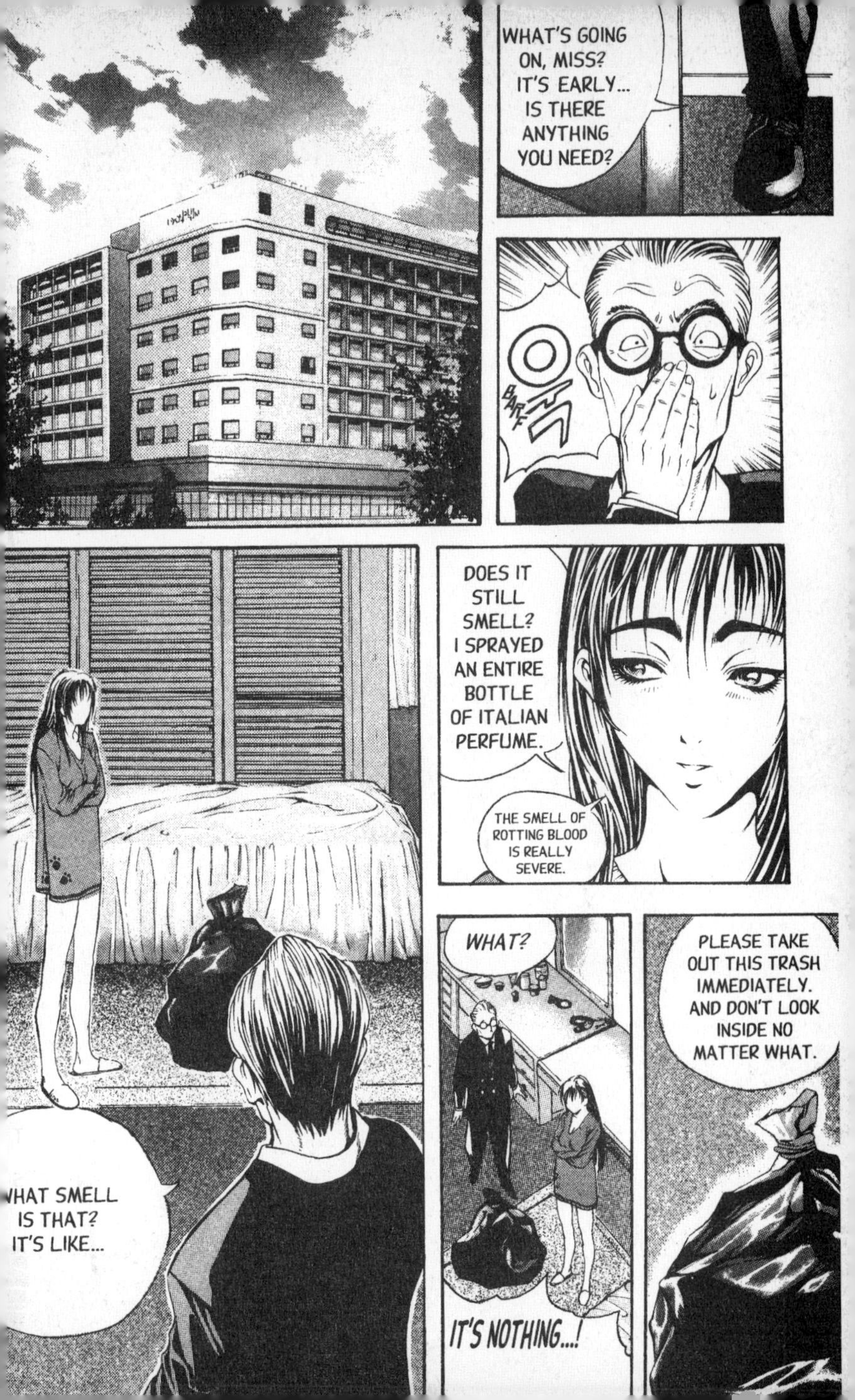
WHAT'S GOING ON, MISS? IT'S EARLY... IS THERE ANYTHING YOU NEED?
BARF
WHAT SMELL IS THAT? IT'S LIKE...
DOES IT STILL SMELL? I SPRAYED AN ENTIRE BOTTLE OF ITALIAN PERFUME.
THE SMELL OF ROTTING BLOOD IS REALLY SEVERE.
WHAT?
IT'S NOTHING...!
PLEASE TAKE OUT THIS TRASH IMMEDIATELY. AND DON'T LOOK INSIDE NO MATTER WHAT.

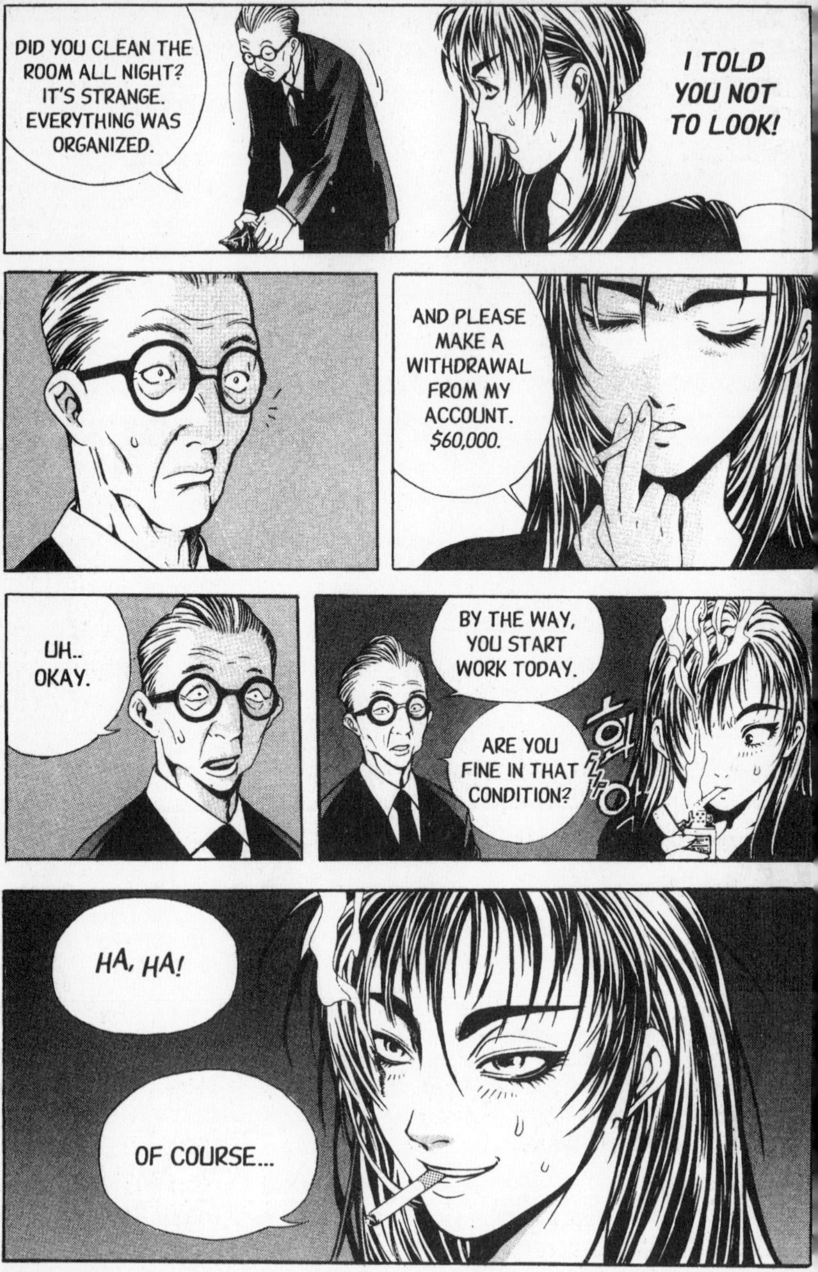
DID YOU CLEAN THE ROOM ALL NIGHT? IT'S STRANGE. EVERYTHING WAS ORGANIZED.
I TOLD YOU NOT TO LOOK!
AND PLEASE MAKE A WITHDRAWAL FROM MY ACCOUNT. $60,000.
UH.. OKAY.
BY THE WAY, YOU START WORK TODAY.
ARE YOU FINE IN THAT CONDITION?
HA, HA!
OF COURSE...

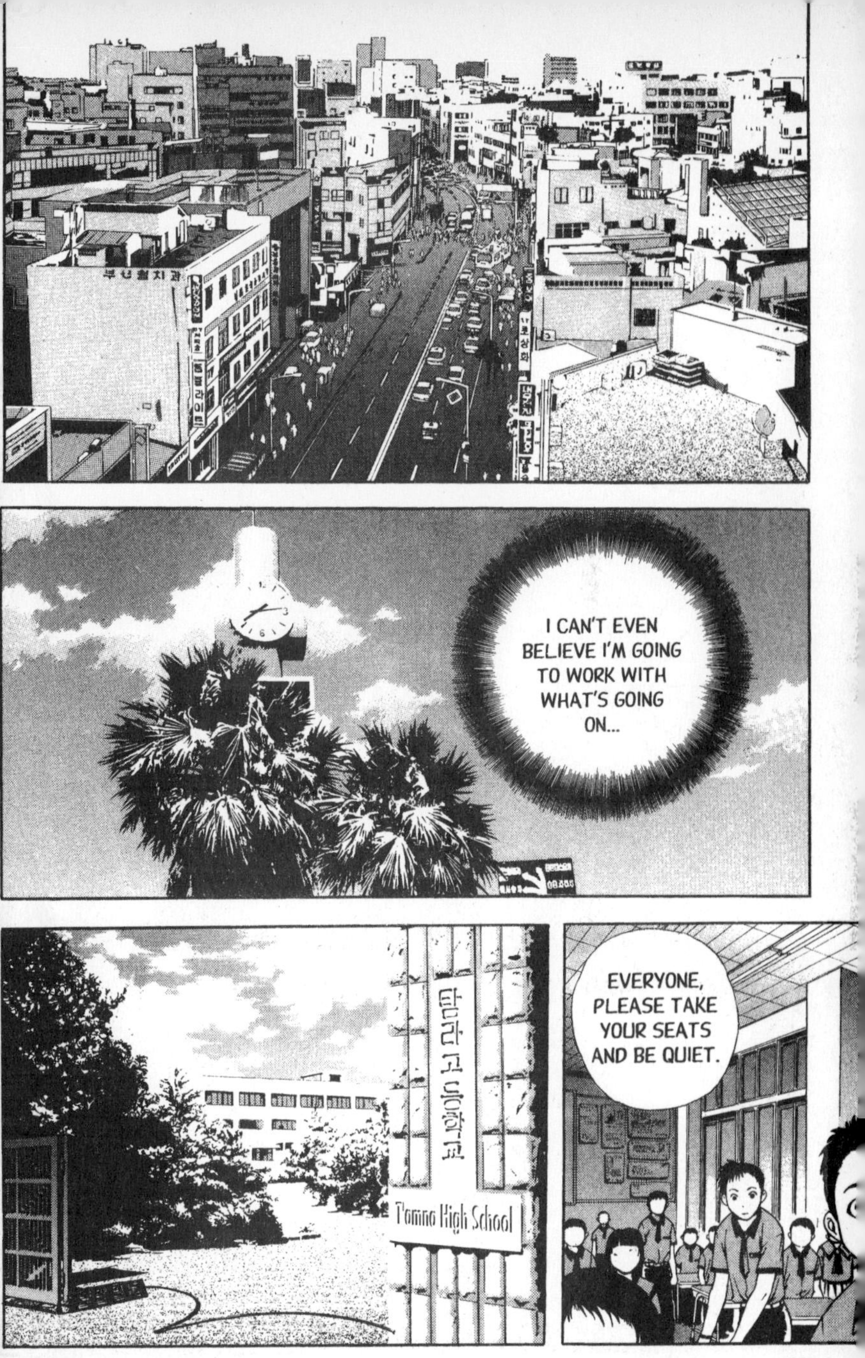
I CAN'T EVEN BELIEVE I'M GOING TO WORK WITH WHAT'S GOING ON...
탐라고등학교
Tamna High School
EVERYONE, PLEASE TAKE YOUR SEATS AND BE QUIET.

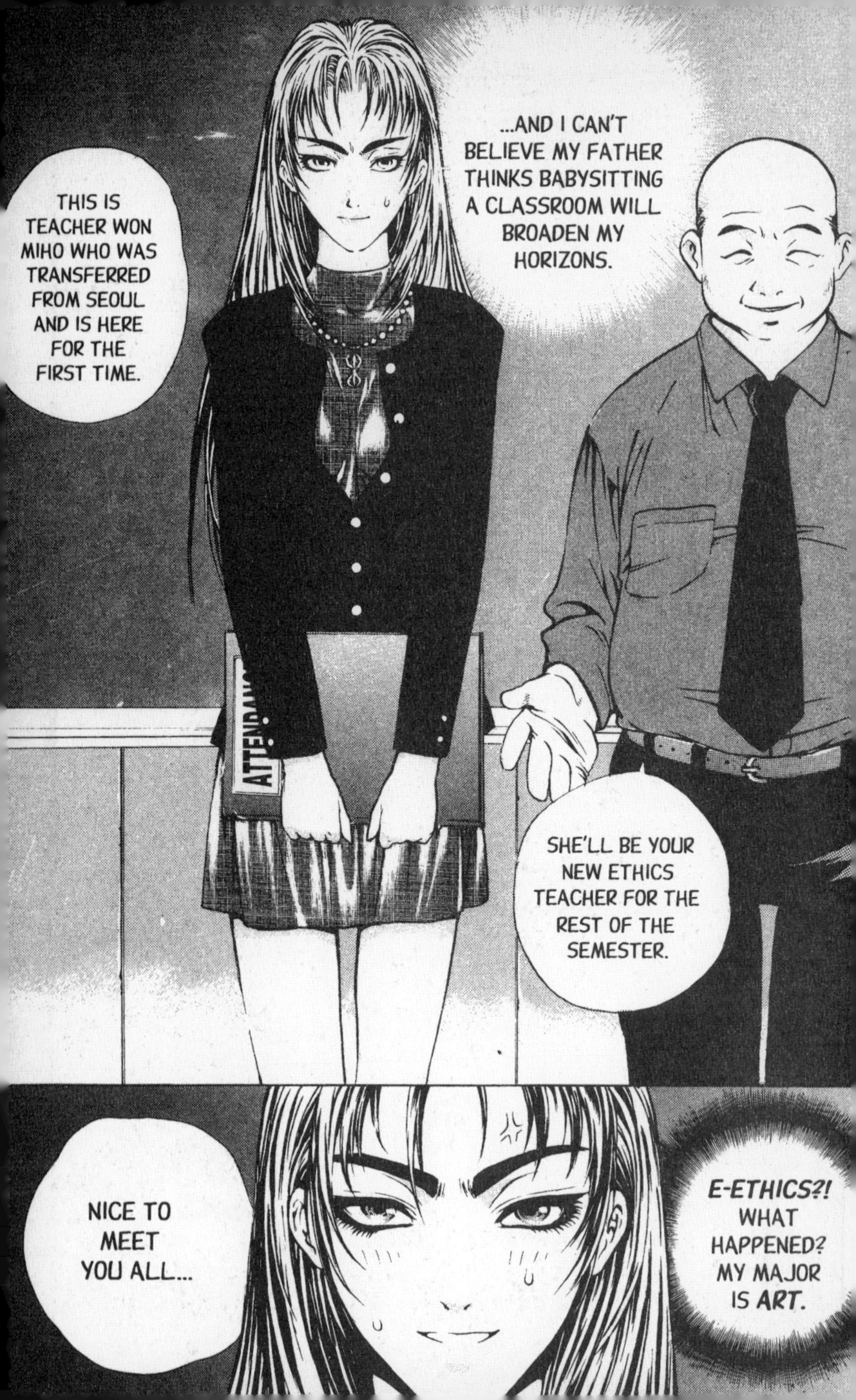
THIS IS TEACHER WON MIHO WHO WAS TRANSFERRED FROM SEOUL AND IS HERE FOR THE FIRST TIME.
...AND I CAN'T BELIEVE MY FATHER THINKS BABYSITTING A CLASSROOM WILL BROADEN MY HORIZONS.
ATTENDANCE
SHE'LL BE YOUR NEW ETHICS TEACHER FOR THE REST OF THE SEMESTER.
NICE TO MEET YOU ALL...
E-ETHICS?! WHAT HAPPENED? MY MAJOR IS ART.

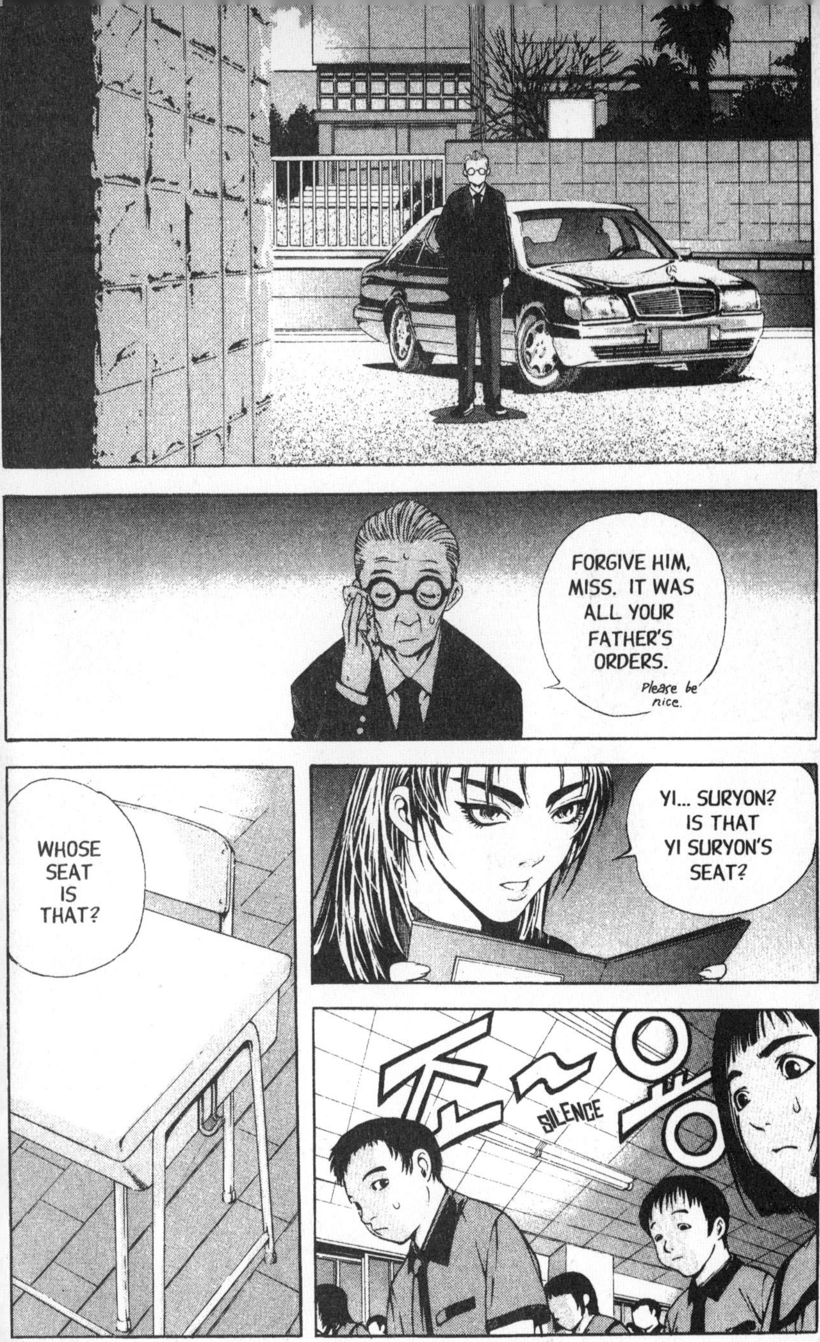
FORGIVE HIM, MISS. IT WAS ALL YOUR FATHER'S ORDERS.
Please be nice.
WHOSE SEAT IS THAT?
YI... SURYON? IS THAT YI SURYON'S SEAT?
SILENCE

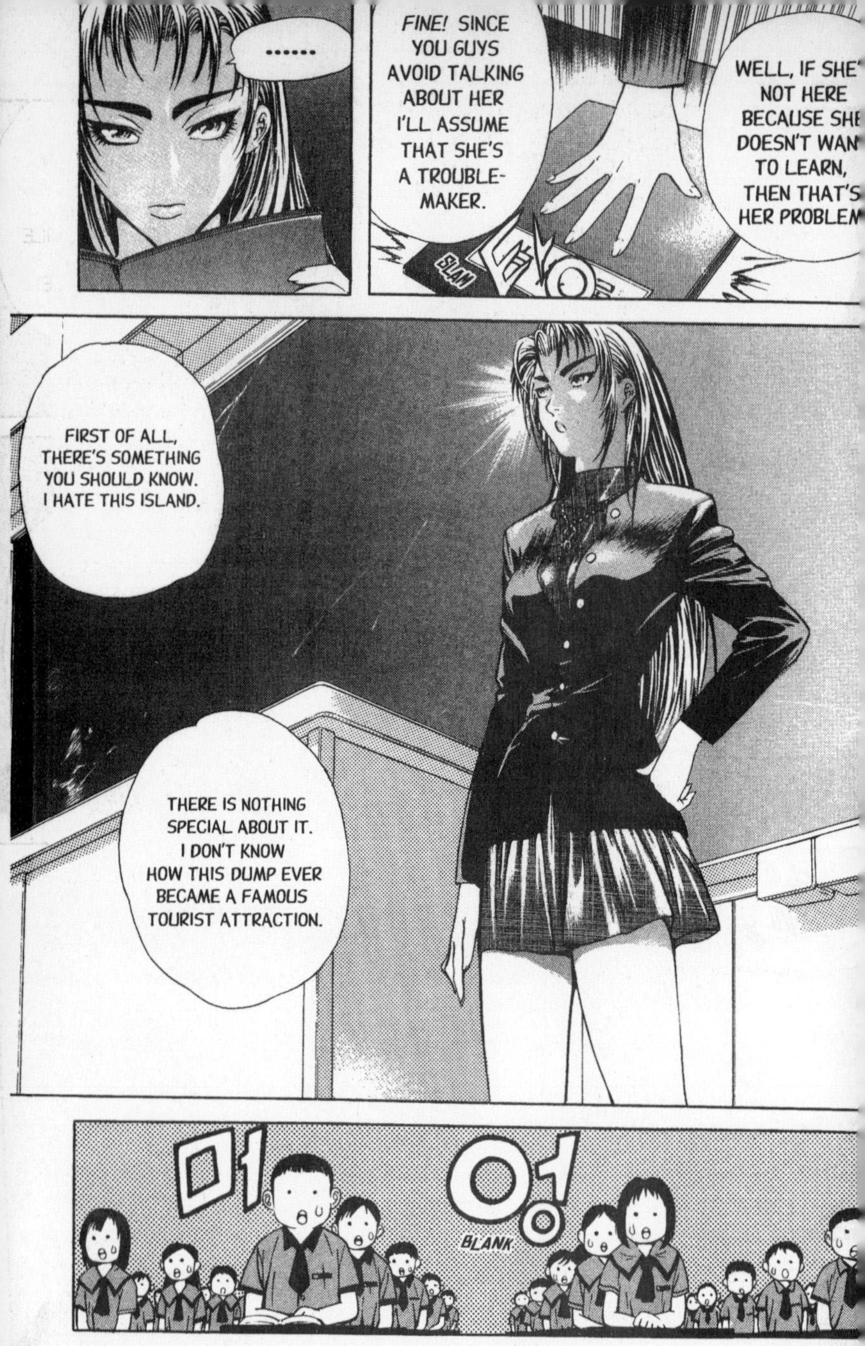
......
FINE! SINCE YOU GUYS AVOID TALKING ABOUT HER I'LL ASSUME THAT SHE'S A TROUBLE-MAKER.
SLAM
WELL, IF SHE' NOT HERE BECAUSE SHE DOESN'T WAN TO LEARN, THEN THAT'S HER PROBLEM
FIRST OF ALL, THERE'S SOMETHING YOU SHOULD KNOW. I HATE THIS ISLAND.
THERE IS NOTHING SPECIAL ABOUT IT. I DON'T KNOW HOW THIS DUMP EVER BECAME A FAMOUS TOURIST ATTRACTION.
미 이
BLANK

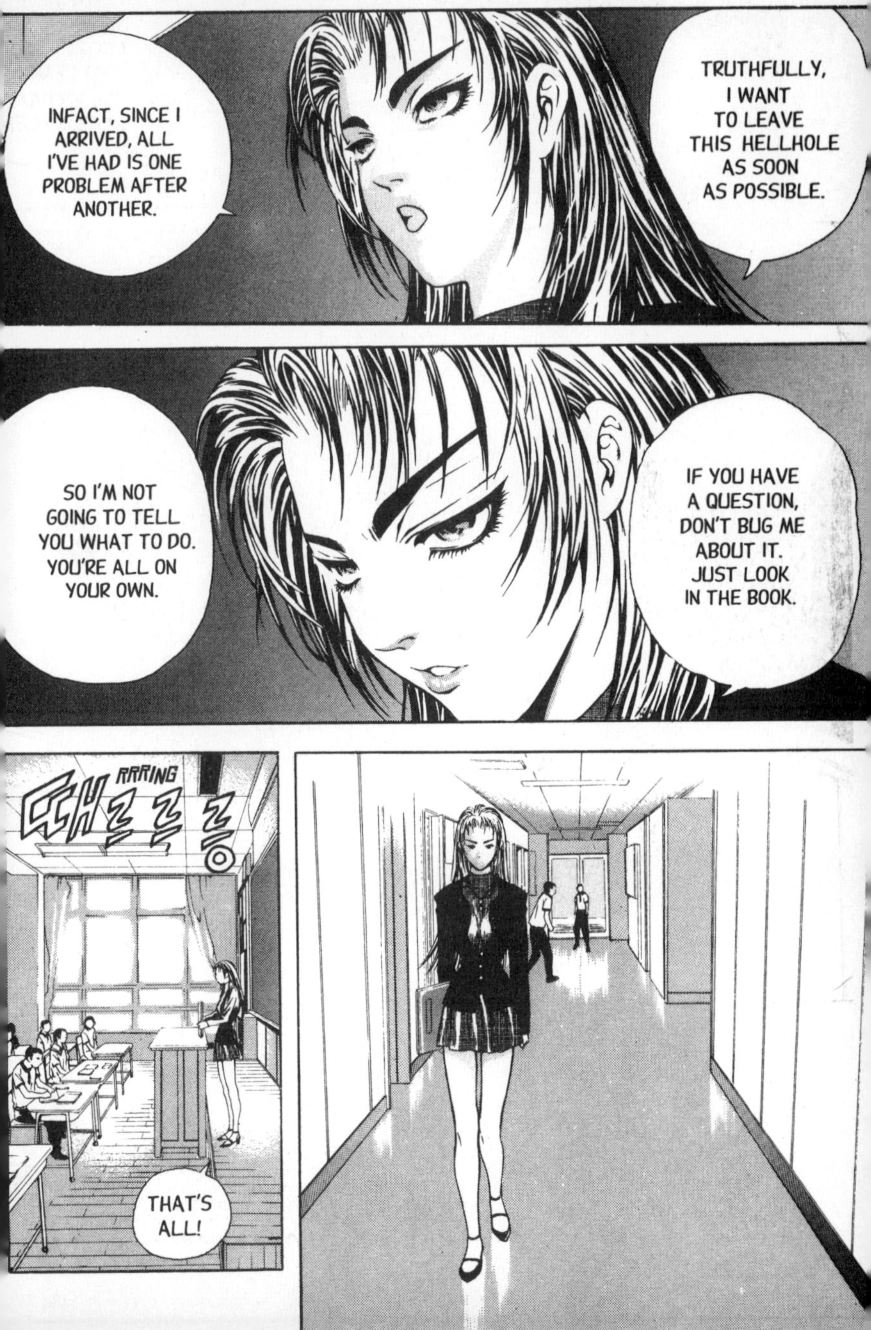
INFACT, SINCE I ARRIVED, ALL I'VE HAD IS ONE PROBLEM AFTER ANOTHER.
TRUTHFULLY, I WANT TO LEAVE THIS HELLHOLE AS SOON AS POSSIBLE.
SO I'M NOT GOING TO TELL YOU WHAT TO DO. YOU'RE ALL ON YOUR OWN.
IF YOU HAVE A QUESTION, DON'T BUG ME ABOUT IT. JUST LOOK IN THE BOOK.
RRRING
CHZZZ
THAT'S ALL!

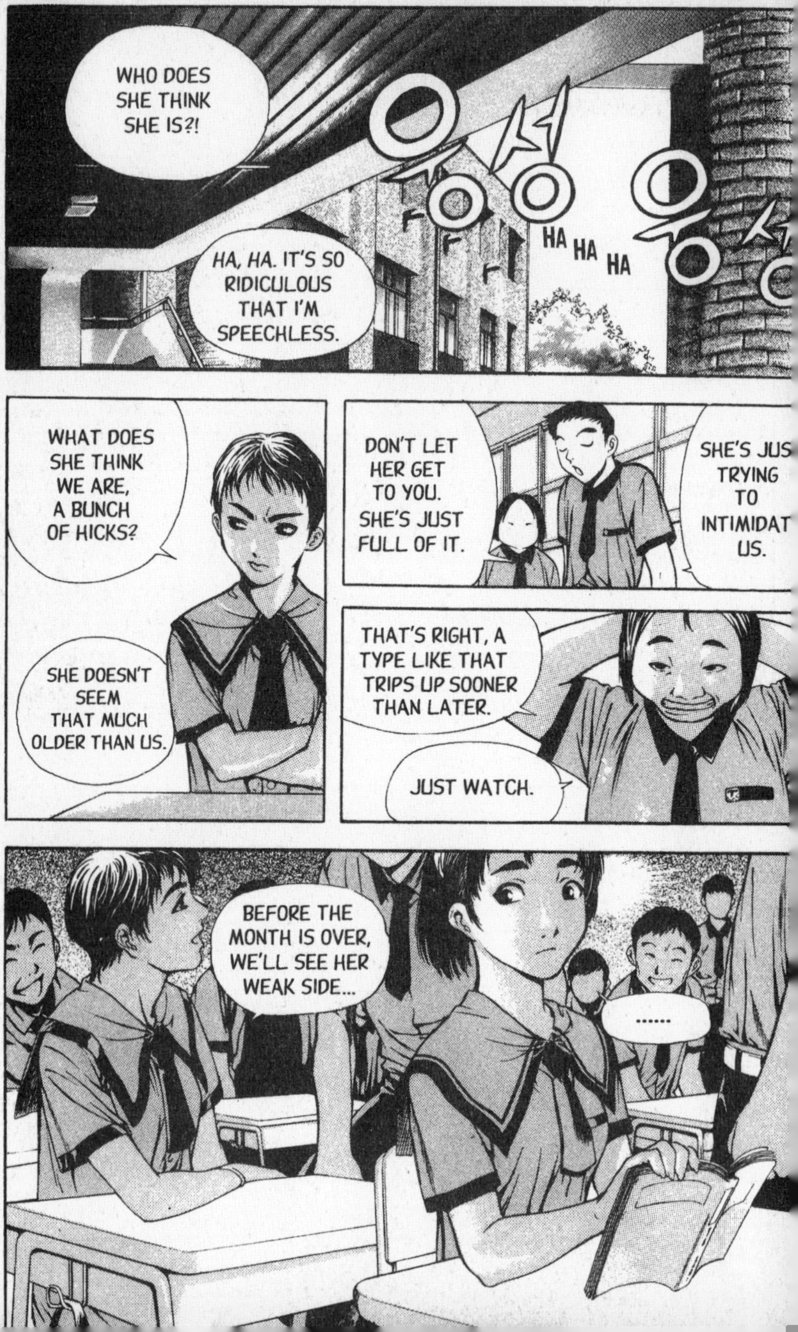
WHO DOES SHE THINK SHE IS?!
HA HA HA
HA, HA. IT'S SO RIDICULOUS THAT I'M SPEECHLESS.
WHAT DOES SHE THINK WE ARE, A BUNCH OF HICKS?
SHE DOESN'T SEEM THAT MUCH OLDER THAN US.
DON'T LET HER GET TO YOU. SHE'S JUST FULL OF IT.
SHE'S JUS TRYING TO INTIMIDAT US.
THAT'S RIGHT, A TYPE LIKE THAT TRIPS UP SOONER THAN LATER.
JUST WATCH.
BEFORE THE MONTH IS OVER, WE'LL SEE HER WEAK SIDE...
......

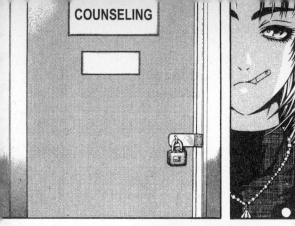

COUNSELING

비 ㅇ 그 SPIN

TEACHER, ETHICS. ALL THAT IS FINE, I GUESS. BUT HOW COME I HAVE TO DO THIS, TOO?

철 컹 CLICK CLICK CLICK 철 컹

UH, TEACHER.

IT'S ABOUT SURYON WHO'S ABSENT TODAY.

AH, YOU'RE FROM MY CLASS. IT'S OK, CAN'T BE BOTHERED BY A STUDENT WHO'S ABSENT.

MISS WON...

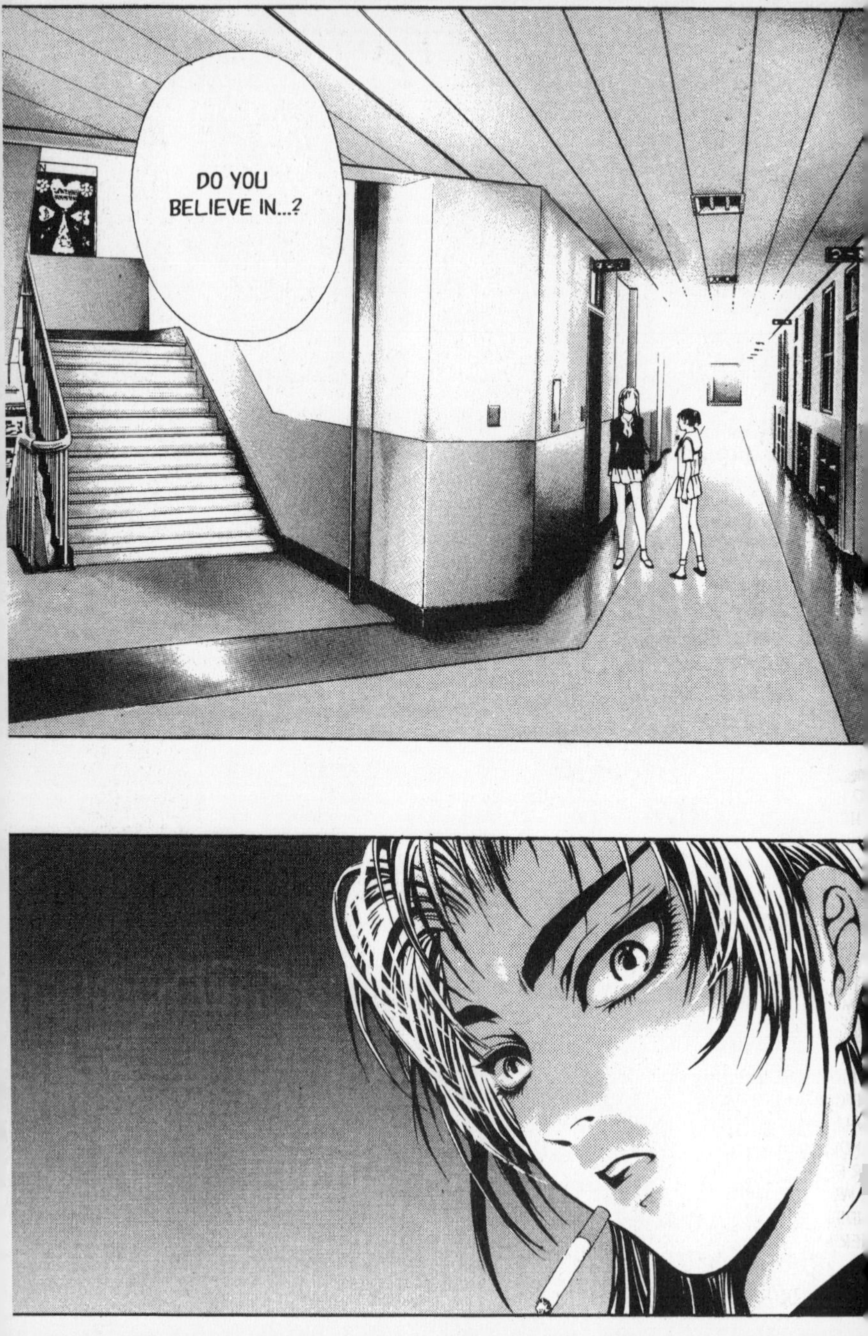
DO YOU BELIEVE IN...?

CHAPTER 3

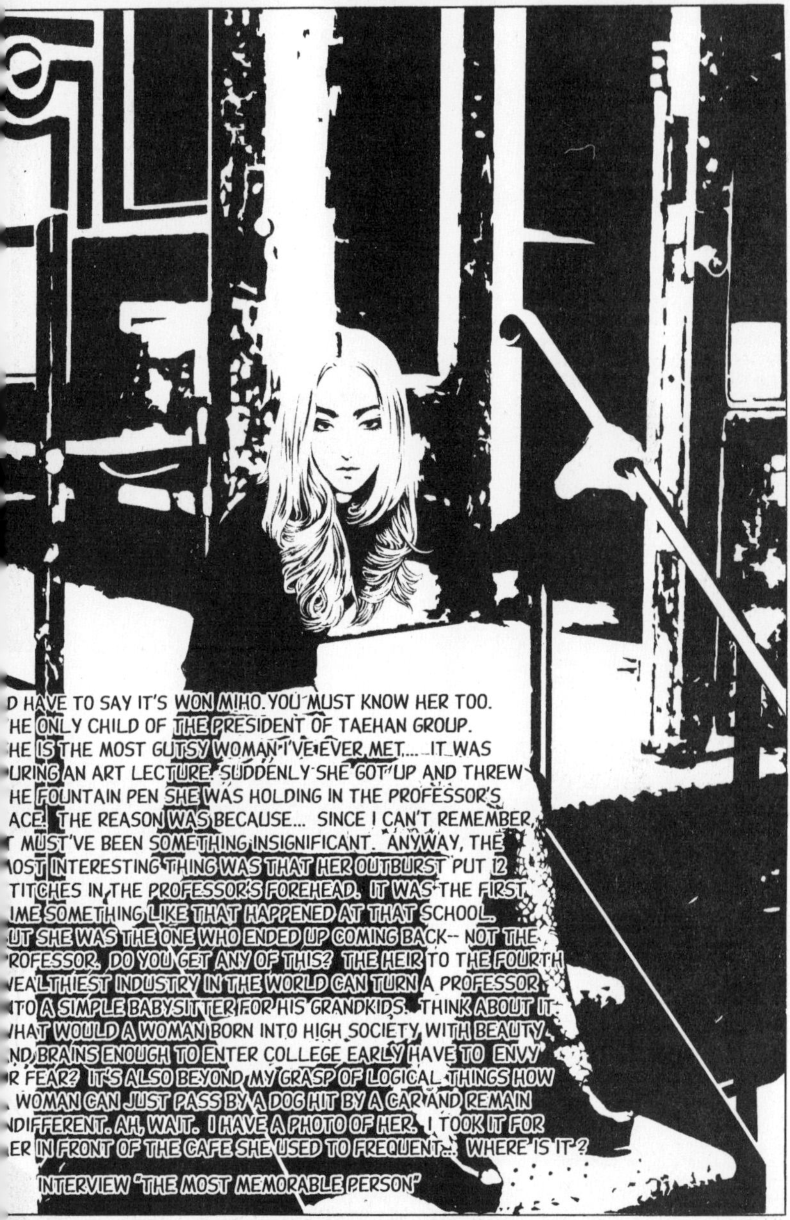
D HAVE TO SAY IT'S WON MIHO. YOU MUST KNOW HER TOO.
HE ONLY CHILD OF THE PRESIDENT OF TAEHAN GROUP.
HE IS THE MOST GUTSY WOMAN I'VE EVER MET.... IT WAS
URING AN ART LECTURE. SUDDENLY SHE GOT UP AND THREW
HE FOUNTAIN PEN SHE WAS HOLDING IN THE PROFESSOR'S
ACE! THE REASON WAS BECAUSE... SINCE I CAN'T REMEMBER,
T MUST'VE BEEN SOMETHING INSIGNIFICANT. ANYWAY, THE
OST INTERESTING THING WAS THAT HER OUTBURST PUT 12
TITCHES IN THE PROFESSOR'S FOREHEAD. IT WAS THE FIRST
IME SOMETHING LIKE THAT HAPPENED AT THAT SCHOOL.
UT SHE WAS THE ONE WHO ENDED UP COMING BACK-- NOT THE
ROFESSOR. DO YOU GET ANY OF THIS? THE HEIR TO THE FOURTH
EALTHIEST INDUSTRY IN THE WORLD CAN TURN A PROFESSOR
TO A SIMPLE BABYSITTER FOR HIS GRANDKIDS. THINK ABOUT IT.
HAT WOULD A WOMAN BORN INTO HIGH SOCIETY WITH BEAUTY
ND BRAINS ENOUGH TO ENTER COLLEGE EARLY HAVE TO ENVY
R FEAR? IT'S ALSO BEYOND MY GRASP OF LOGICAL THINGS HOW
WOMAN CAN JUST PASS BY A DOG HIT BY A CAR AND REMAIN
NDIFFERENT. AH, WAIT. I HAVE A PHOTO OF HER. I TOOK IT FOR
ER IN FRONT OF THE CAFE SHE USED TO FREQUENT... WHERE IS IT?
INTERVIEW "THE MOST MEMORABLE PERSON"

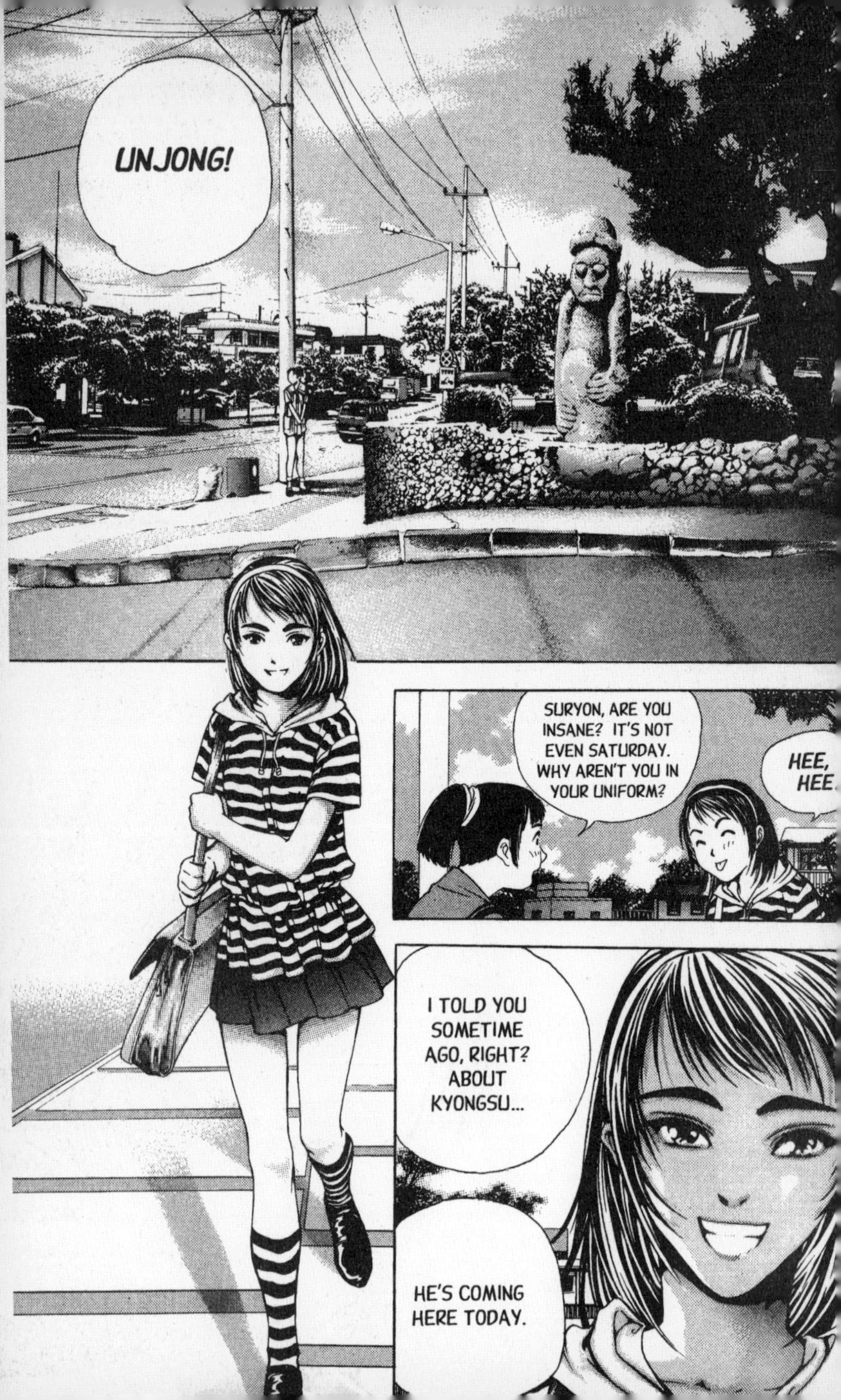
UNJONG!
SURYON, ARE YOU INSANE? IT'S NOT EVEN SATURDAY. WHY AREN'T YOU IN YOUR UNIFORM?
HEE, HEE.
I TOLD YOU SOMETIME AGO, RIGHT? ABOUT KYONGSU...
HE'S COMING HERE TODAY.

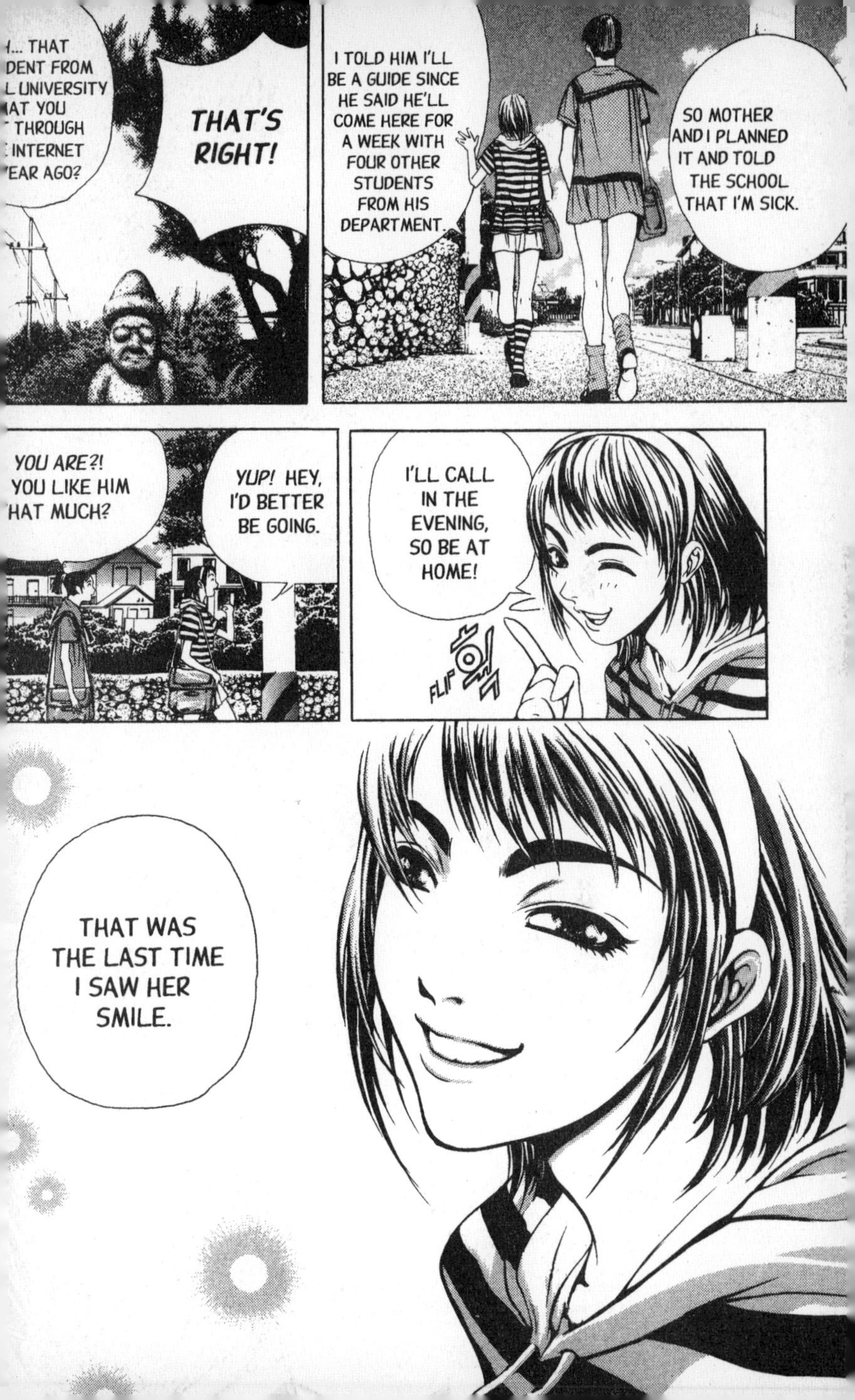

H... THAT
DENT FROM
L UNIVERSITY
AT YOU
T THROUGH
INTERNET
EAR AGO?
THAT'S RIGHT!
I TOLD HIM I'LL BE A GUIDE SINCE HE SAID HE'LL COME HERE FOR A WEEK WITH FOUR OTHER STUDENTS FROM HIS DEPARTMENT.
SO MOTHER AND I PLANNED IT AND TOLD THE SCHOOL THAT I'M SICK.
YOU ARE?! YOU LIKE HIM HAT MUCH?
YUP! HEY, I'D BETTER BE GOING.
I'LL CALL IN THE EVENING, SO BE AT HOME!
FLIP
THAT WAS THE LAST TIME I SAW HER SMILE.

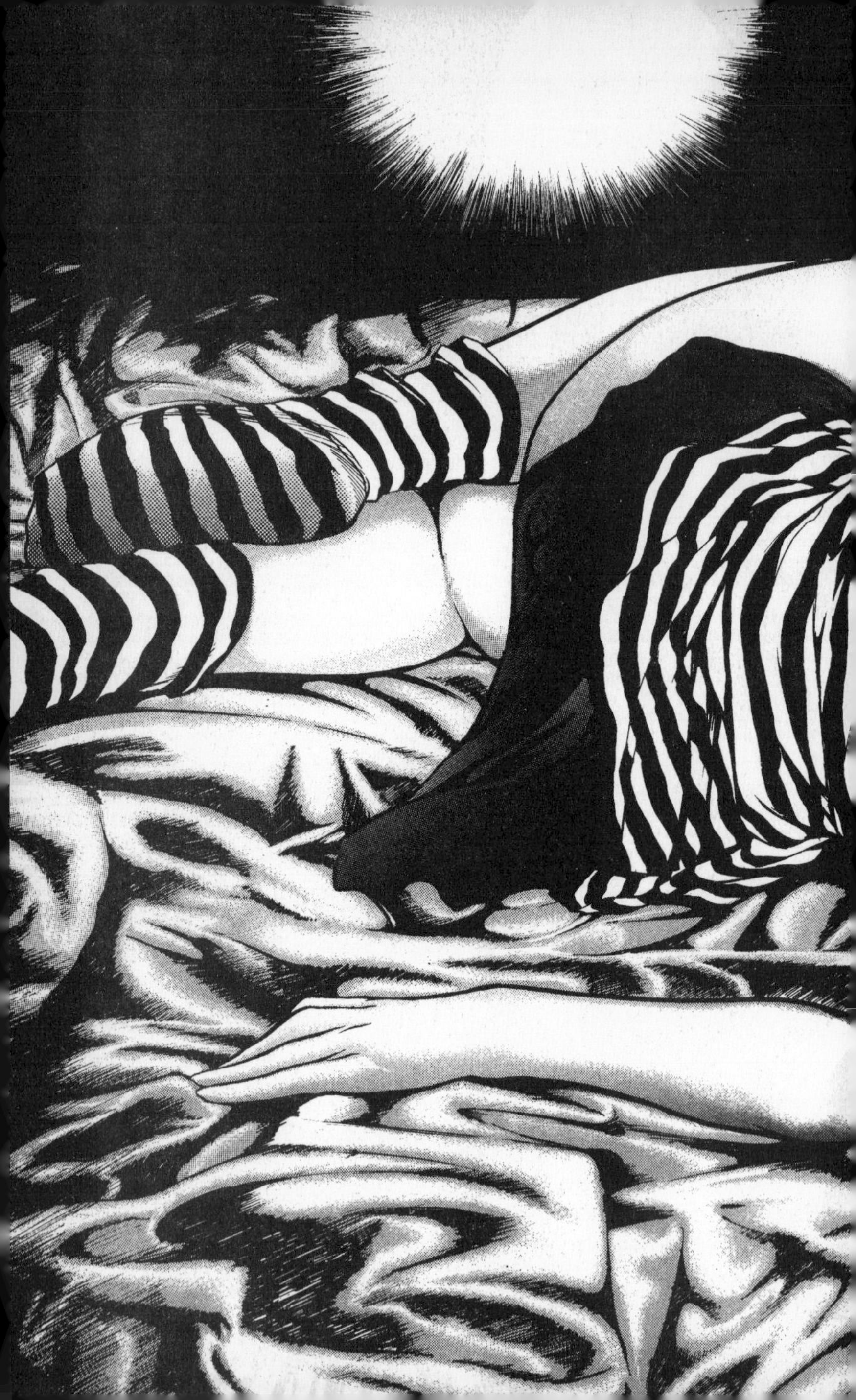

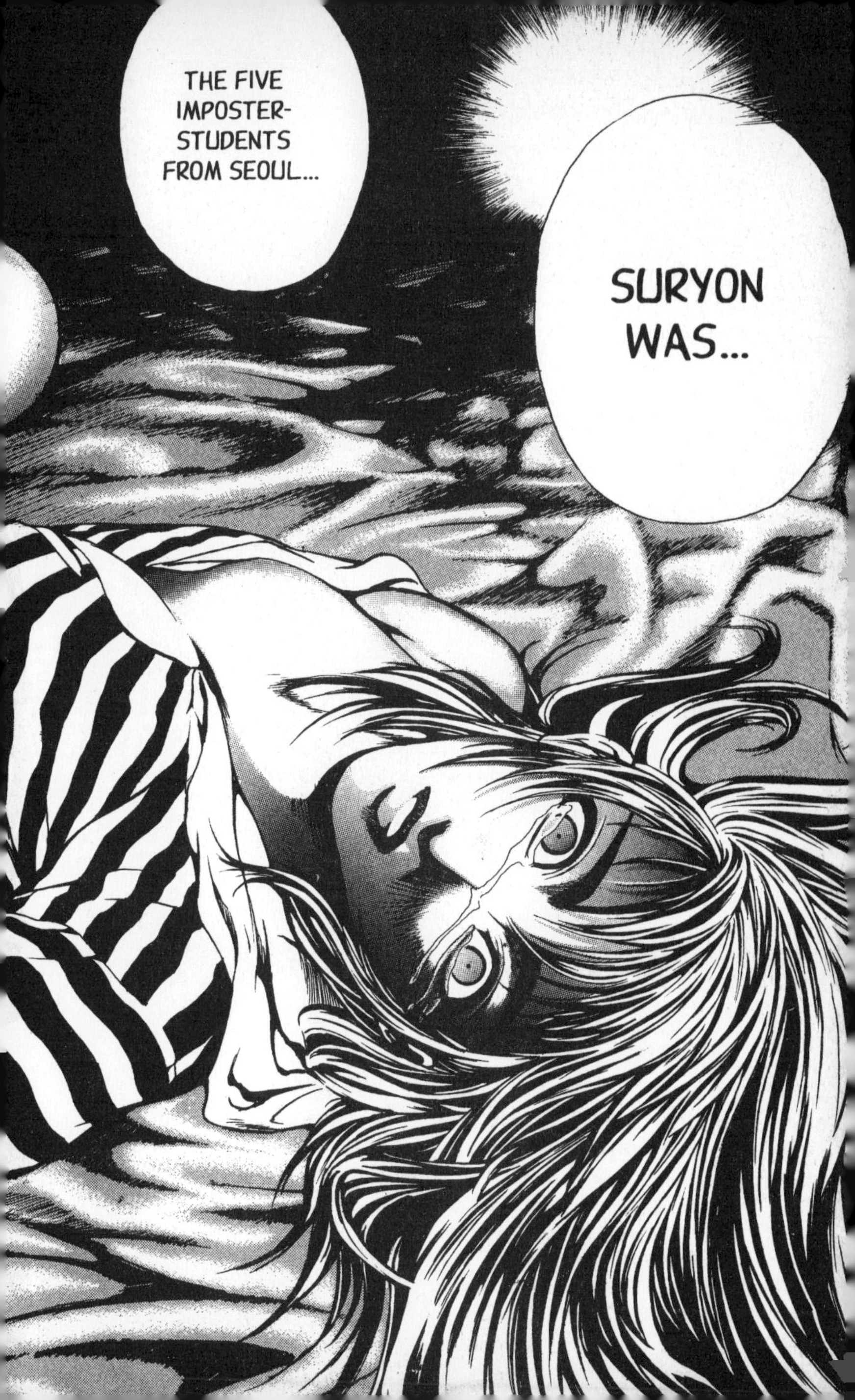
THE FIVE IMPOSTER-STUDENTS FROM SEOUL...
SURYON WAS...

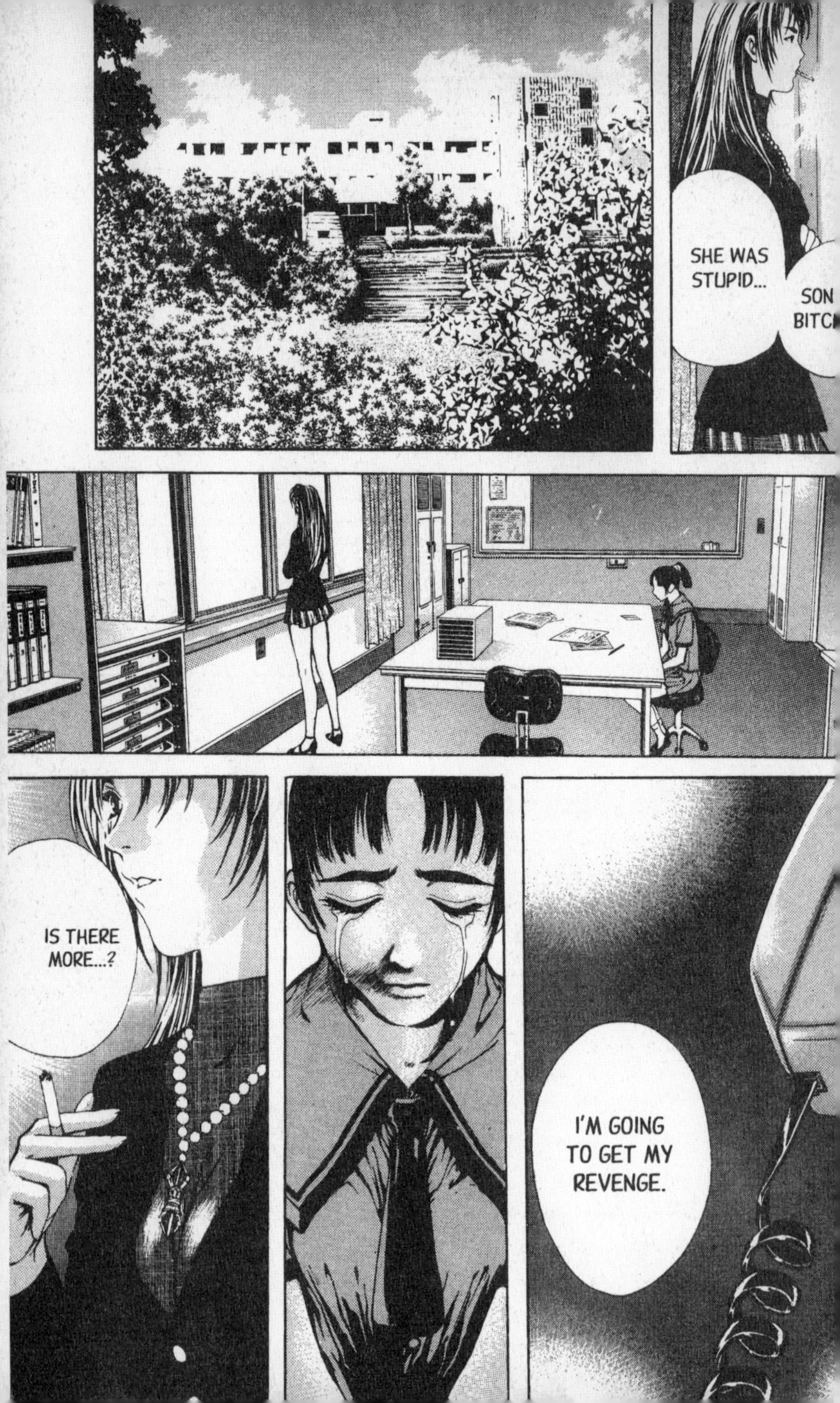
SHE WAS STUPID...
SON BITC
IS THERE MORE...?
I'M GOING TO GET MY REVENGE.

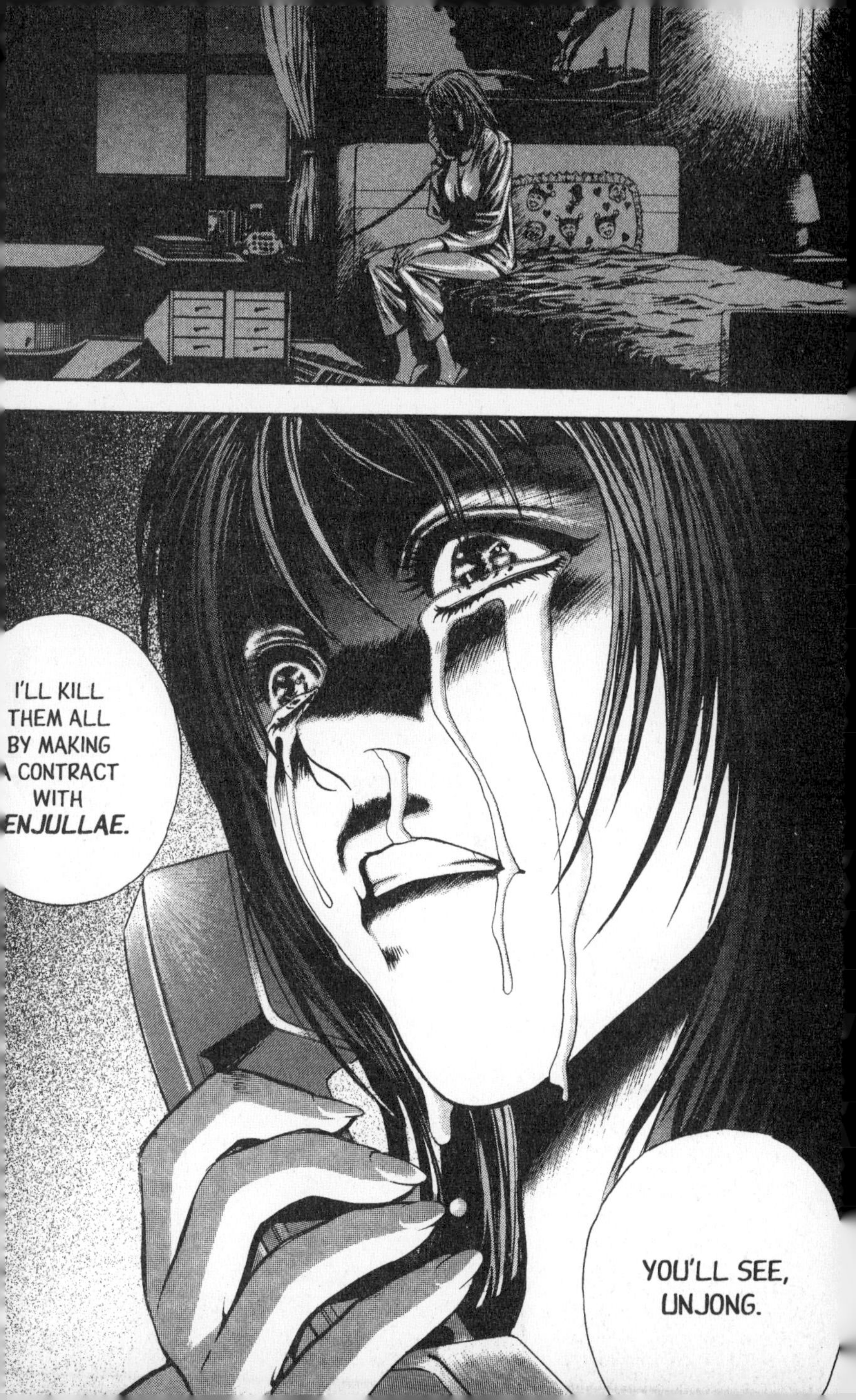
I'LL KILL THEM ALL BY MAKING A CONTRACT WITH ENJULLAE.
YOU'LL SEE, UNJONG.

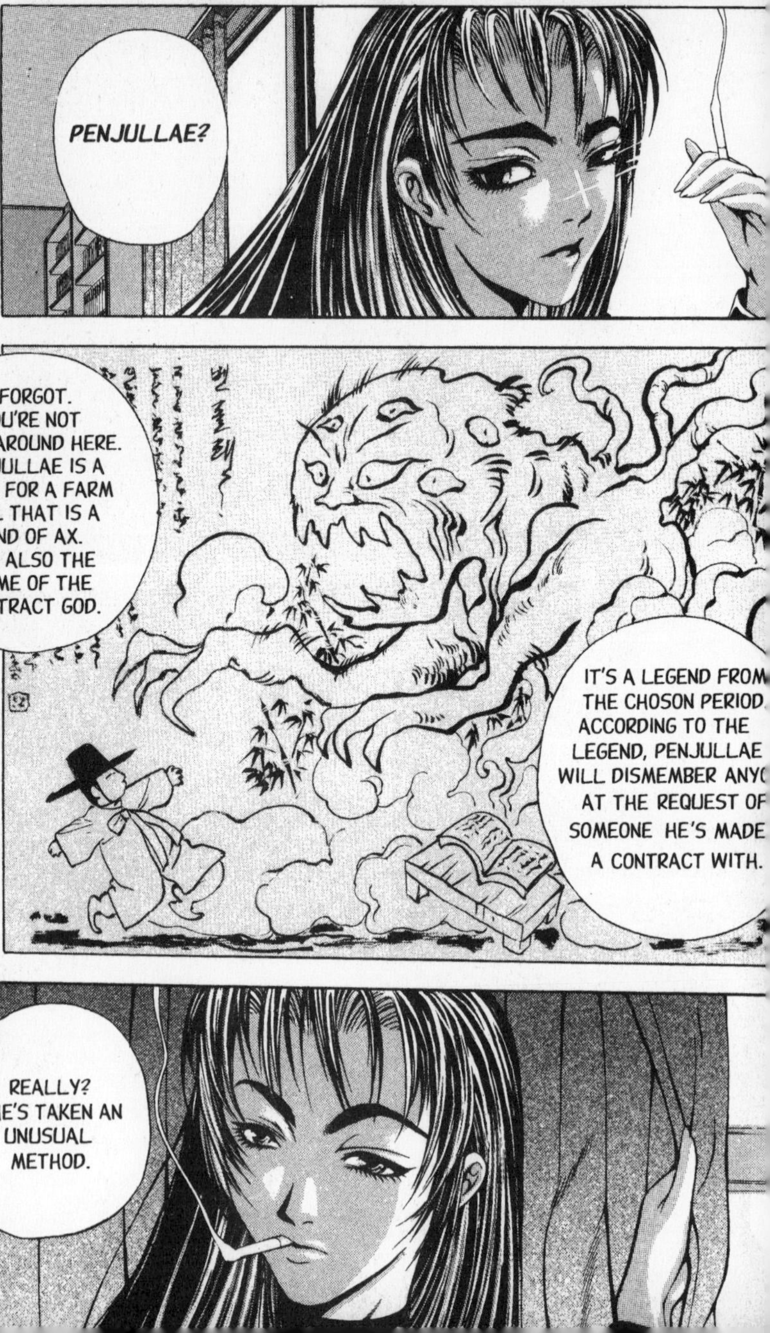
PENJULLAE?
I FORGOT. YOU'RE NOT FROM AROUND HERE. PENJULLAE IS A WORD FOR A FARM TOOL THAT IS A KIND OF AX. IT'S ALSO THE NAME OF THE CONTRACT GOD.
IT'S A LEGEND FROM THE CHOSON PERIOD. ACCORDING TO THE LEGEND, PENJULLAE WILL DISMEMBER ANY AT THE REQUEST OF SOMEONE HE'S MADE A CONTRACT WITH.
REALLY? SHE'S TAKEN AN UNUSUAL METHOD.

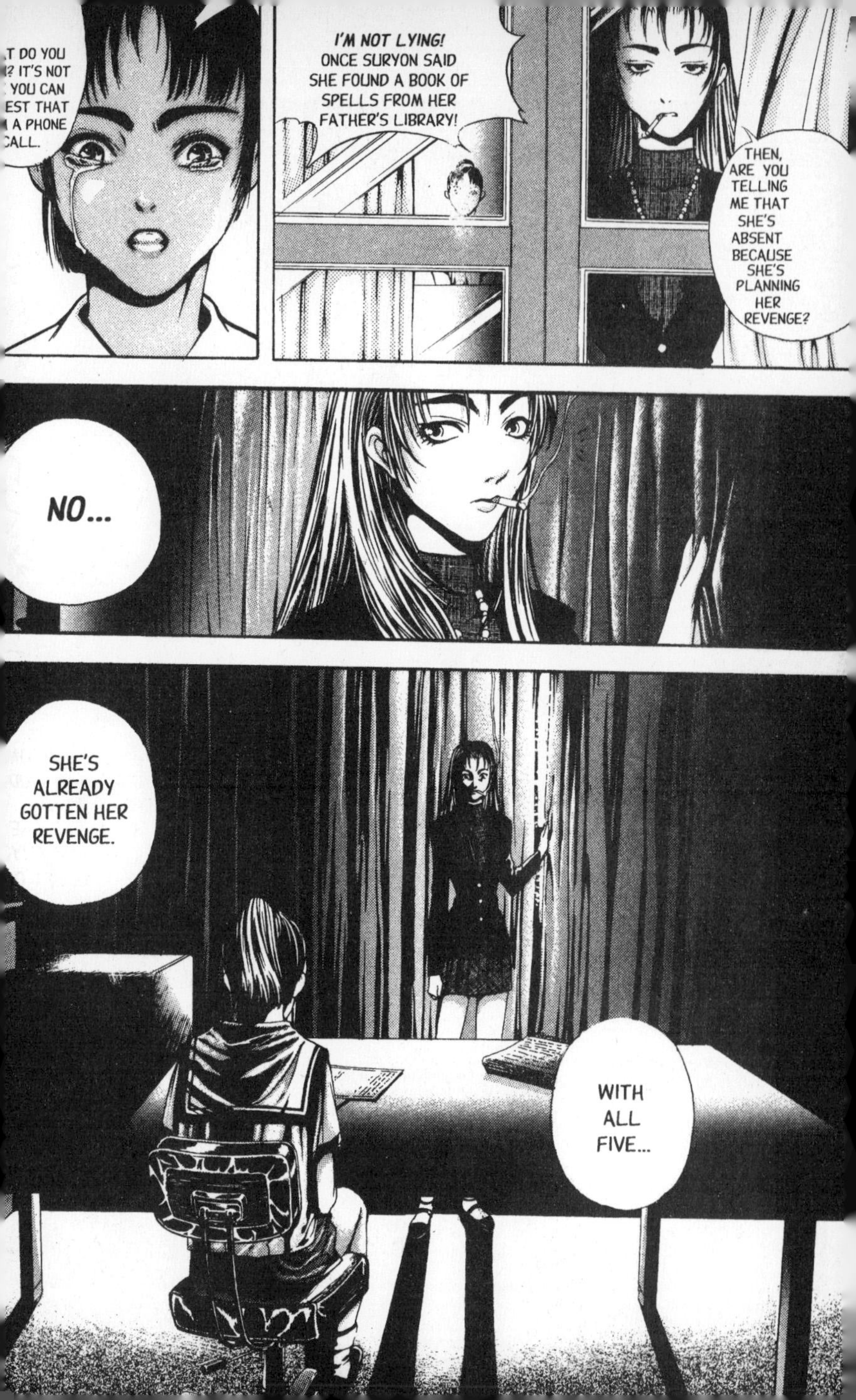
T DO YOU ? IT'S NOT YOU CAN EST THAT A PHONE CALL.
I'M NOT LYING! ONCE SURYON SAID SHE FOUND A BOOK OF SPELLS FROM HER FATHER'S LIBRARY!
THEN, ARE YOU TELLING ME THAT SHE'S ABSENT BECAUSE SHE'S PLANNING HER REVENGE?
NO...
SHE'S ALREADY GOTTEN HER REVENGE.
WITH ALL FIVE...

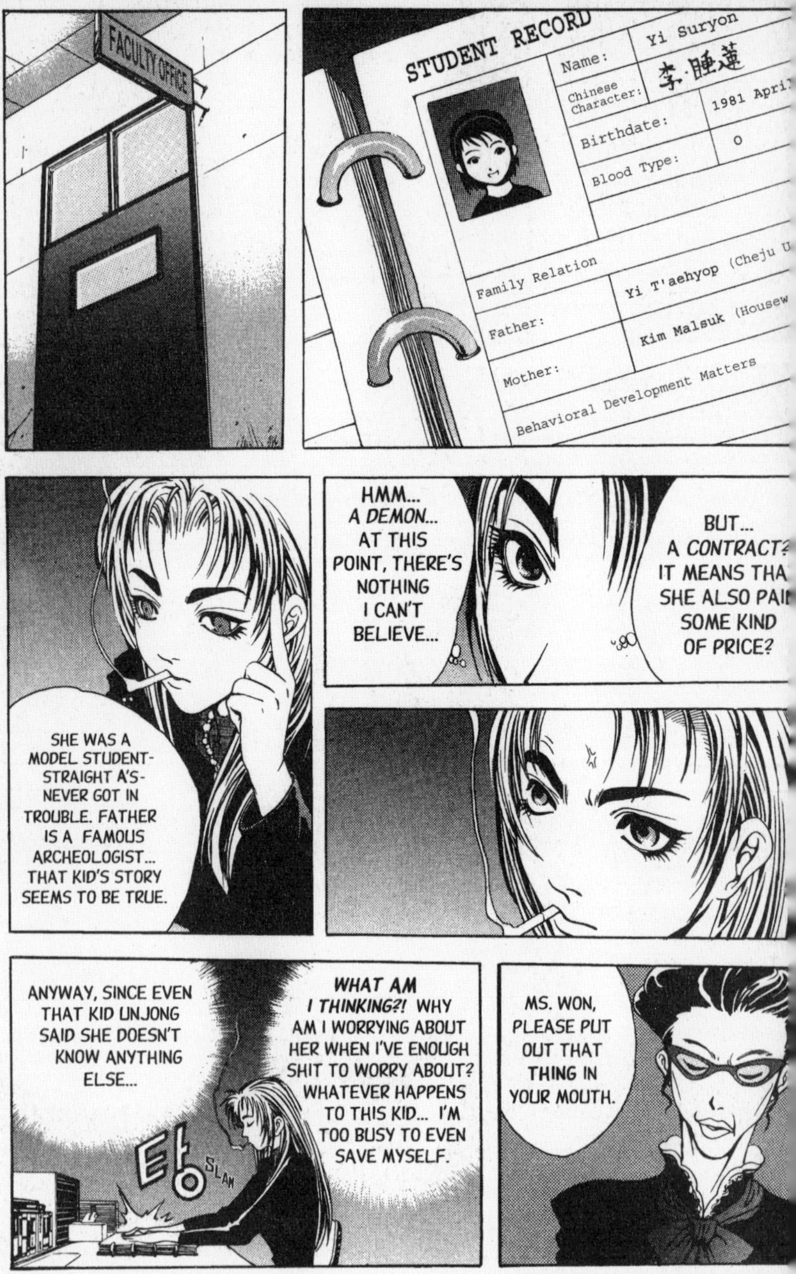
FACULTY OFFICE
STUDENT RECORD
Name: Yi Suryon
Chinese Character: 李·睡蓮
Birthdate: 1981 April
Blood Type: O
Family Relation
Father: Yi T'aehyop (Cheju U
Mother: Kim Malsuk (Housew
Behavioral Development Matters
SHE WAS A MODEL STUDENT- STRAIGHT A'S- NEVER GOT IN TROUBLE. FATHER IS A FAMOUS ARCHEOLOGIST... THAT KID'S STORY SEEMS TO BE TRUE.
HMM... A *DEMON*... AT THIS POINT, THERE'S NOTHING I CAN'T BELIEVE...
BUT... A *CONTRACT?* IT MEANS THA SHE ALSO PAI SOME KIND OF PRICE?
ANYWAY, SINCE EVEN THAT KID UNJONG SAID SHE DOESN'T KNOW ANYTHING ELSE...
SLAM
WHAT AM I THINKING?! WHY AM I WORRYING ABOUT HER WHEN I'VE ENOUGH SHIT TO WORRY ABOUT? WHATEVER HAPPENS TO THIS KID... I'M TOO BUSY TO EVEN SAVE MYSELF.
MS. WON, PLEASE PUT OUT THAT THING IN YOUR MOUTH.

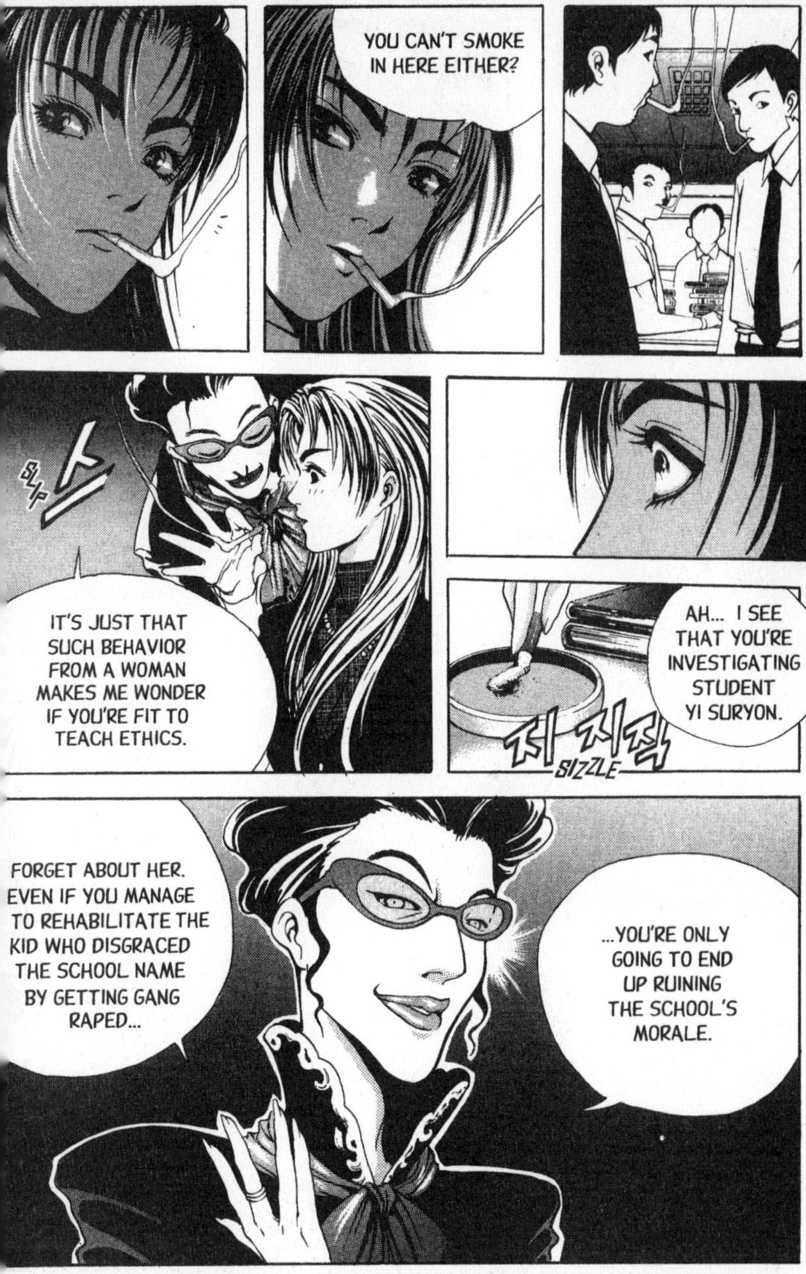
YOU CAN'T SMOKE IN HERE EITHER?
SLIP
IT'S JUST THAT SUCH BEHAVIOR FROM A WOMAN MAKES ME WONDER IF YOU'RE FIT TO TEACH ETHICS.
AH... I SEE THAT YOU'RE INVESTIGATING STUDENT YI SURYON.
치지직
SIZZLE
FORGET ABOUT HER. EVEN IF YOU MANAGE TO REHABILITATE THE KID WHO DISGRACED THE SCHOOL NAME BY GETTING GANG RAPED...
...YOU'RE ONLY GOING TO END UP RUINING THE SCHOOL'S MORALE.

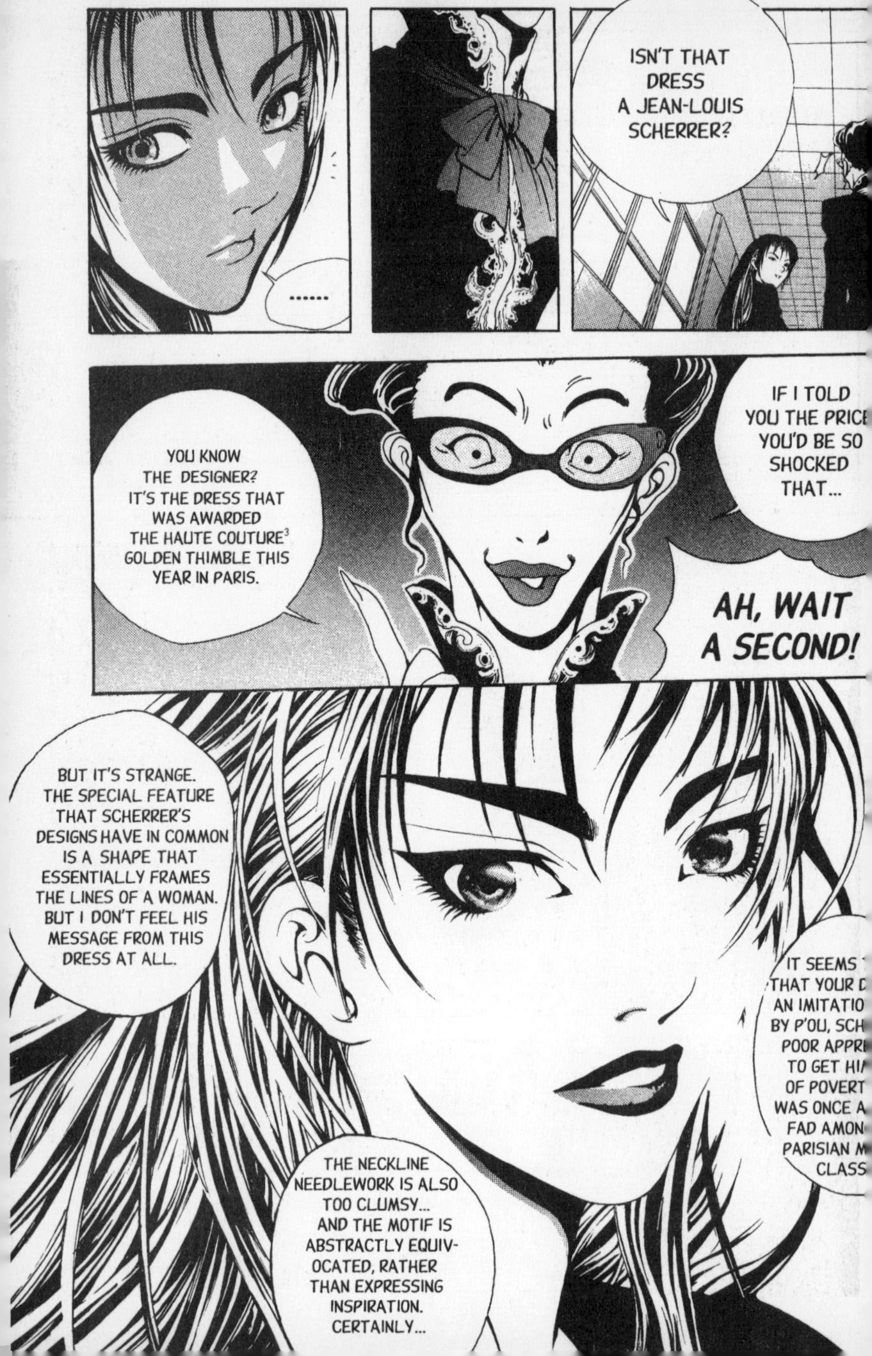
......
ISN'T THAT DRESS A JEAN-LOUIS SCHERRER?
YOU KNOW THE DESIGNER? IT'S THE DRESS THAT WAS AWARDED THE HAUTE COUTURE[3] GOLDEN THIMBLE THIS YEAR IN PARIS.
IF I TOLD YOU THE PRIC YOU'D BE SO SHOCKED THAT...
AH, WAIT A SECOND!
BUT IT'S STRANGE. THE SPECIAL FEATURE THAT SCHERRER'S DESIGNS HAVE IN COMMON IS A SHAPE THAT ESSENTIALLY FRAMES THE LINES OF A WOMAN. BUT I DON'T FEEL HIS MESSAGE FROM THIS DRESS AT ALL.
IT SEEMS THAT YOUR AN IMITATIO BY P'OU, SCH POOR APPR TO GET HI OF POVERT WAS ONCE A FAD AMON PARISIAN CLASS
THE NECKLINE NEEDLEWORK IS ALSO TOO CLUMSY... AND THE MOTIF IS ABSTRACTLY EQUIV-OCATED, RATHER THAN EXPRESSING INSPIRATION. CERTAINLY...

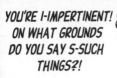

YOU'RE I-IMPERTINENT! ON WHAT GROUNDS DO YOU SAY S-SUCH THINGS?!

GO HOME AND CHECK THE TAG.

JEAN-LOUIS'S INITIALS WOULD BE S.L. INSTEAD OF S.R.

I'M CONFIDENT BECAUSE I GAVE IT TO MY MAID AS A PRESENT.

KIK
KIK
KIK

I APPRECIATE YOUR KNOWLEDGE OF FASHION, MS. WON! BUT I KNOW ONE THING FOR SURE...

A WOMAN LIKE YOU WILL STIR UP DELINQUENCY IN A PROBLEM CHILD, FAR FROM GIVING HER PROPER GUIDANCE!

THAT BITCH...

79

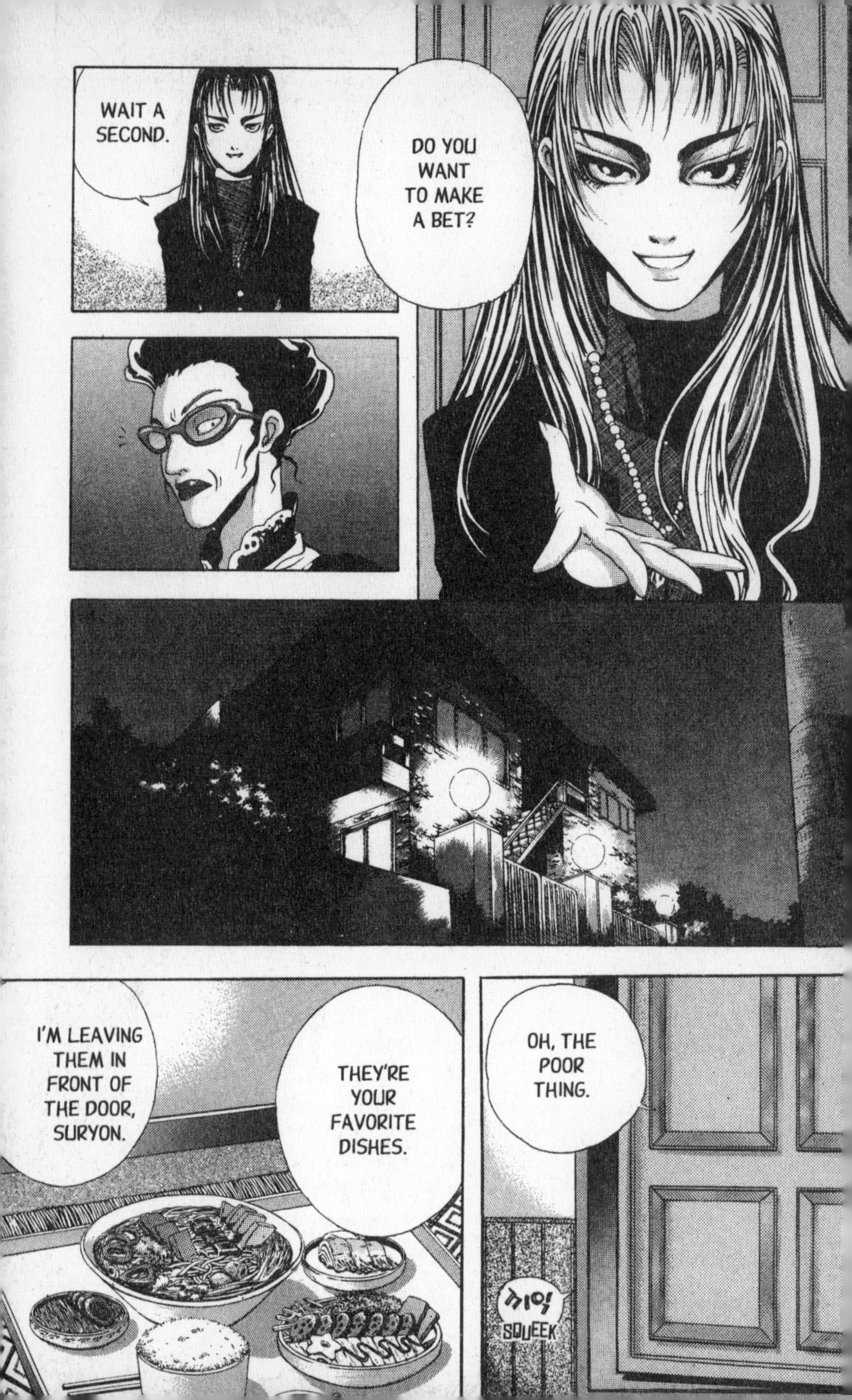
WAIT A SECOND.
DO YOU WANT TO MAKE A BET?
I'M LEAVING THEM IN FRONT OF THE DOOR, SURYON.
THEY'RE YOUR FAVORITE DISHES.
OH, THE POOR THING.
끼익
SQUEEK

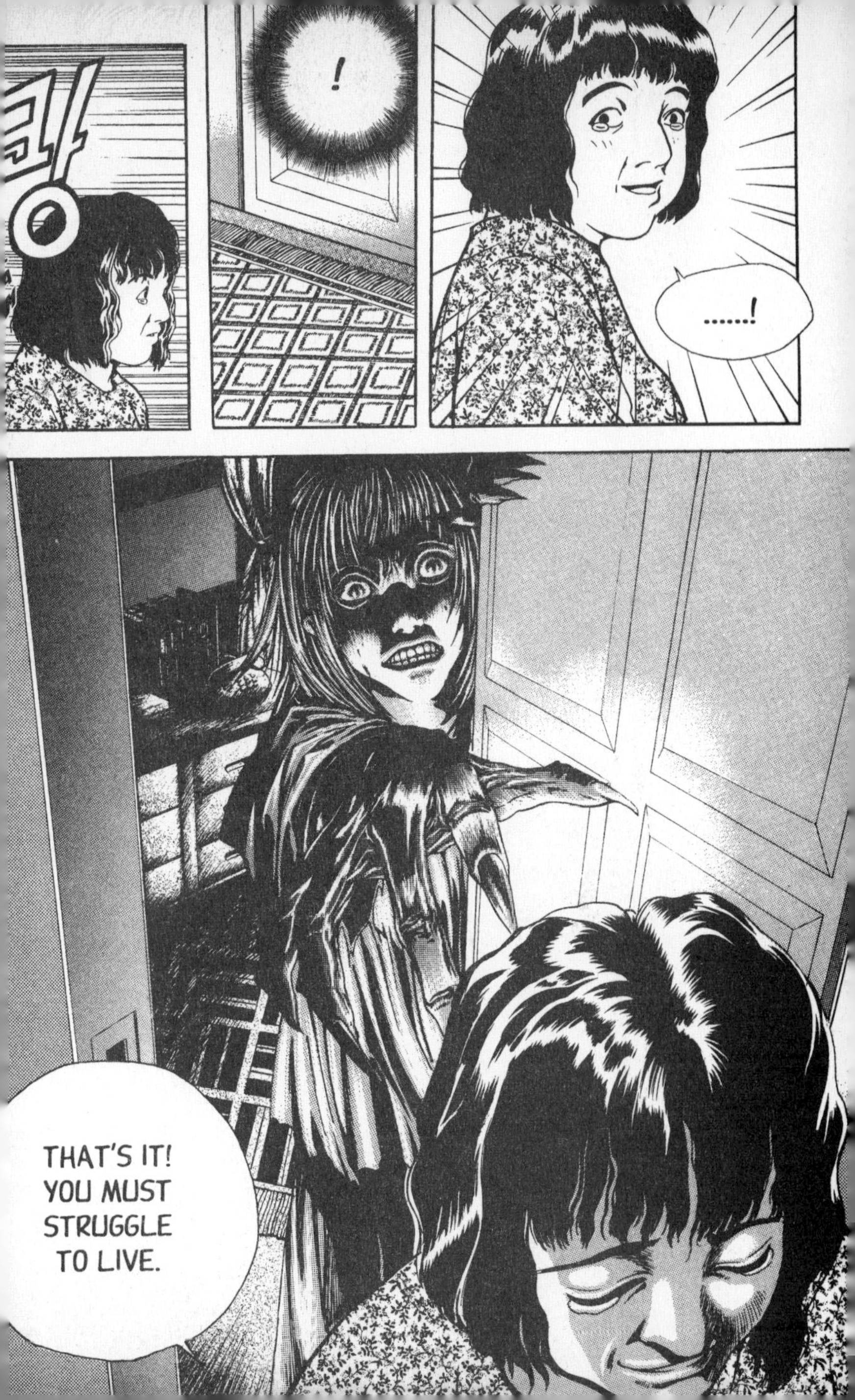
!
......!
THAT'S IT! YOU MUST STRUGGLE TO LIVE.

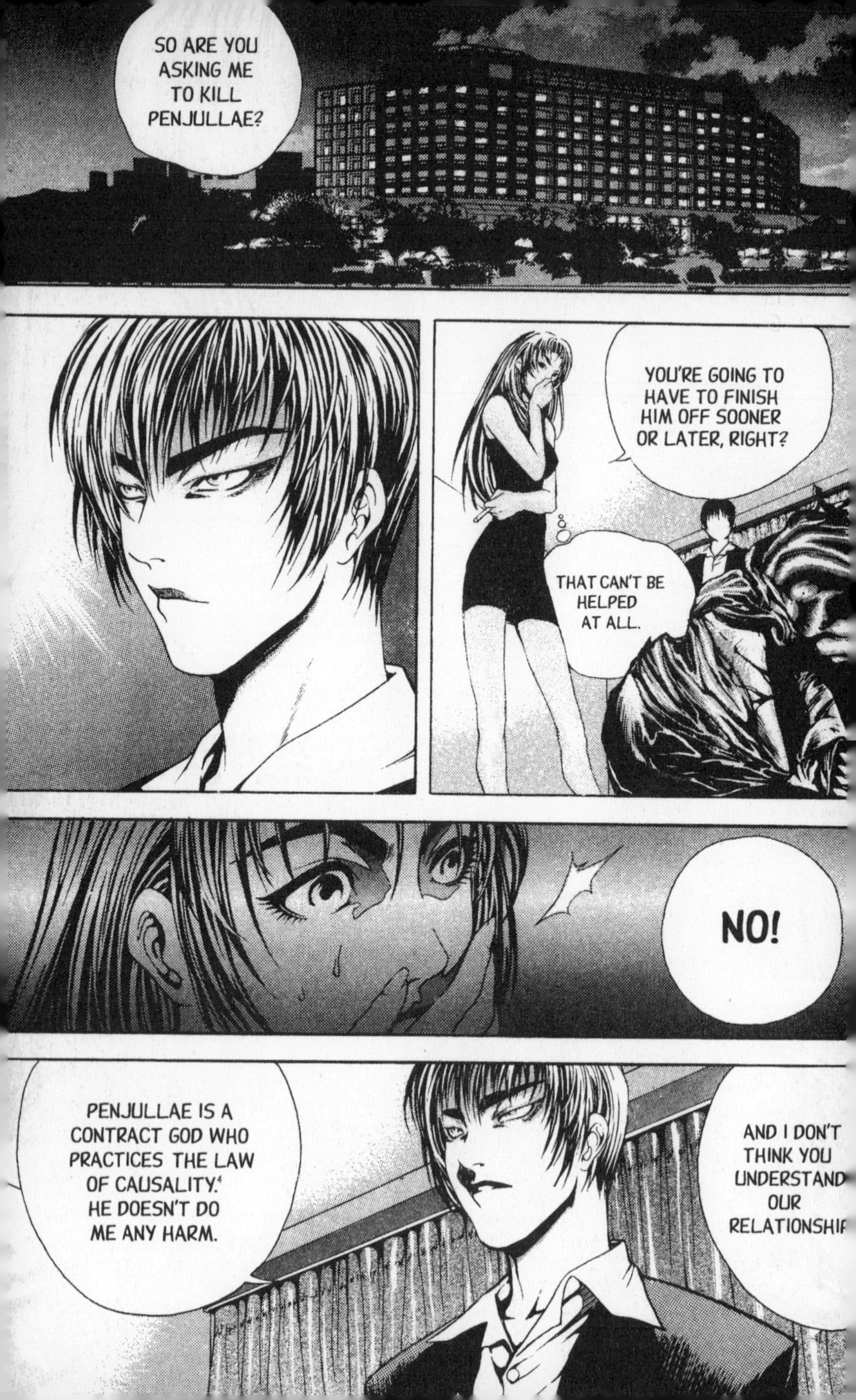
SO ARE YOU ASKING ME TO KILL PENJULLAE?
YOU'RE GOING TO HAVE TO FINISH HIM OFF SOONER OR LATER, RIGHT?
THAT CAN'T BE HELPED AT ALL.
NO!
PENJULLAE IS A CONTRACT GOD WHO PRACTICES THE LAW OF CAUSALITY.[4] HE DOESN'T DO ME ANY HARM.
AND I DON'T THINK YOU UNDERSTAND OUR RELATIONSHIP

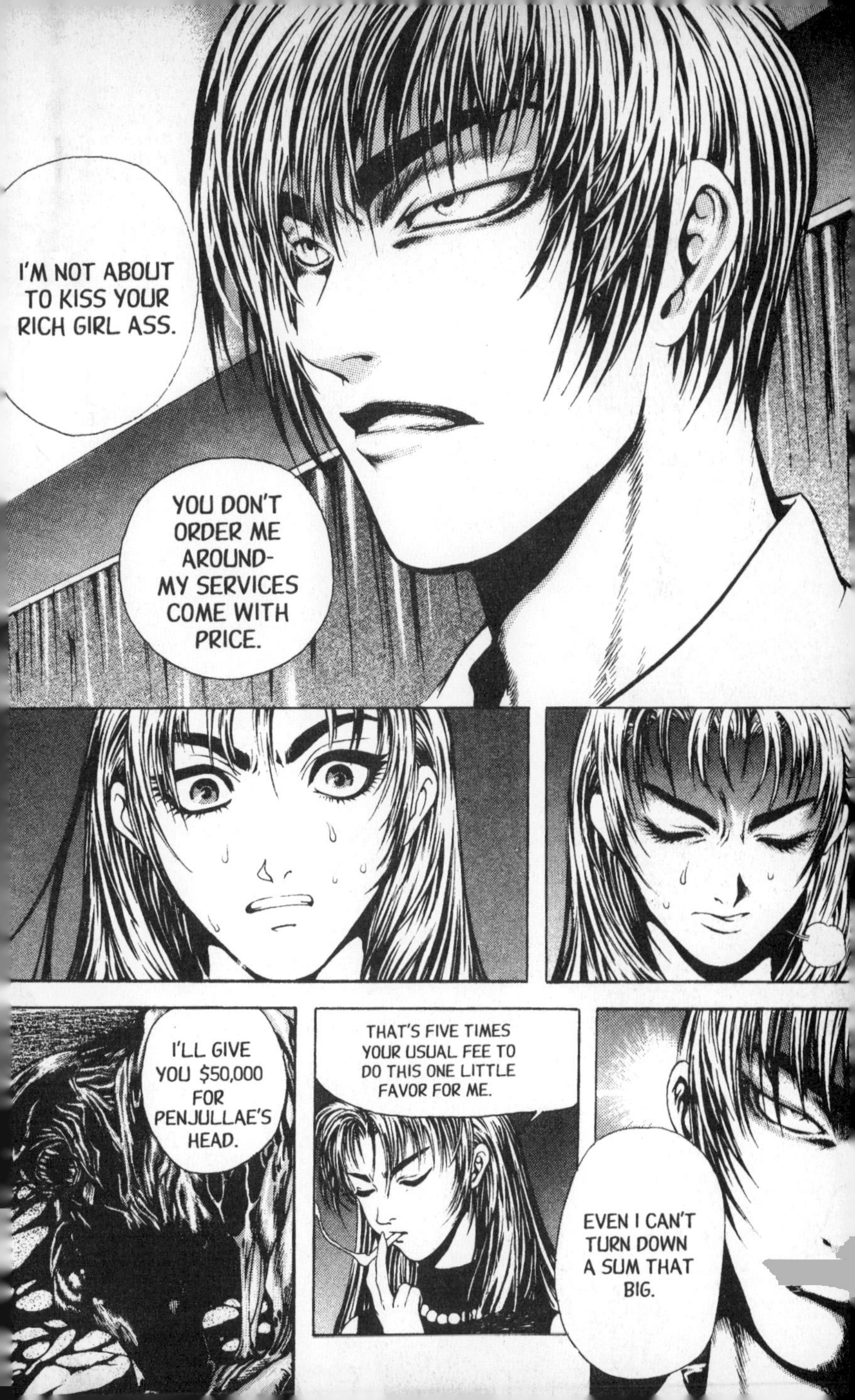
I'M NOT ABOUT TO KISS YOUR RICH GIRL ASS.
YOU DON'T ORDER ME AROUND- MY SERVICES COME WITH PRICE.
I'LL GIVE YOU $50,000 FOR PENJULLAE'S HEAD.
THAT'S FIVE TIMES YOUR USUAL FEE TO DO THIS ONE LITTLE FAVOR FOR ME.
EVEN I CAN'T TURN DOWN A SUM THAT BIG.

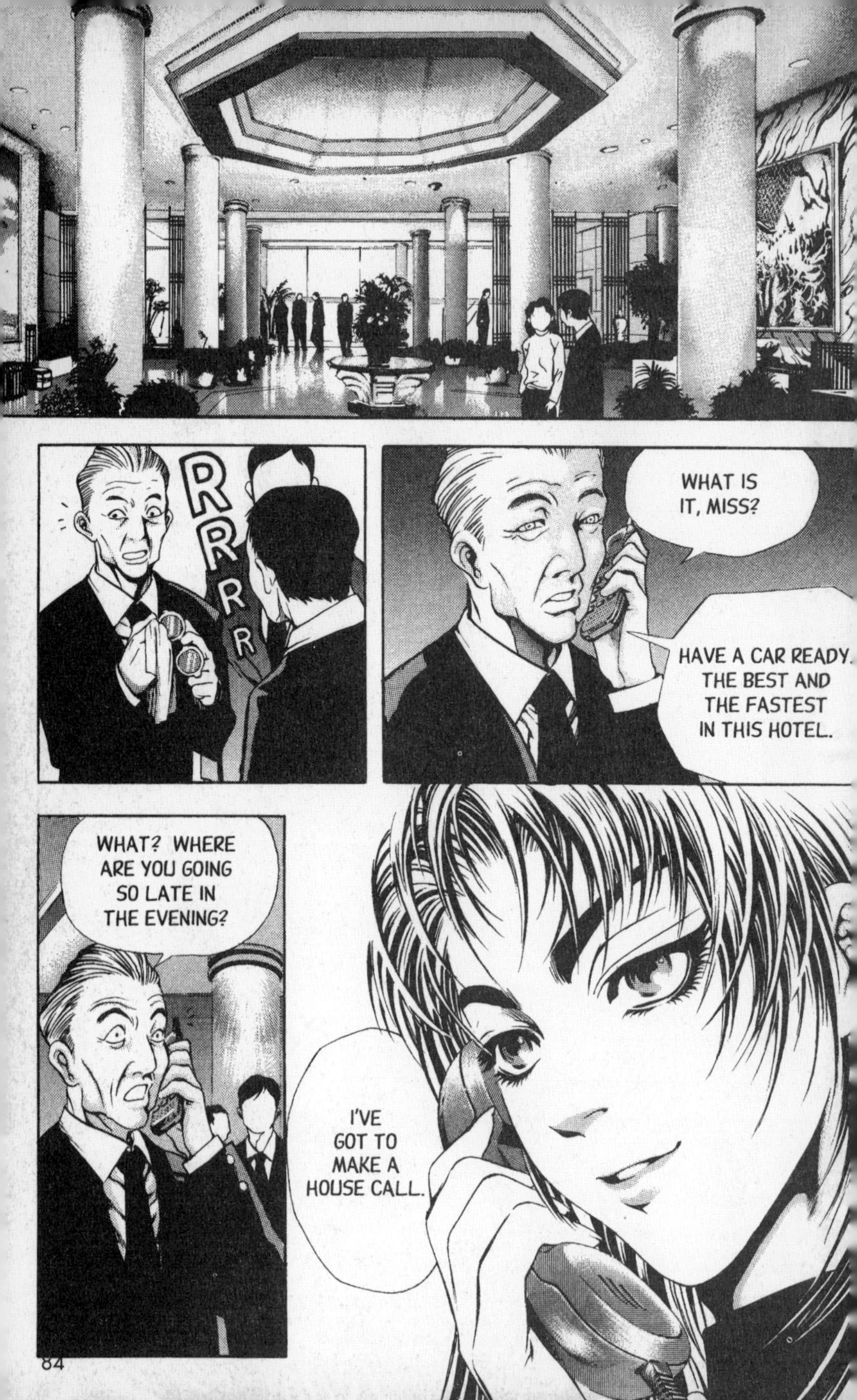
RRRR
WHAT IS IT, MISS?
HAVE A CAR READY. THE BEST AND THE FASTEST IN THIS HOTEL.
WHAT? WHERE ARE YOU GOING SO LATE IN THE EVENING?
I'VE GOT TO MAKE A HOUSE CALL.

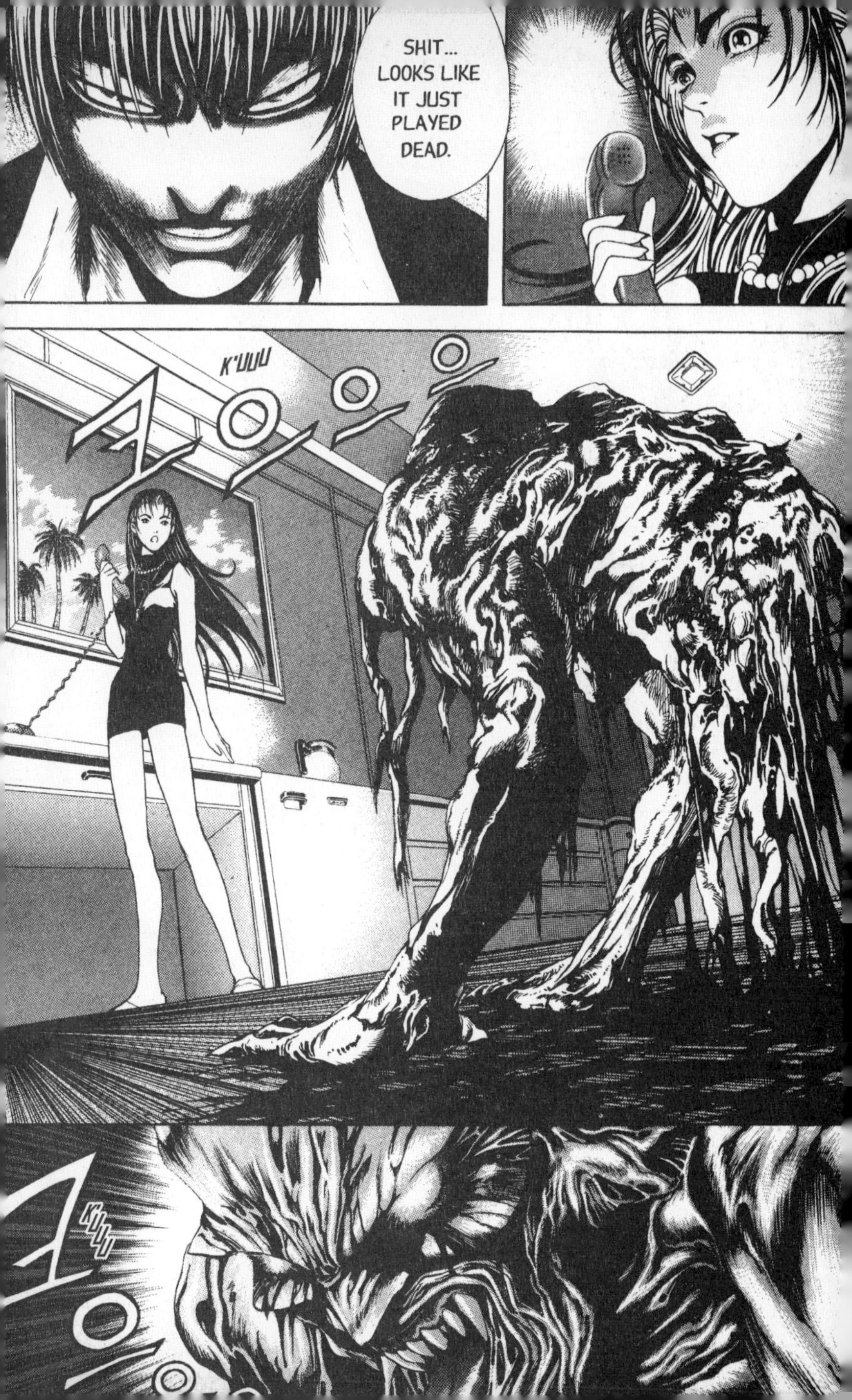
SHIT... LOOKS LIKE IT JUST PLAYED DEAD.
K'UUU
K'UUU

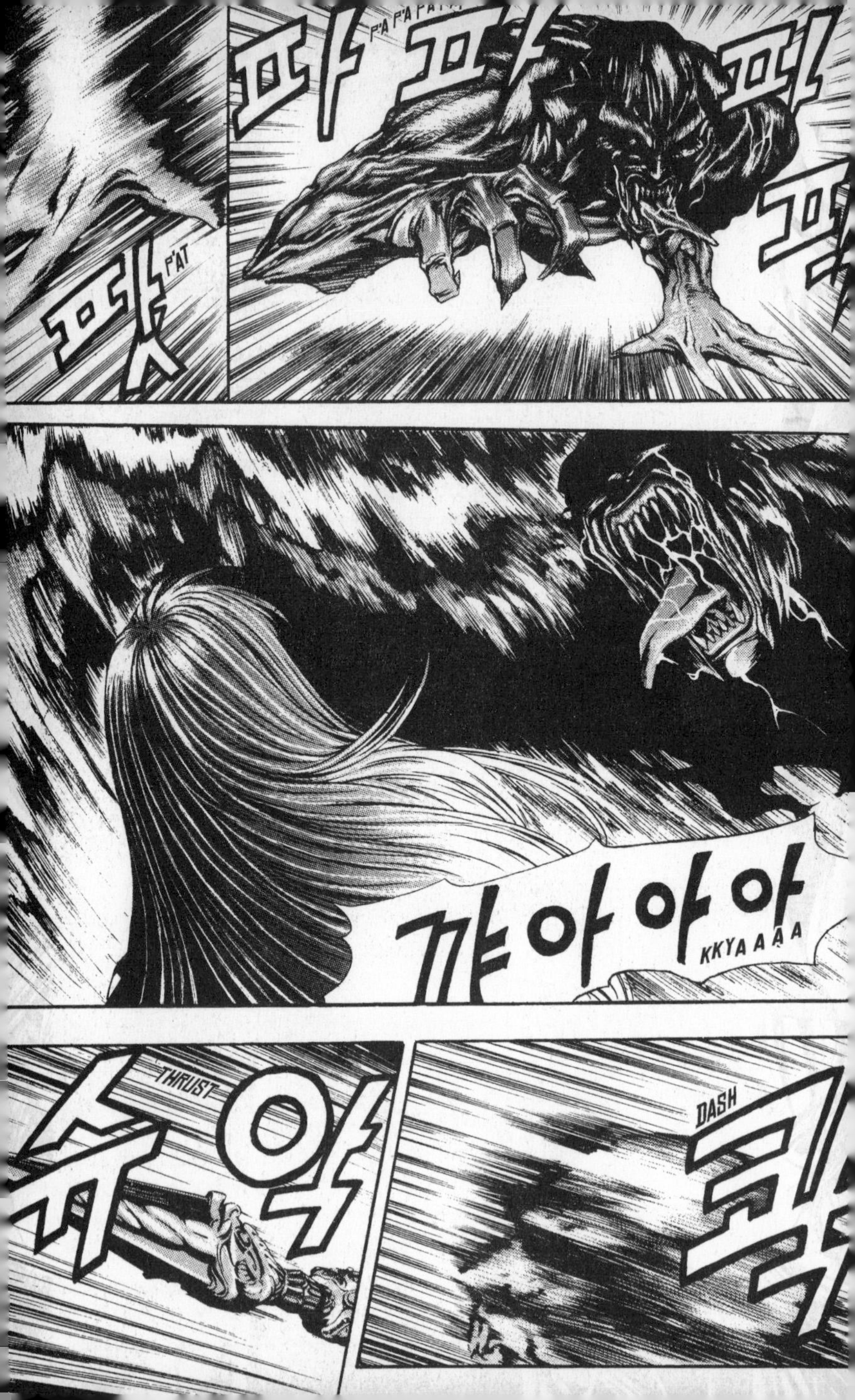
팟
PAT
파 파 파 팟
P'A P'A P'A
꺄아아아
KKYA A A A
THRUST
DASH

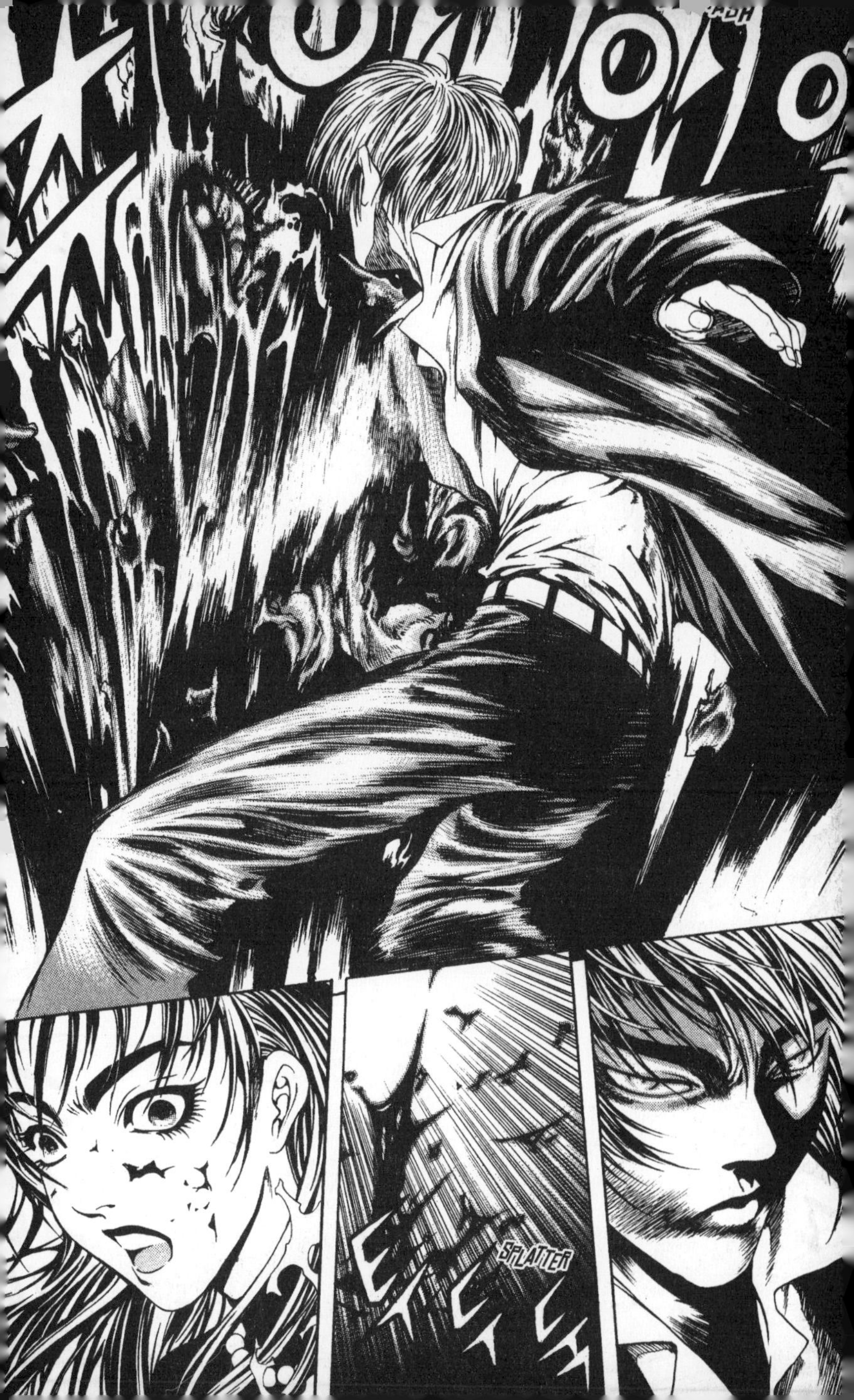
SPLATTER

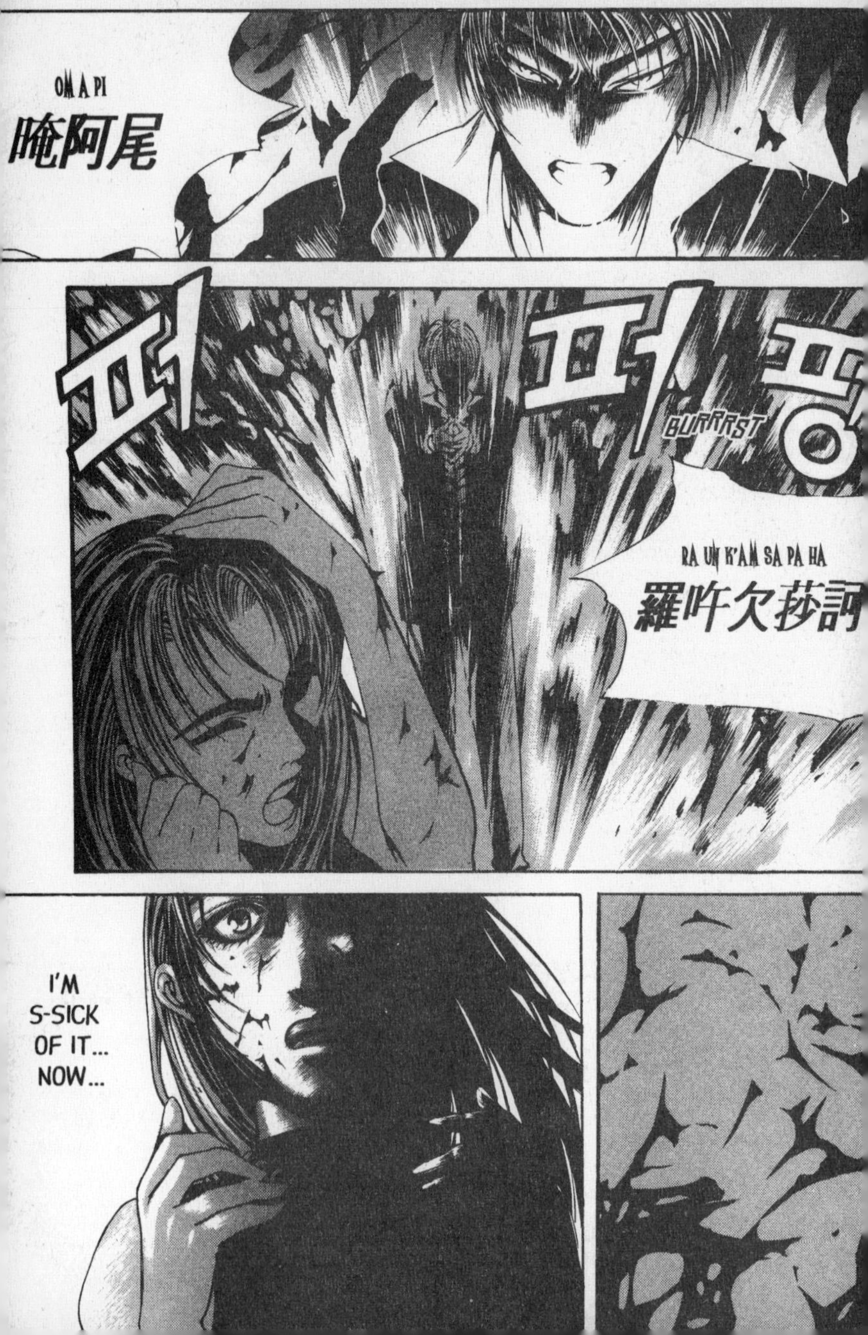
OM A PI
晻阿尾
BURRRST
RA UN K'AM SA PA HA
羅吽欠莎訶
I'M S-SICK OF IT... NOW...

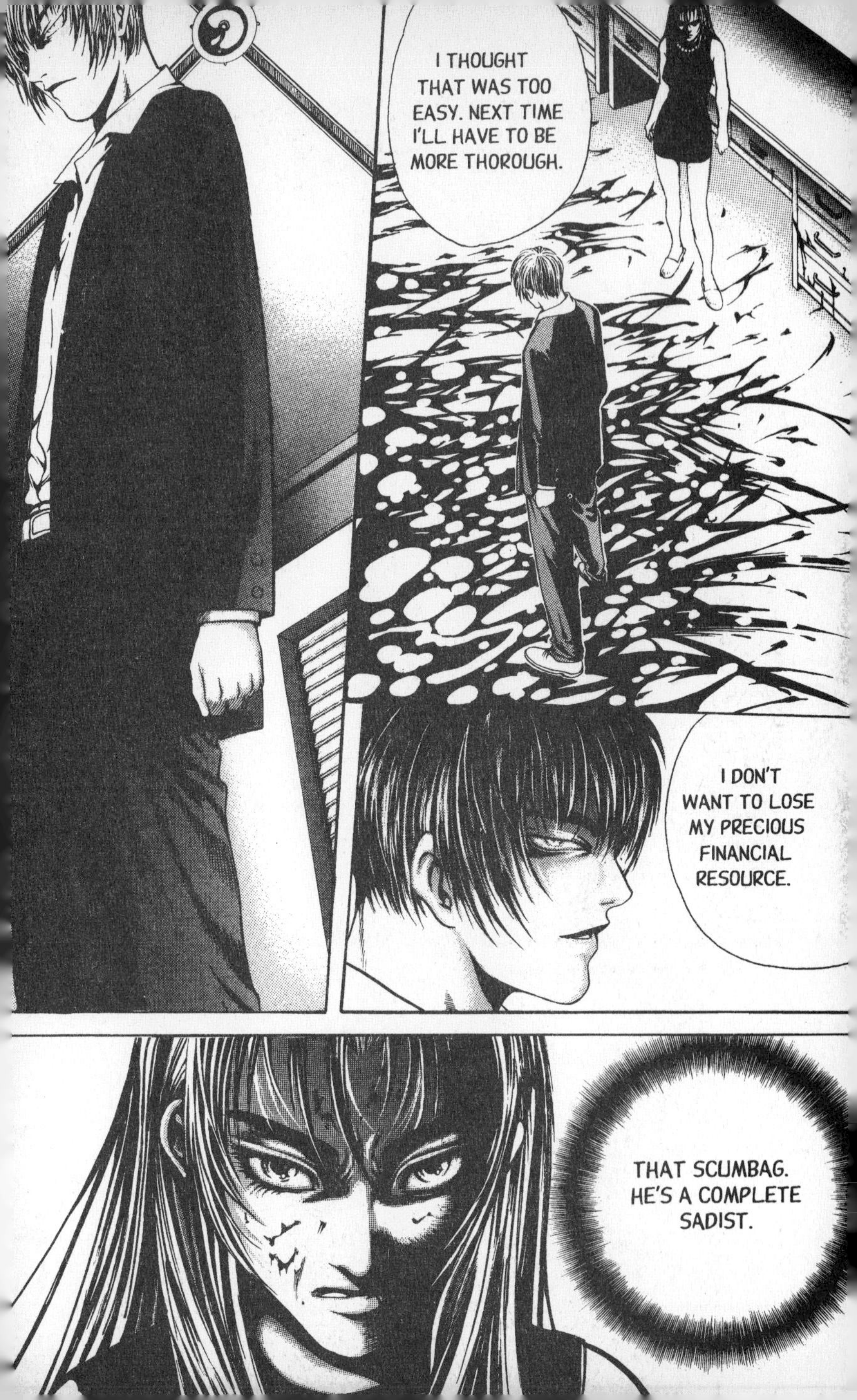
I THOUGHT THAT WAS TOO EASY. NEXT TIME I'LL HAVE TO BE MORE THOROUGH.
I DON'T WANT TO LOSE MY PRECIOUS FINANCIAL RESOURCE.
THAT SCUMBAG. HE'S A COMPLETE SADIST.

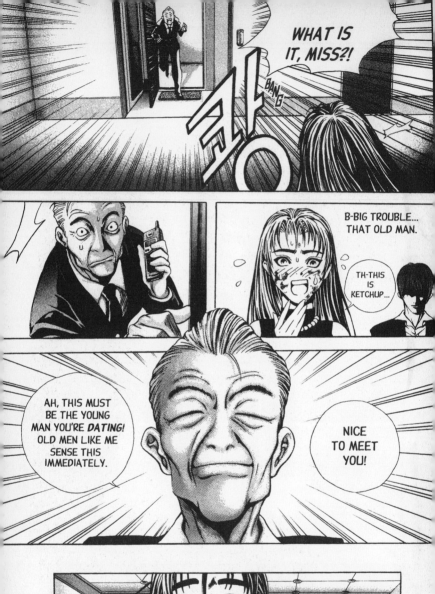

WHAT IS IT, MISS?!

B-BIG TROUBLE... THAT OLD MAN.

TH-THIS IS KETCHUP...

AH, THIS MUST BE THE YOUNG MAN YOU'RE *DATING!* OLD MEN LIKE ME SENSE THIS IMMEDIATELY.

NICE TO MEET YOU!

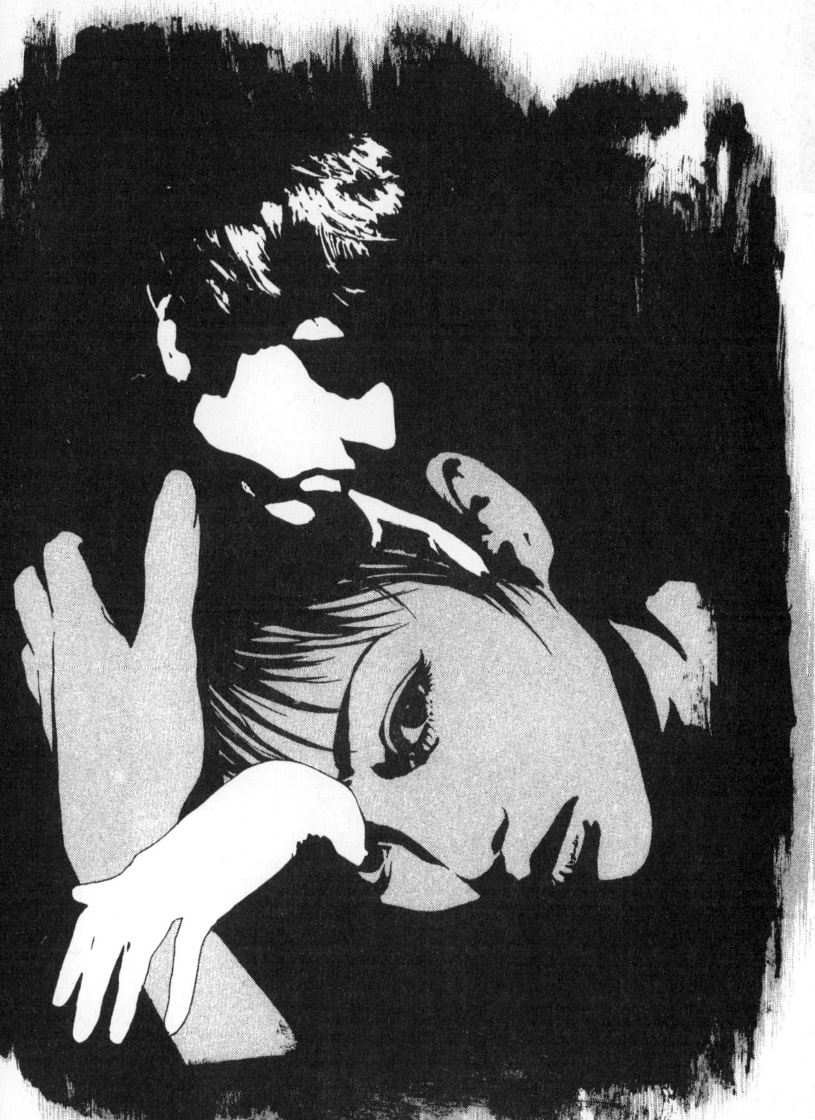

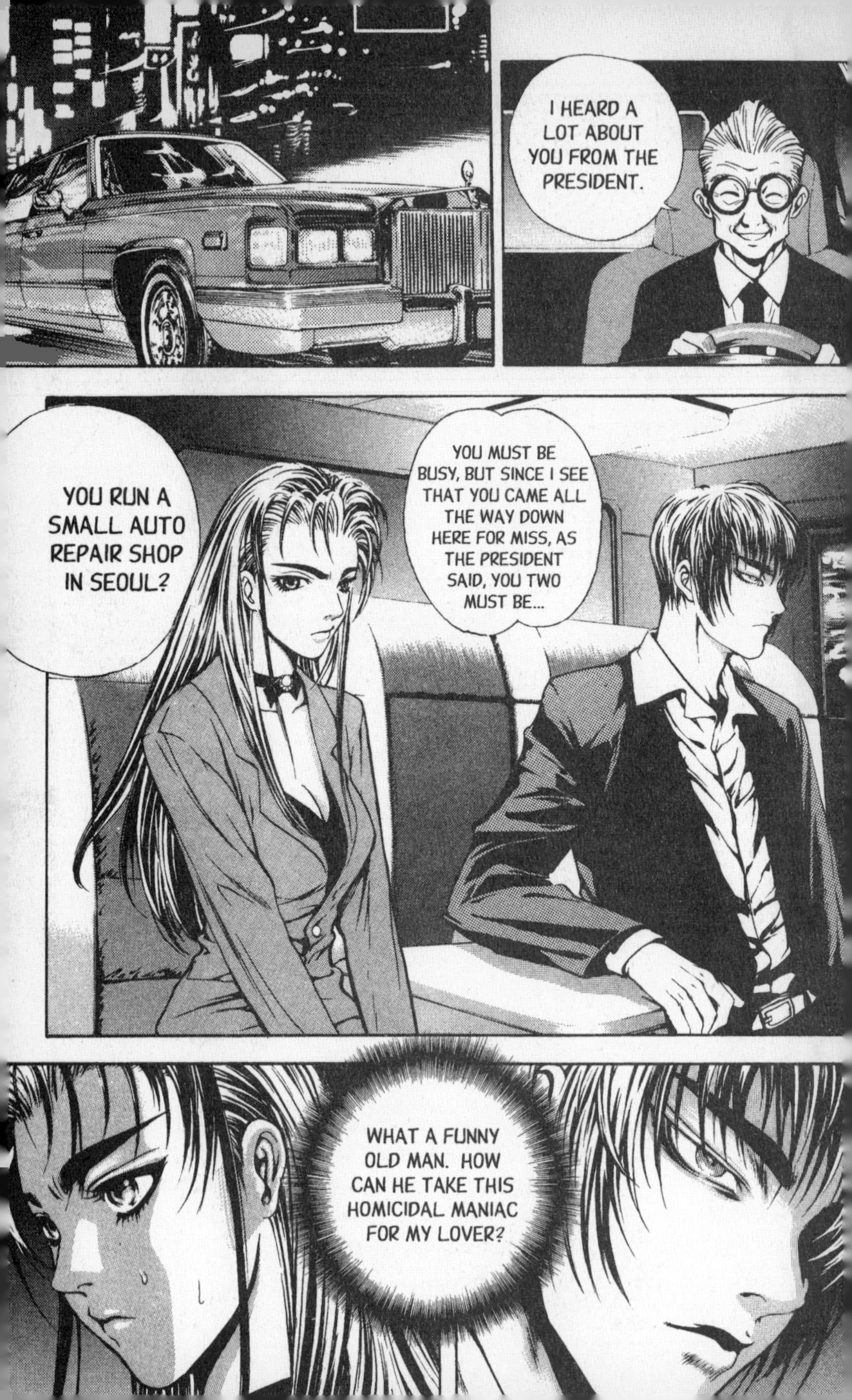
I HEARD A LOT ABOUT YOU FROM THE PRESIDENT.
YOU RUN A SMALL AUTO REPAIR SHOP IN SEOUL?
YOU MUST BE BUSY, BUT SINCE I SEE THAT YOU CAME ALL THE WAY DOWN HERE FOR MISS, AS THE PRESIDENT SAID, YOU TWO MUST BE...
WHAT A FUNNY OLD MAN. HOW CAN HE TAKE THIS HOMICIDAL MANIAC FOR MY LOVER?

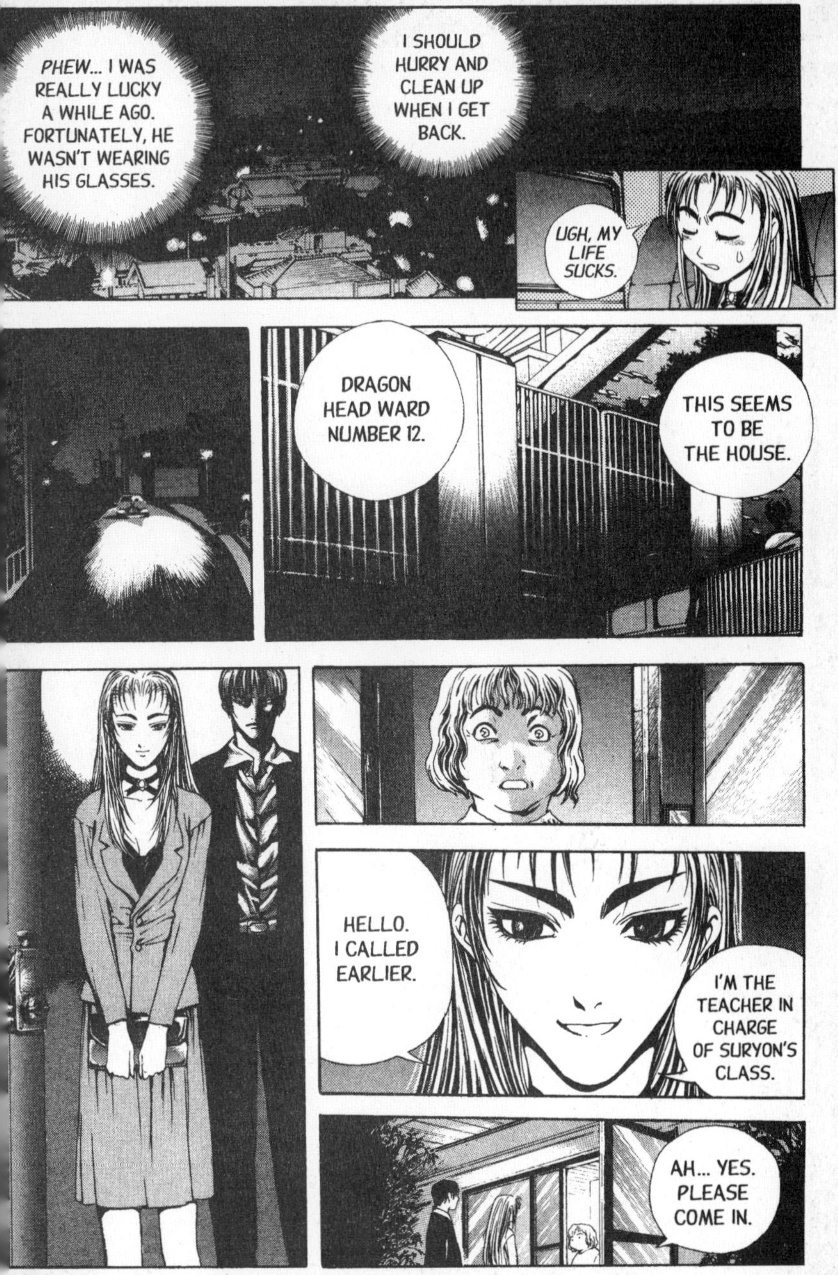
PHEW... I WAS REALLY LUCKY A WHILE AGO. FORTUNATELY, HE WASN'T WEARING HIS GLASSES.
I SHOULD HURRY AND CLEAN UP WHEN I GET BACK.
UGH, MY LIFE SUCKS.
DRAGON HEAD WARD NUMBER 12.
THIS SEEMS TO BE THE HOUSE.
HELLO. I CALLED EARLIER.
I'M THE TEACHER IN CHARGE OF SURYON'S CLASS.
AH... YES. PLEASE COME IN.

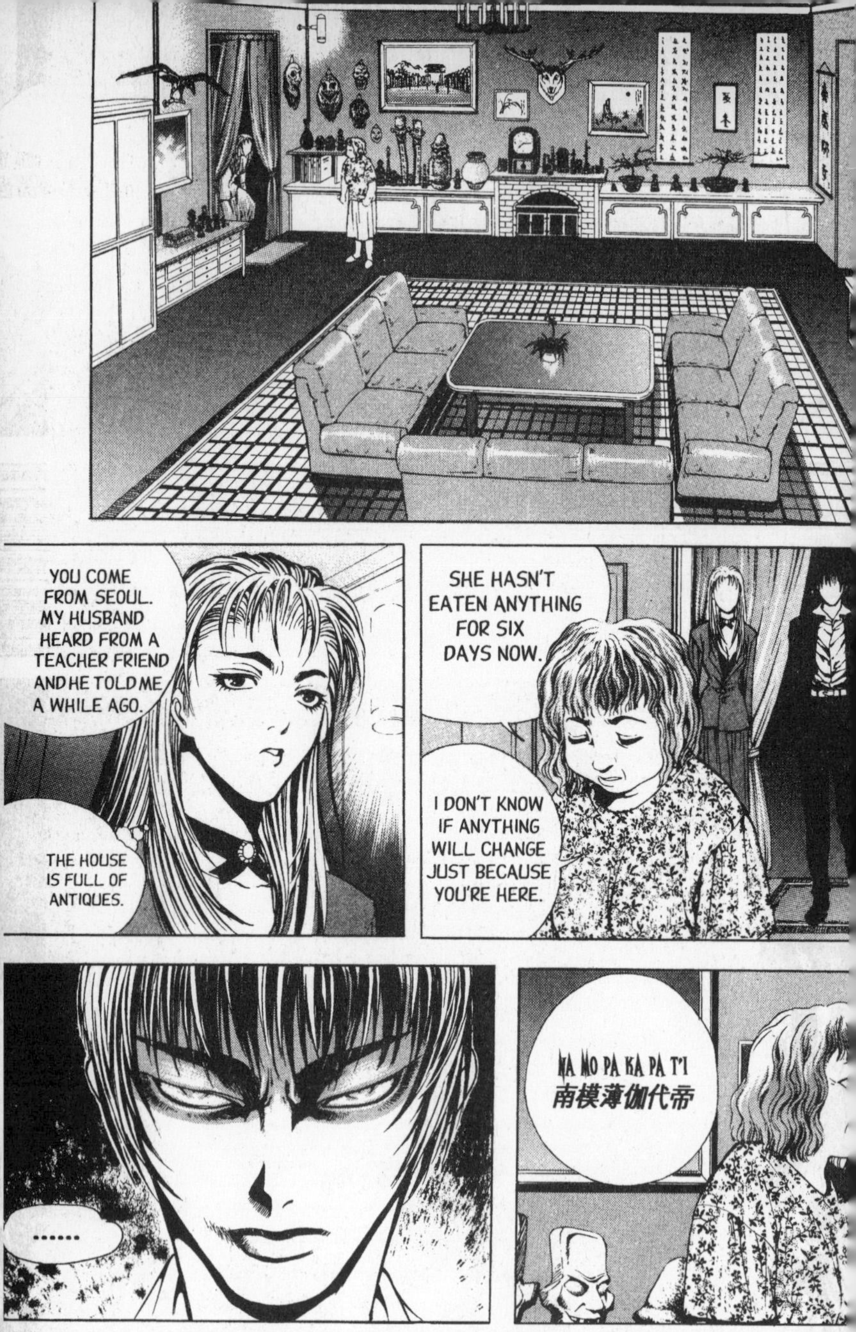
YOU COME FROM SEOUL. MY HUSBAND HEARD FROM A TEACHER FRIEND AND HE TOLD ME A WHILE AGO.
THE HOUSE IS FULL OF ANTIQUES.
SHE HASN'T EATEN ANYTHING FOR SIX DAYS NOW.
I DON'T KNOW IF ANYTHING WILL CHANGE JUST BECAUSE YOU'RE HERE.
......
NA MO PA KA PA T'I
南模薄伽代帝

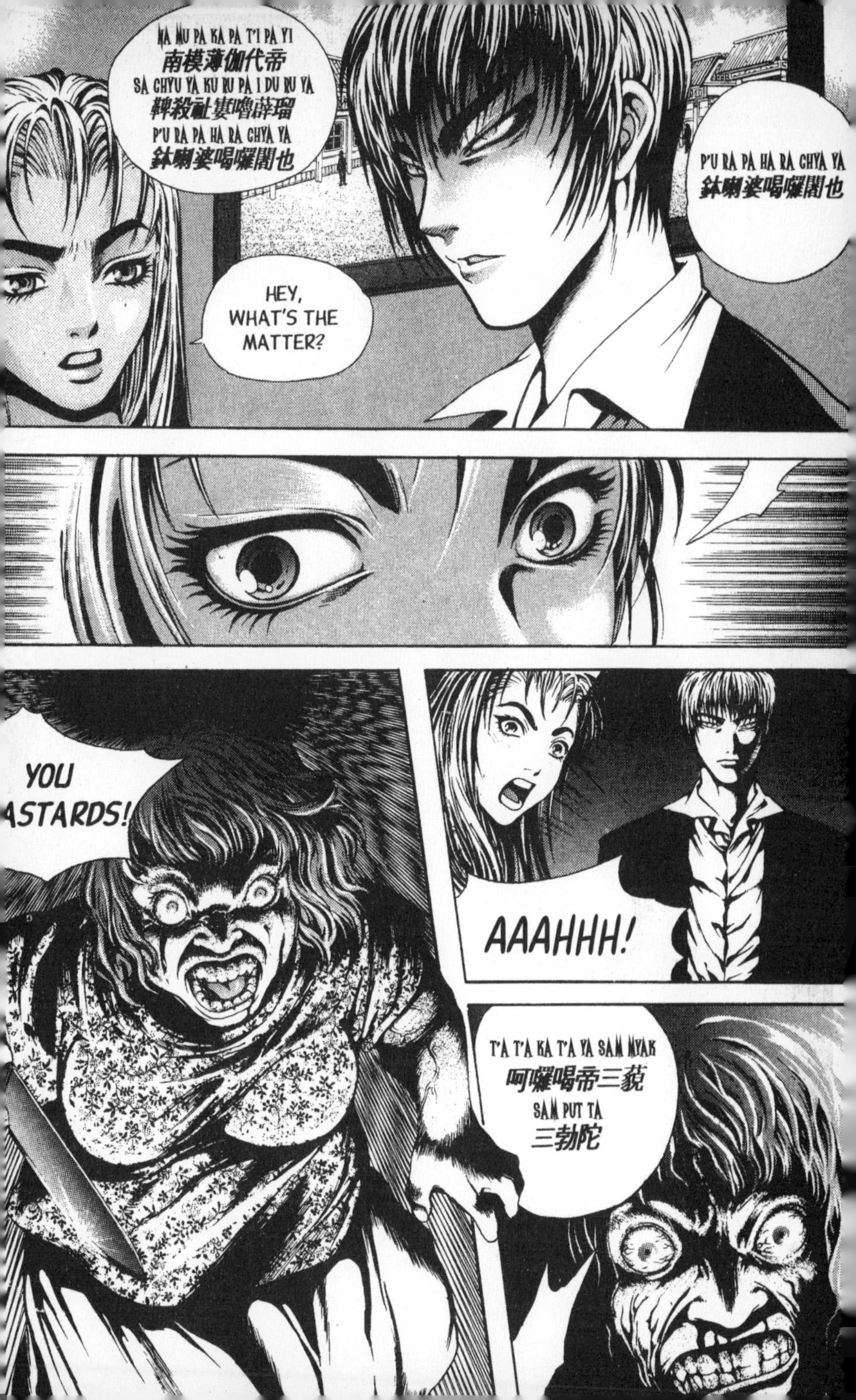
NA MU PA KA PA T'I PA YI
南模薄伽代帝
SA CHYU YA KU RU PA I DU RU YA
韡殺祉婁嚕薜瑠
P'U RA PA HA RA CHYA YA
鉢喇婆喝囉闍也
P'U RA PA HA RA CHYA YA
鉢喇婆喝囉闍也
HEY, WHAT'S THE MATTER?
YOU ASTARDS!
AAAHHH!
T'A T'A KA T'A YA SAM MYAK
呵囉喝帝三藐
SAM PUT TA
三勃陀

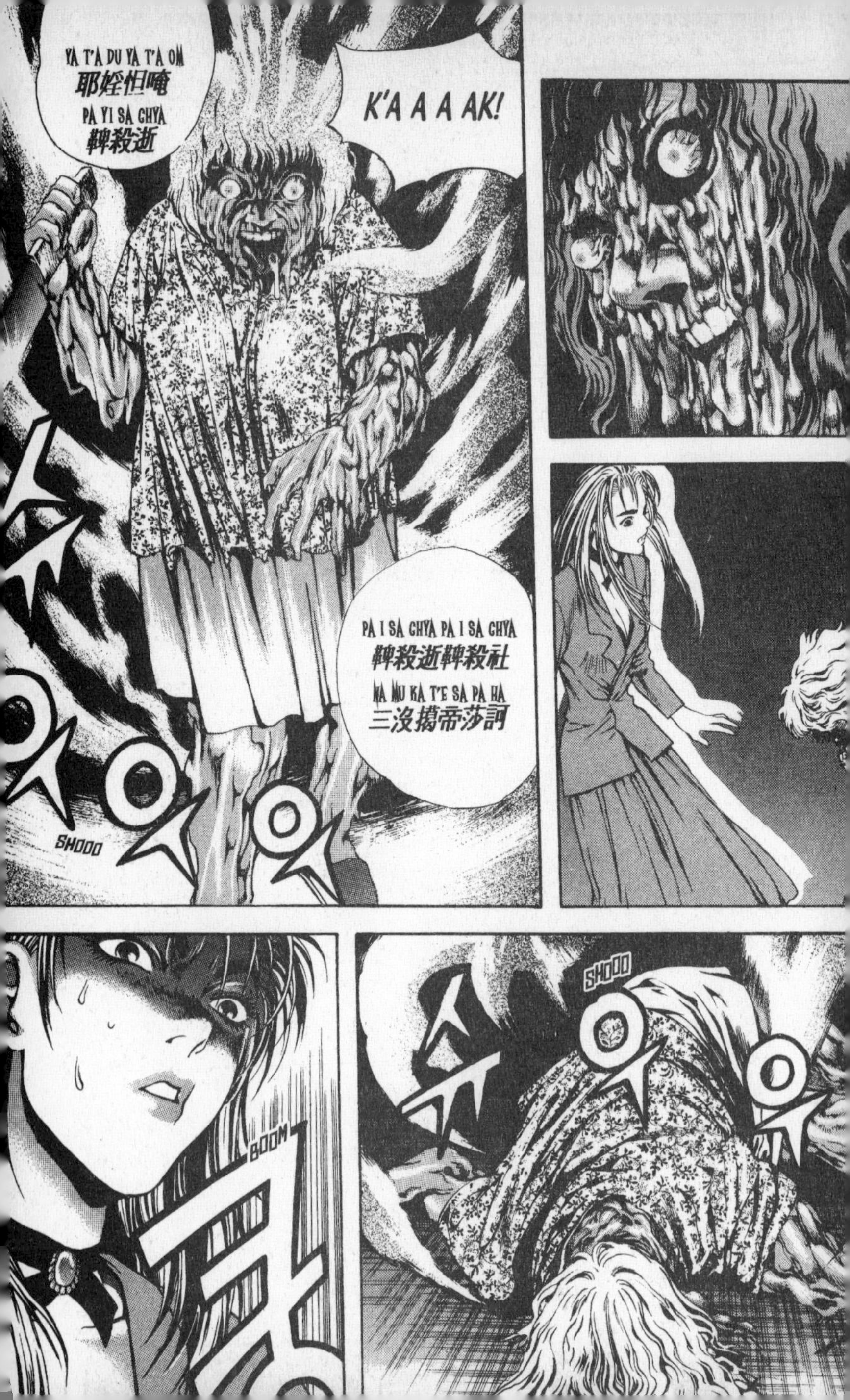

YA T'A DU YA T'A OM
耶姪怛唵
PA YI SA CHYA
鞞殺逝
K'A A A AK!
PA I SA CHYA PA I SA CHYA
鞞殺逝鞞殺社
NA MU KA T'E SA PA HA
三沒揭帝莎訶
SHOOO
BOOM
SHOOO

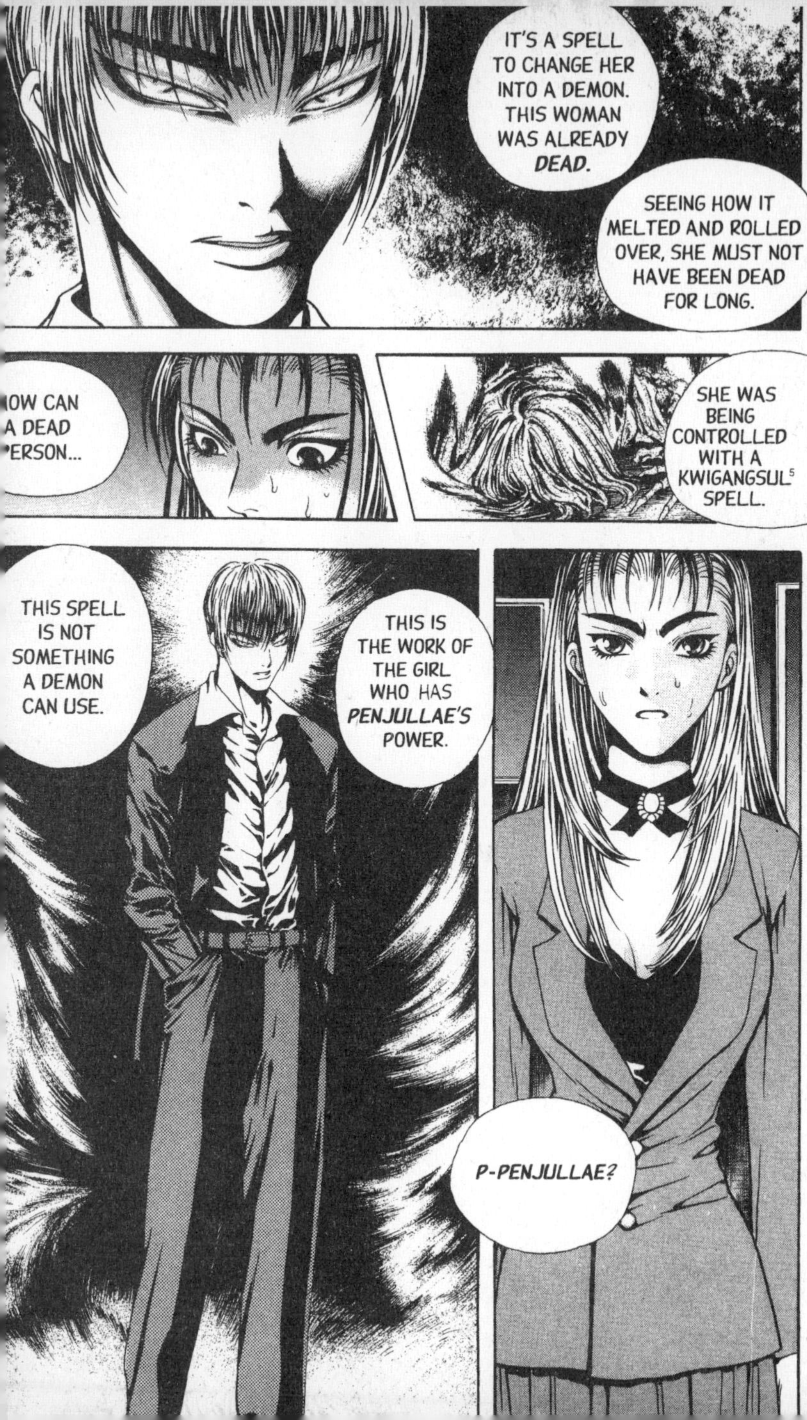
IT'S A SPELL TO CHANGE HER INTO A DEMON. THIS WOMAN WAS ALREADY *DEAD.*
SEEING HOW IT MELTED AND ROLLED OVER, SHE MUST NOT HAVE BEEN DEAD FOR LONG.
OW CAN A DEAD ERSON...
SHE WAS BEING CONTROLLED WITH A KWIGANGSUL[5] SPELL.
THIS SPELL IS NOT SOMETHING A DEMON CAN USE.
THIS IS THE WORK OF THE GIRL WHO HAS *PENJULLAE'S* POWER.
P-PENJULLAE?

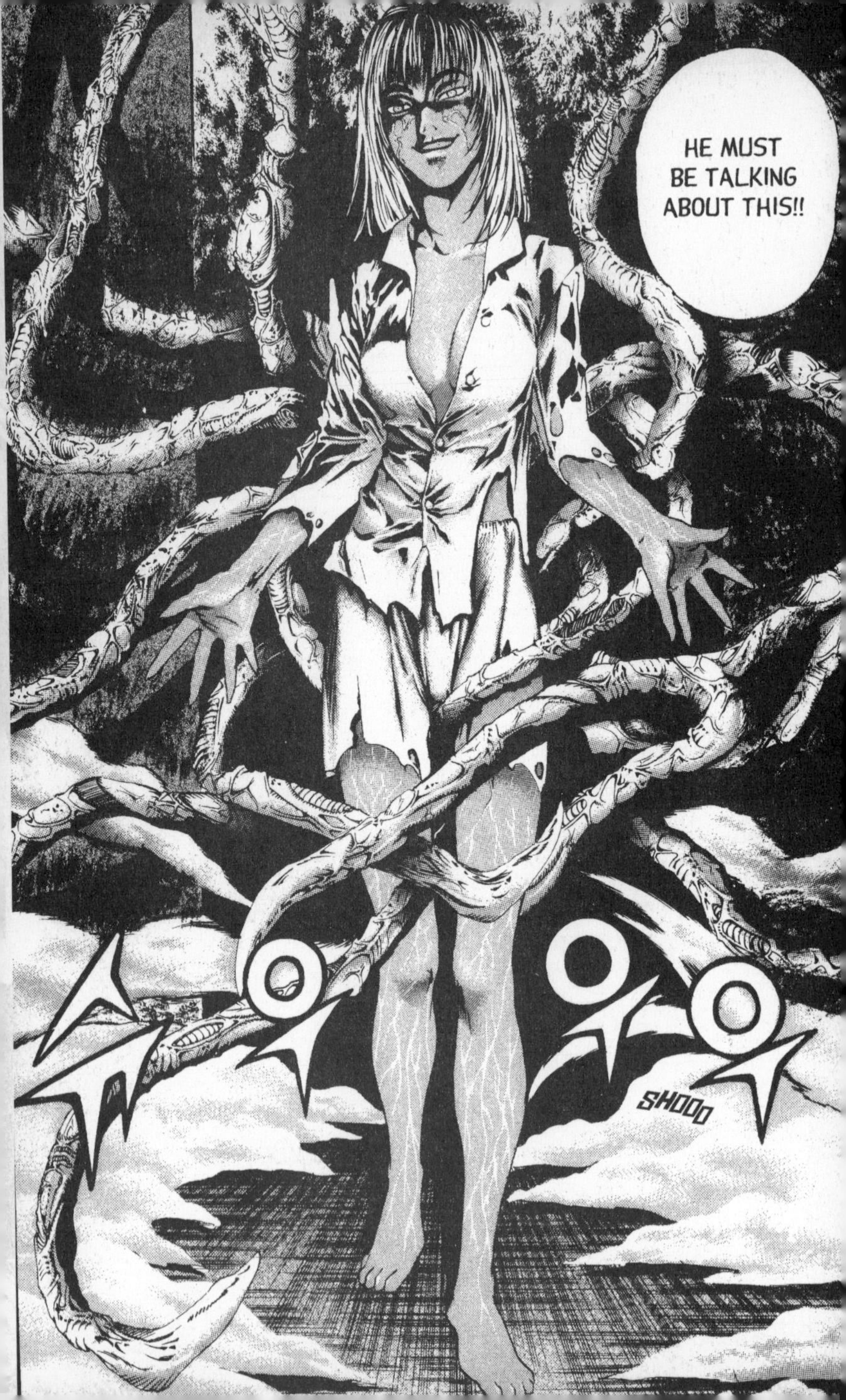
HE MUST BE TALKING ABOUT THIS!!
SHOOO

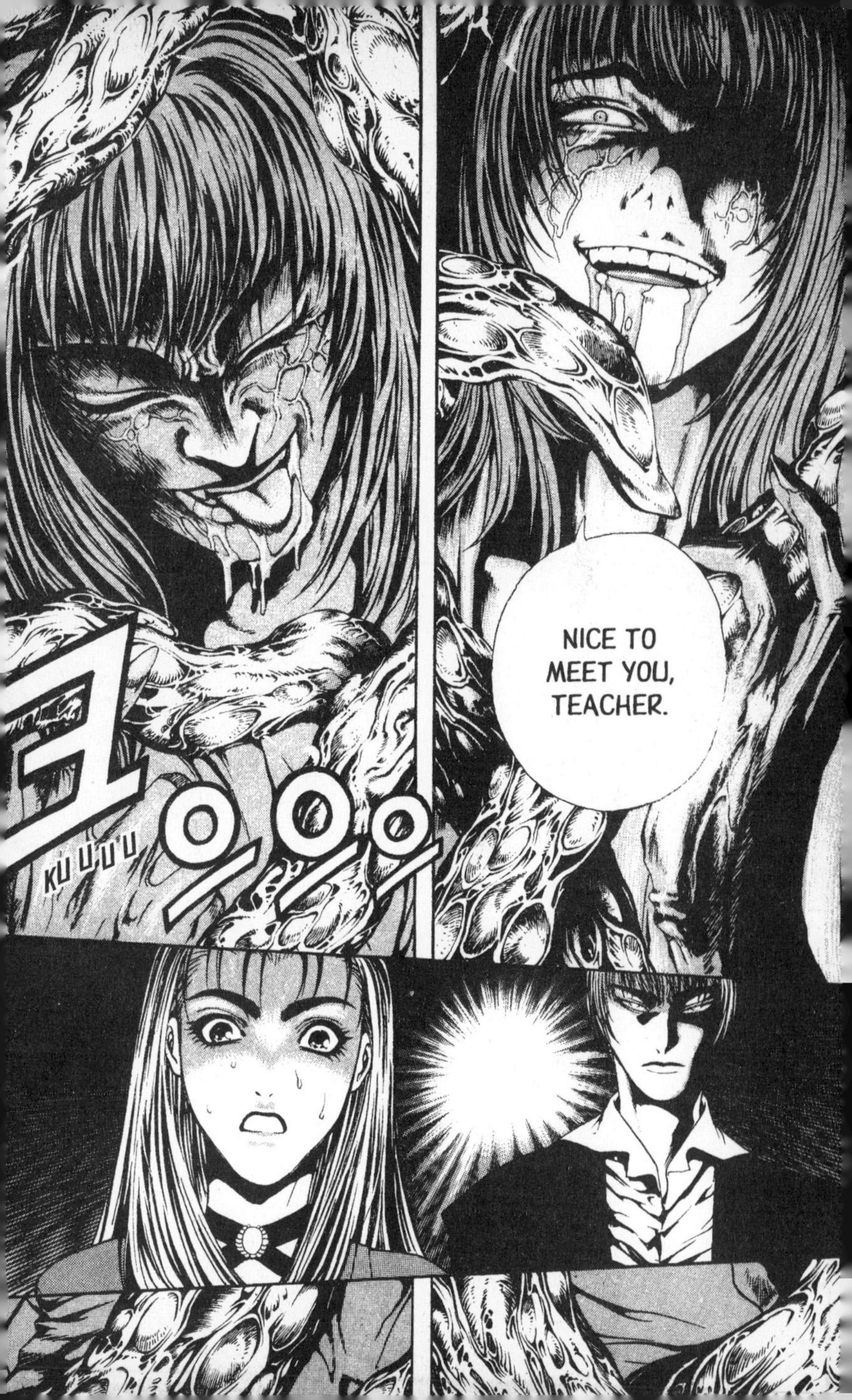
KUUUU
NICE TO MEET YOU, TEACHER.

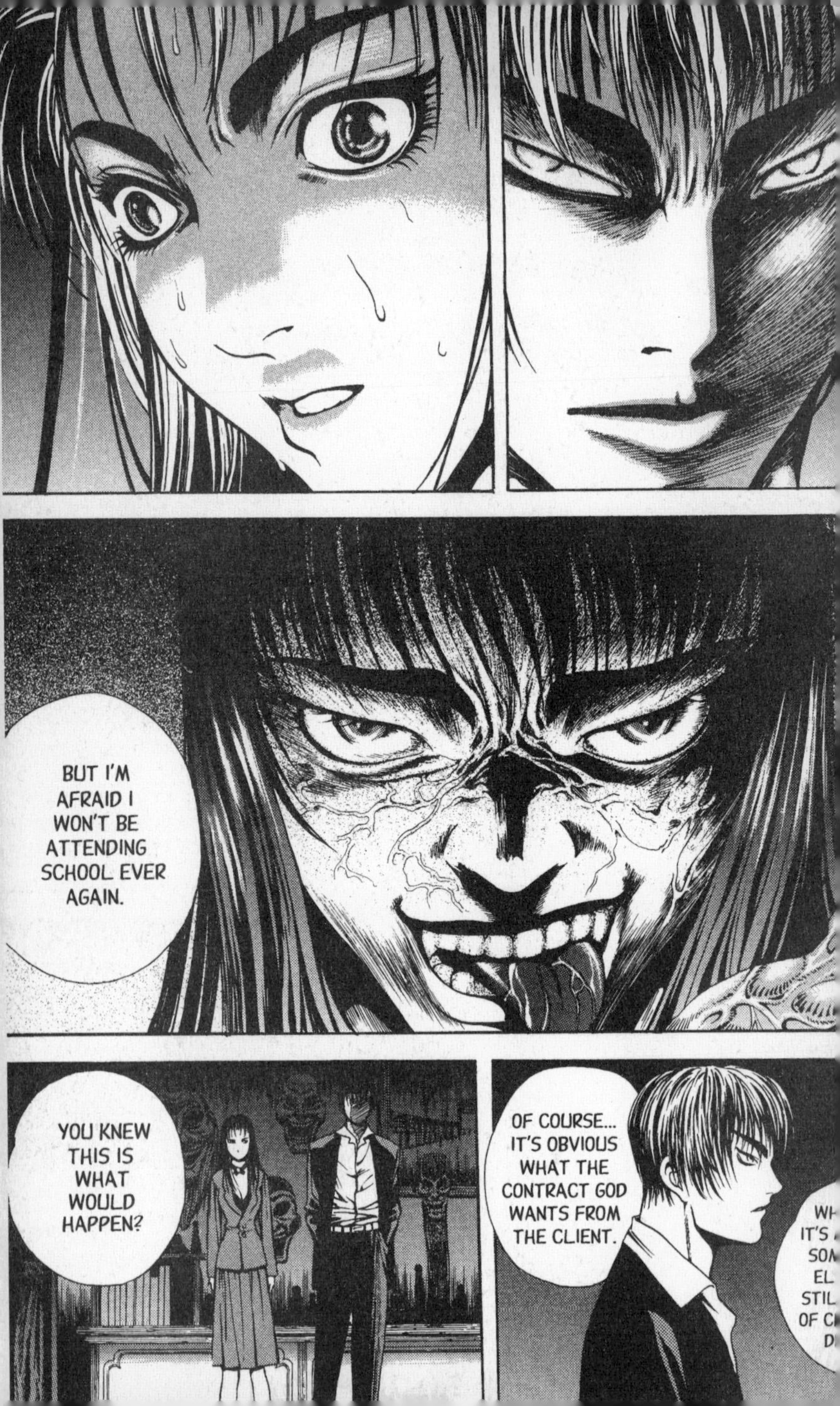
BUT I'M AFRAID I WON'T BE ATTENDING SCHOOL EVER AGAIN.
YOU KNEW THIS IS WHAT WOULD HAPPEN?
OF COURSE... IT'S OBVIOUS WHAT THE CONTRACT GOD WANTS FROM THE CLIENT.

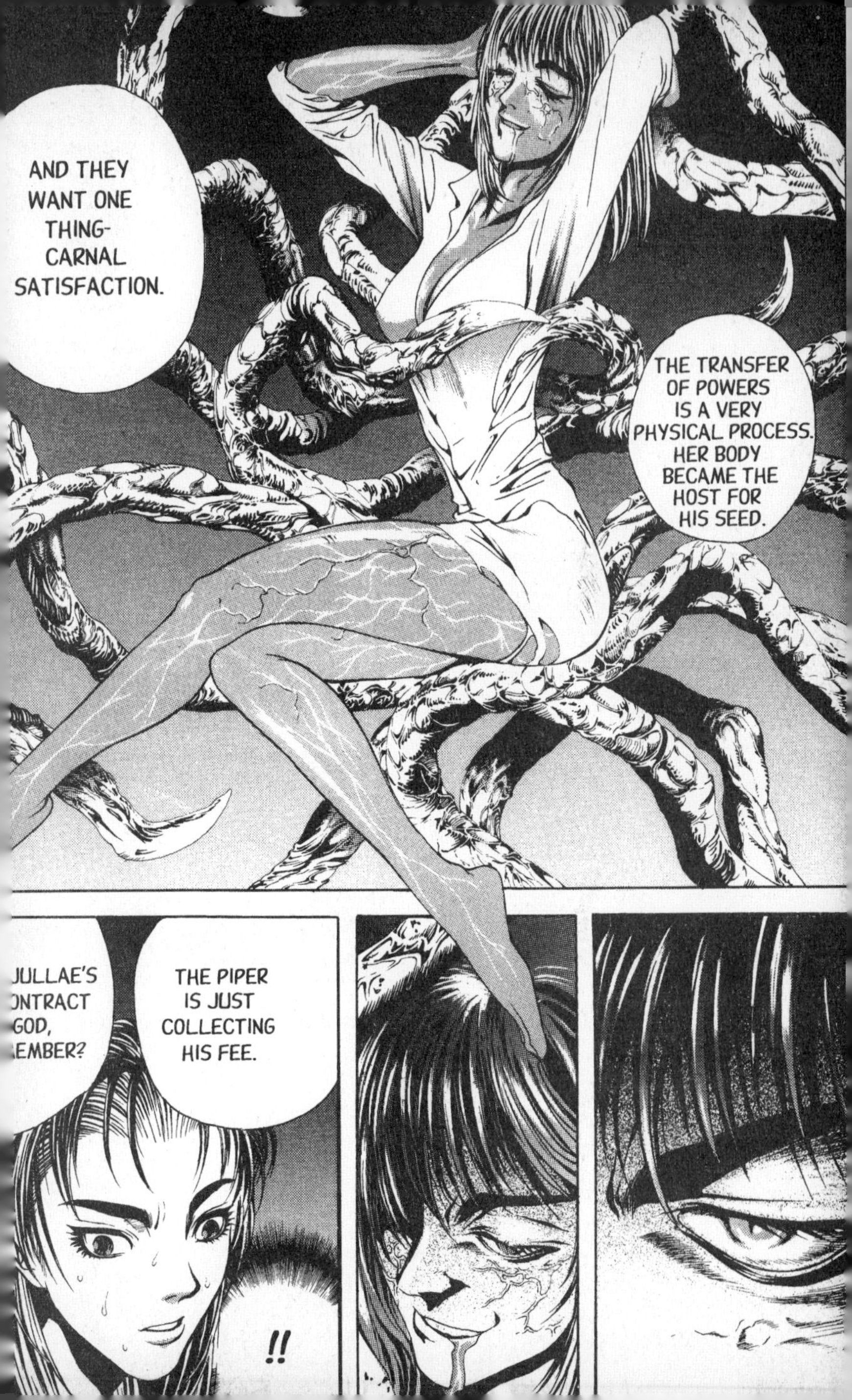
AND THEY WANT ONE THING- CARNAL SATISFACTION.
THE TRANSFER OF POWERS IS A VERY PHYSICAL PROCESS. HER BODY BECAME THE HOST FOR HIS SEED.
JULLAE'S ONTRACT GOD, EMBER?
THE PIPER IS JUST COLLECTING HIS FEE.
!!

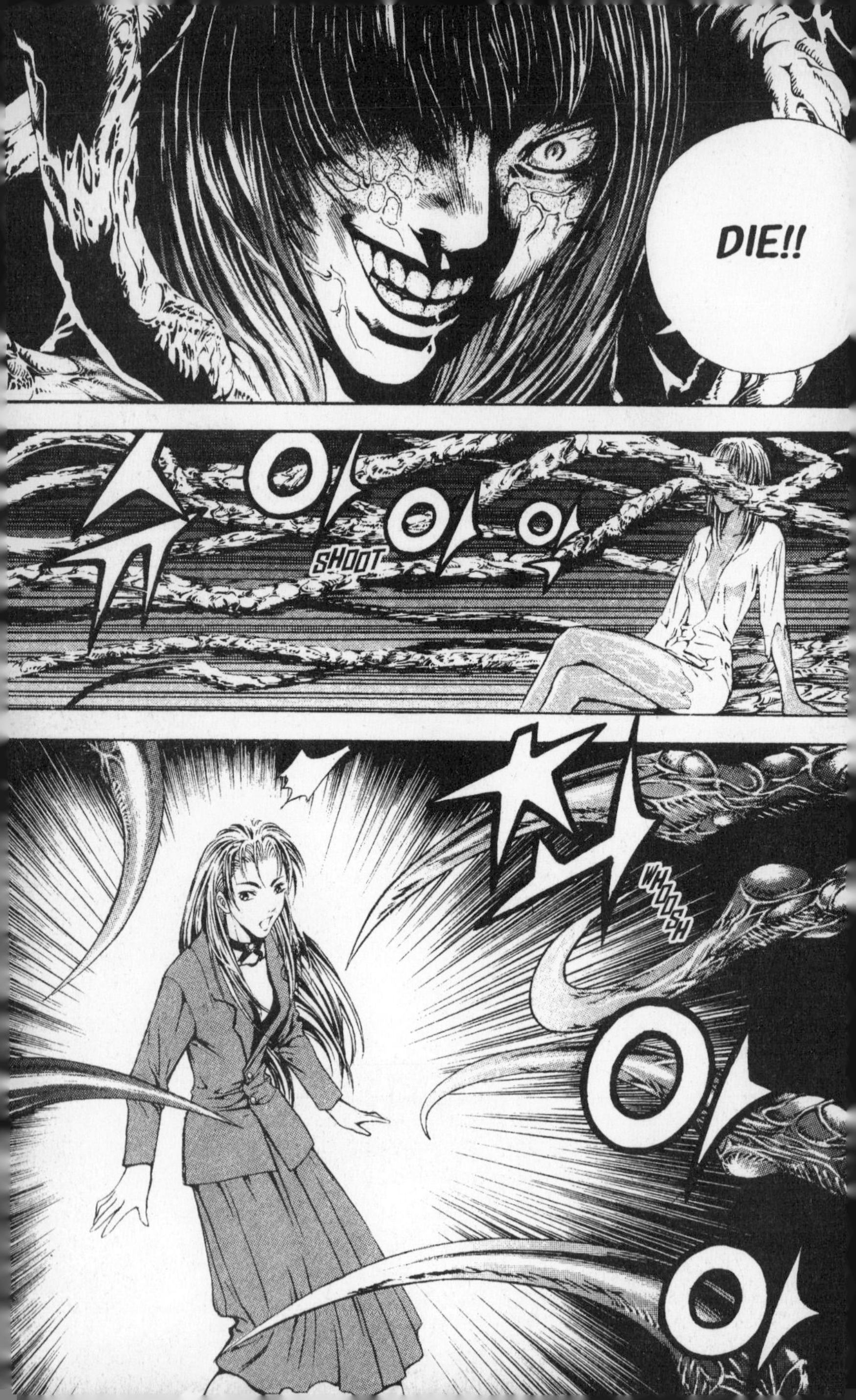
DIE!!
SHOOT
WHOOSH

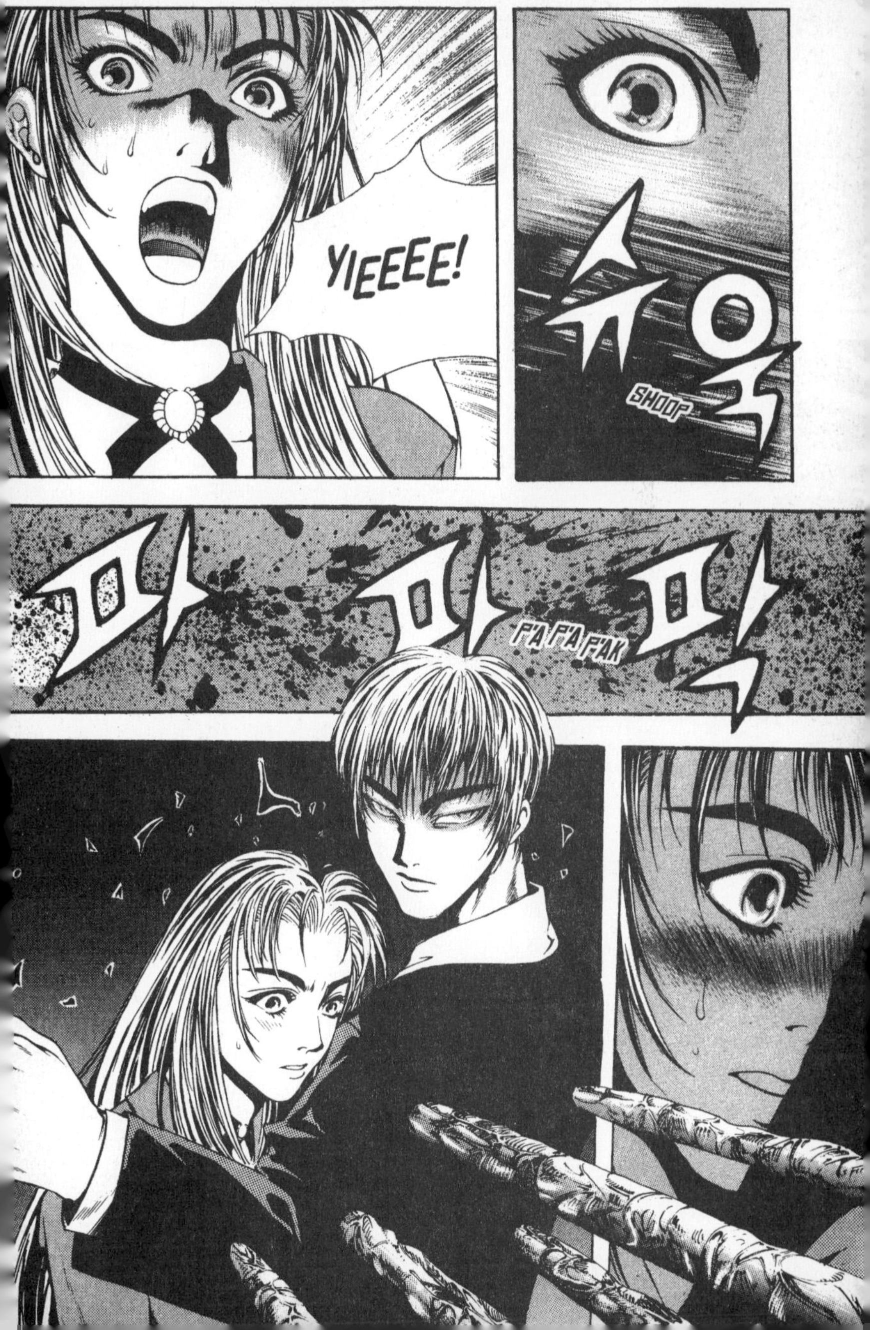
YIEEEE!
SHOOP
P'A P'A P'AK

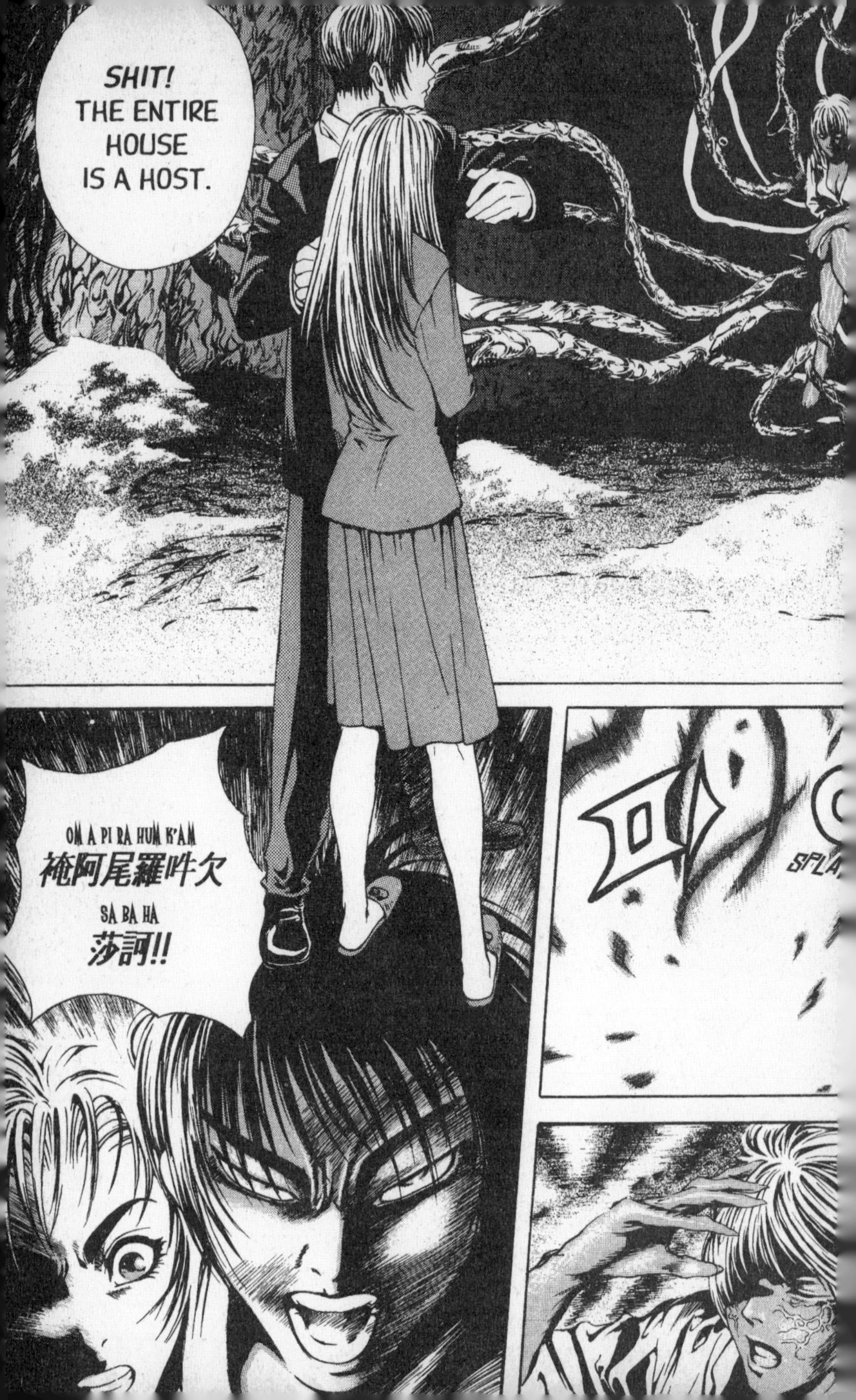
SHIT! THE ENTIRE HOUSE IS A HOST.
OM A PI RA HUM K'AM
唵阿尾羅吽欠
SA BA HA
莎訶!!
SPLA

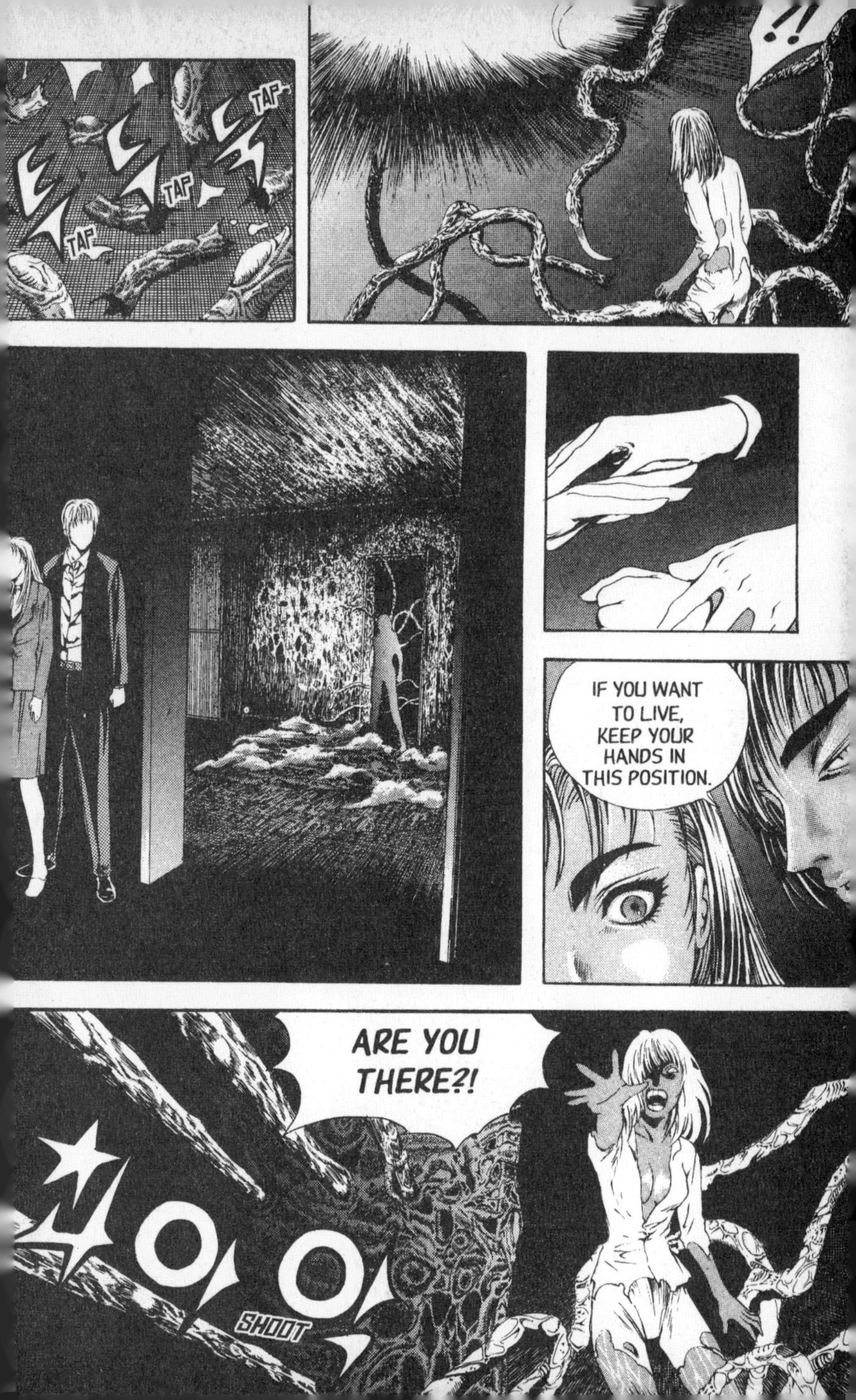
TAP-
TAP
TAP
!!
IF YOU WANT TO LIVE, KEEP YOUR HANDS IN THIS POSITION.
ARE YOU THERE?!
SHOOT

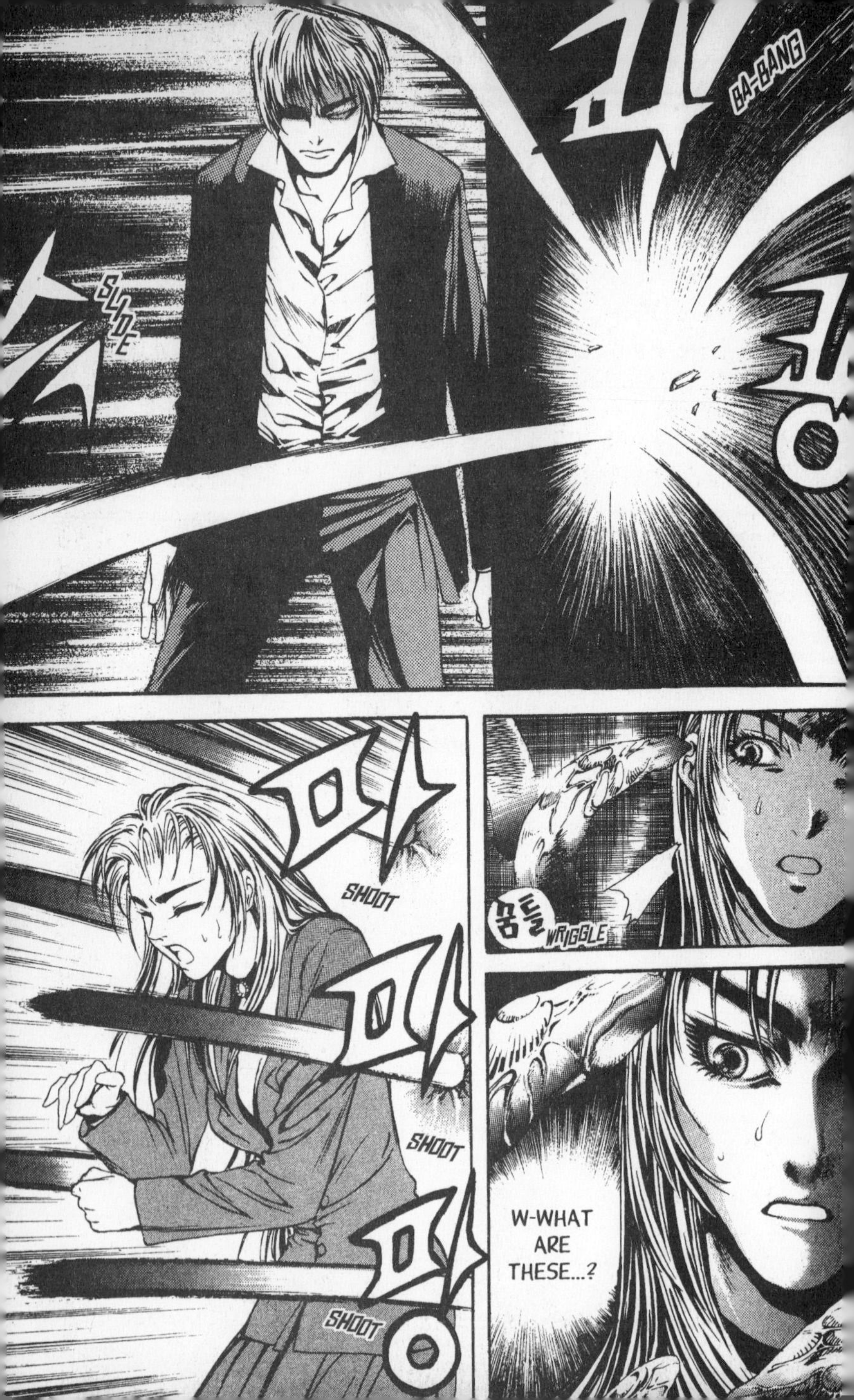
BA-BANG
SLIDE
꿈틀
WRIGGLE
W-WHAT ARE THESE...?
SHOOT
SHOOT
SHOOT

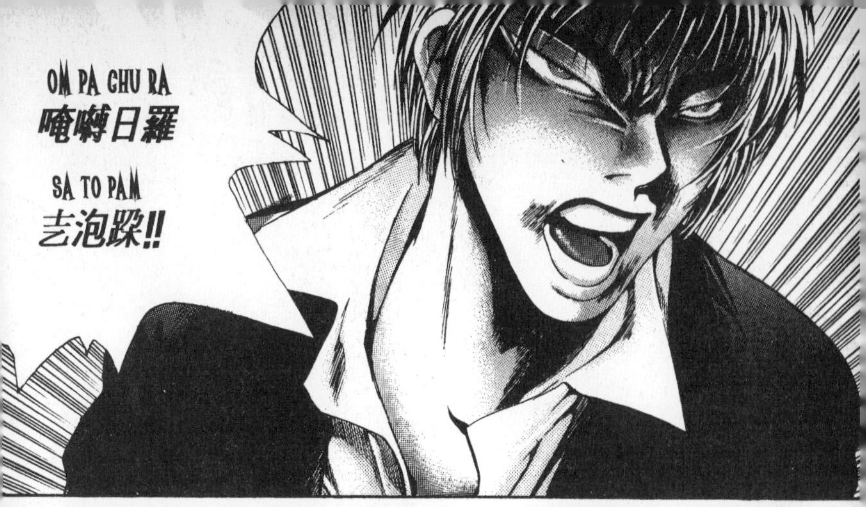
OM PA CHU RA
唵嚩日羅
SA TO PAM
乞泡跺!!

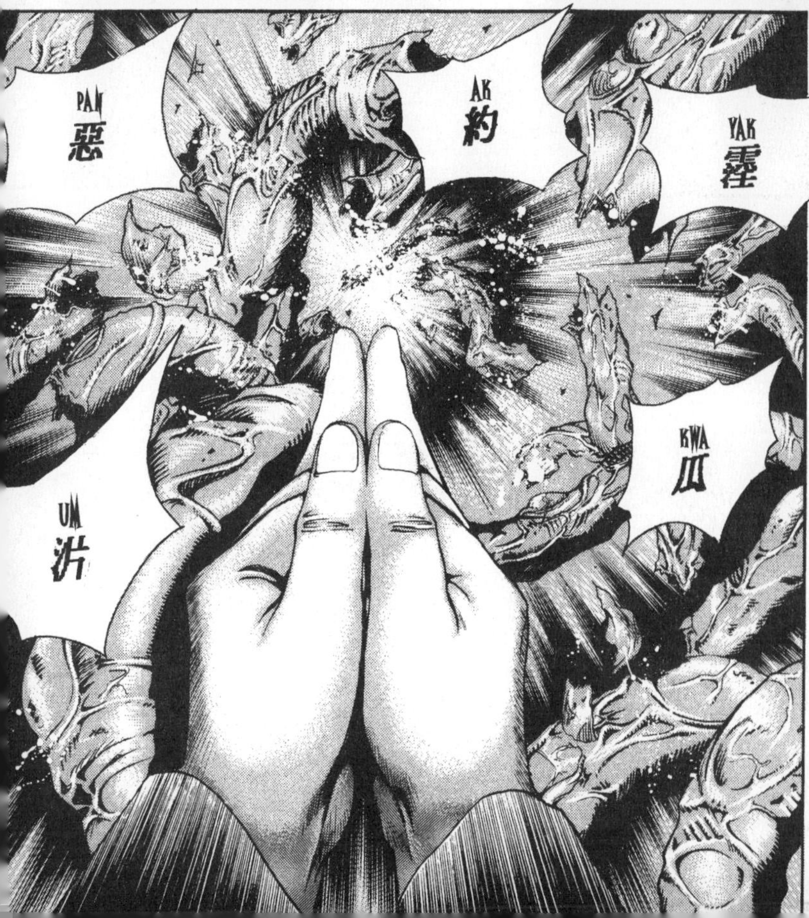
PAN
惡
AK
約
YAK
霆
KWA
瓜
UM
沚

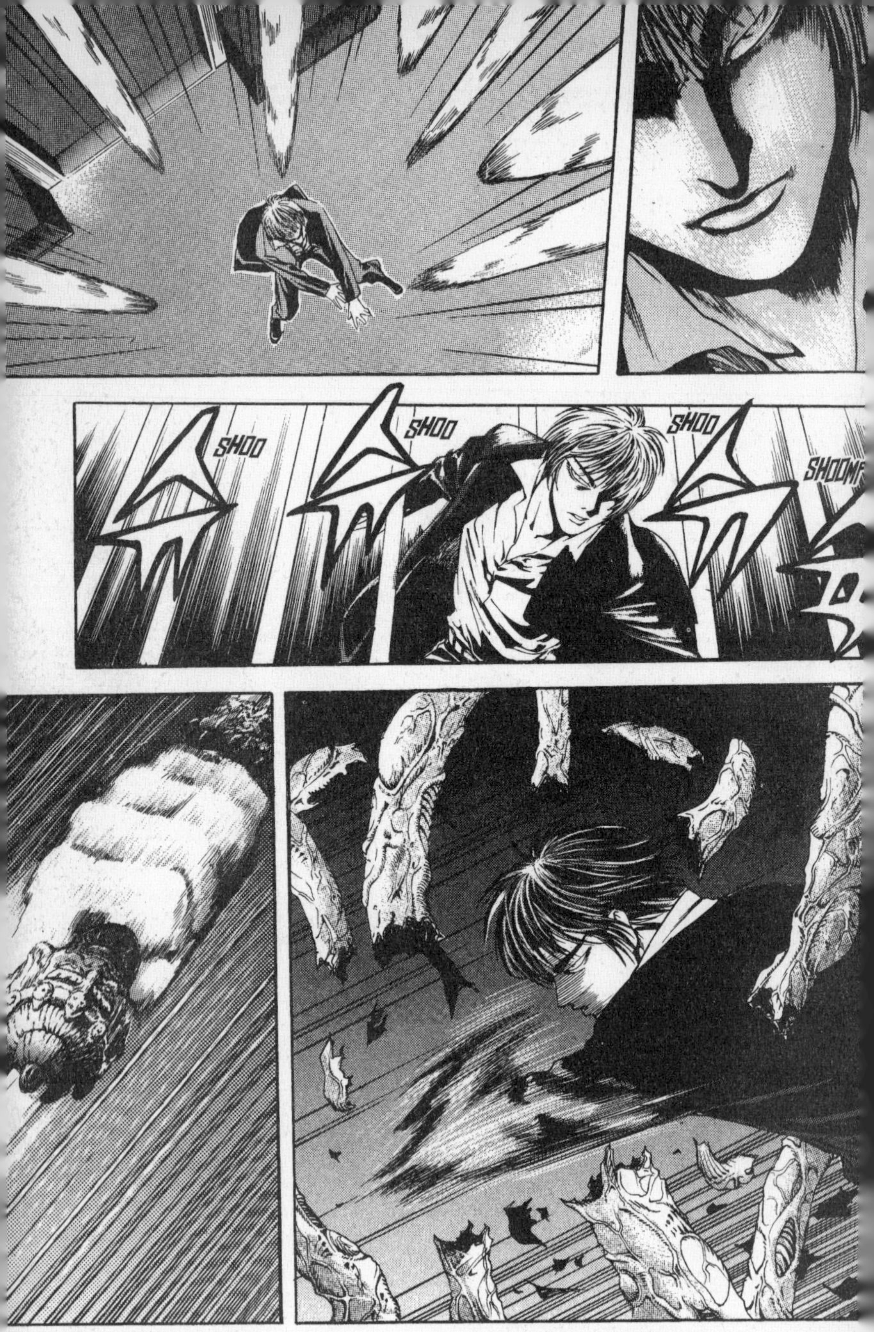
SHOO
SHOO
SHOO
SHOOM

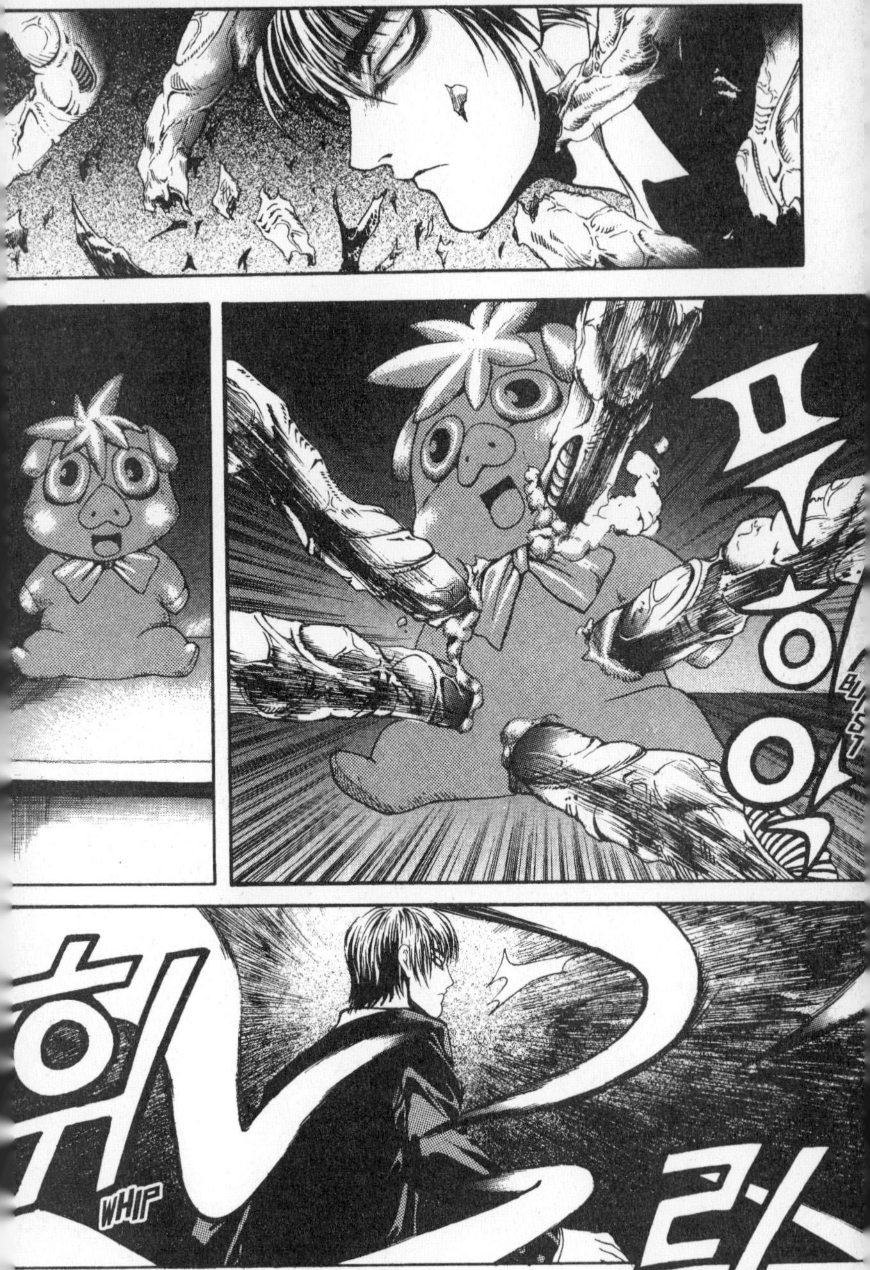
BURST
WHIP

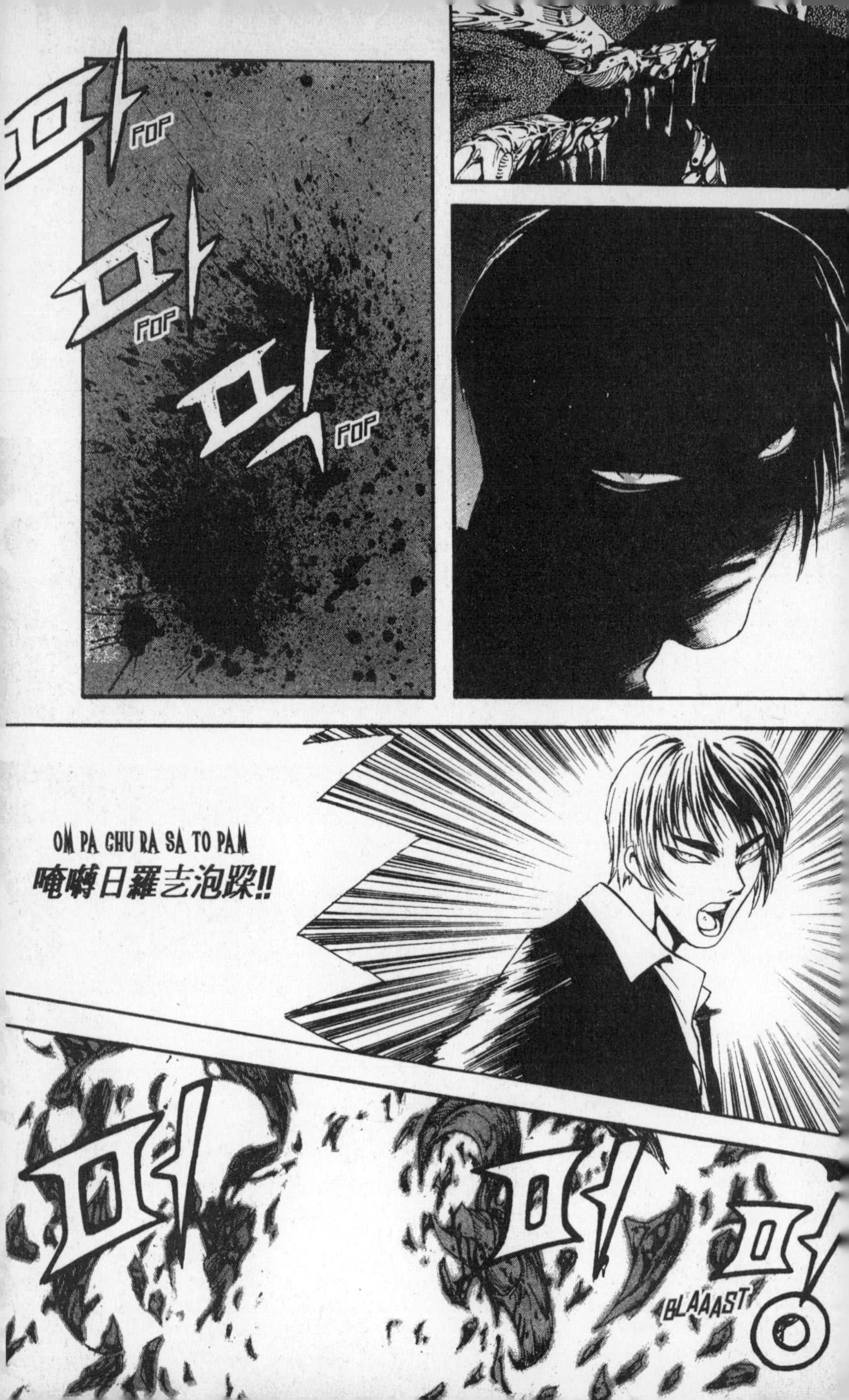
POP
POP
POP
OM PA CHU RA SA TO PAM
唵嚩日羅乞泡蹤!!
BLAAAST

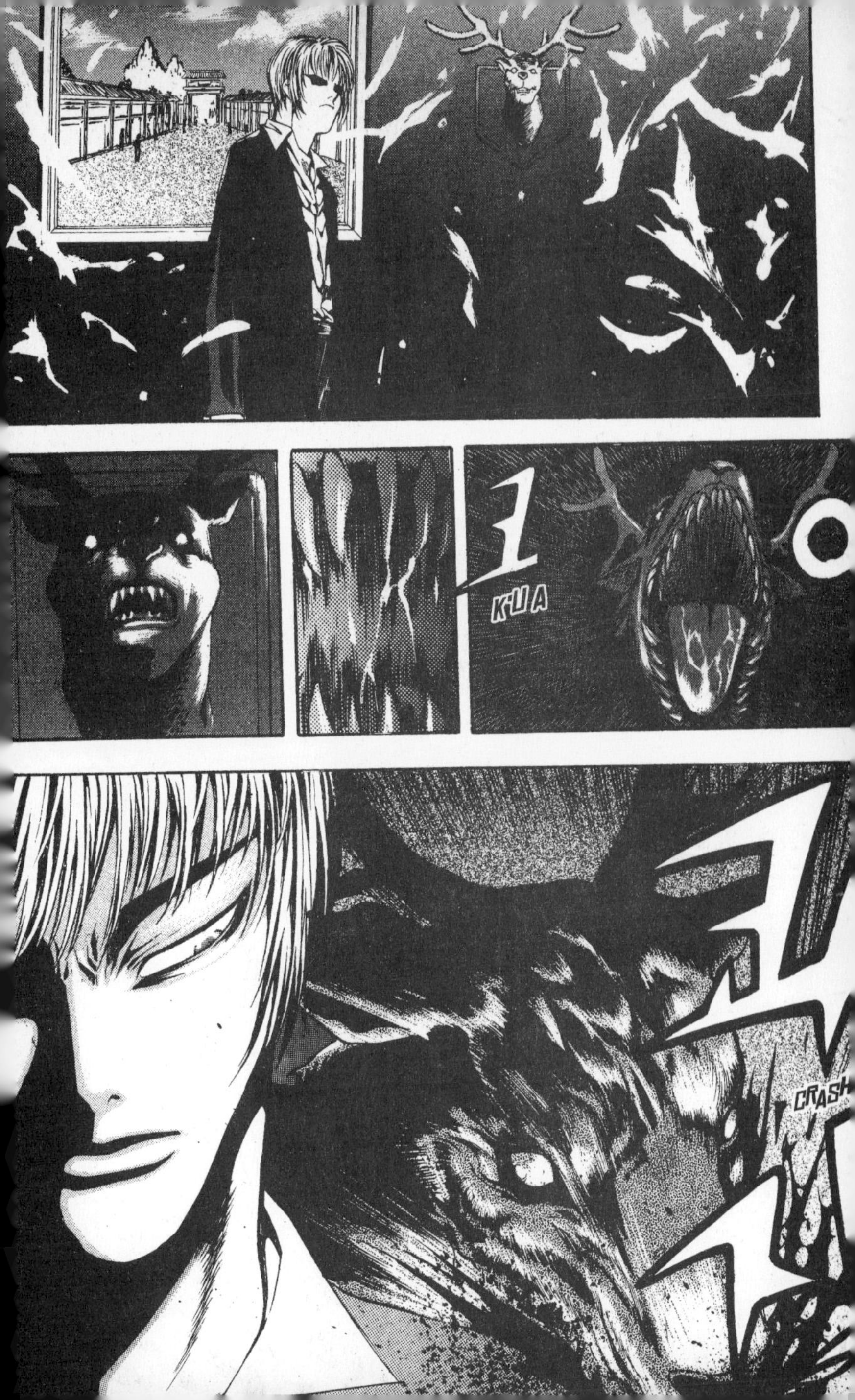
K'U A
CRASH

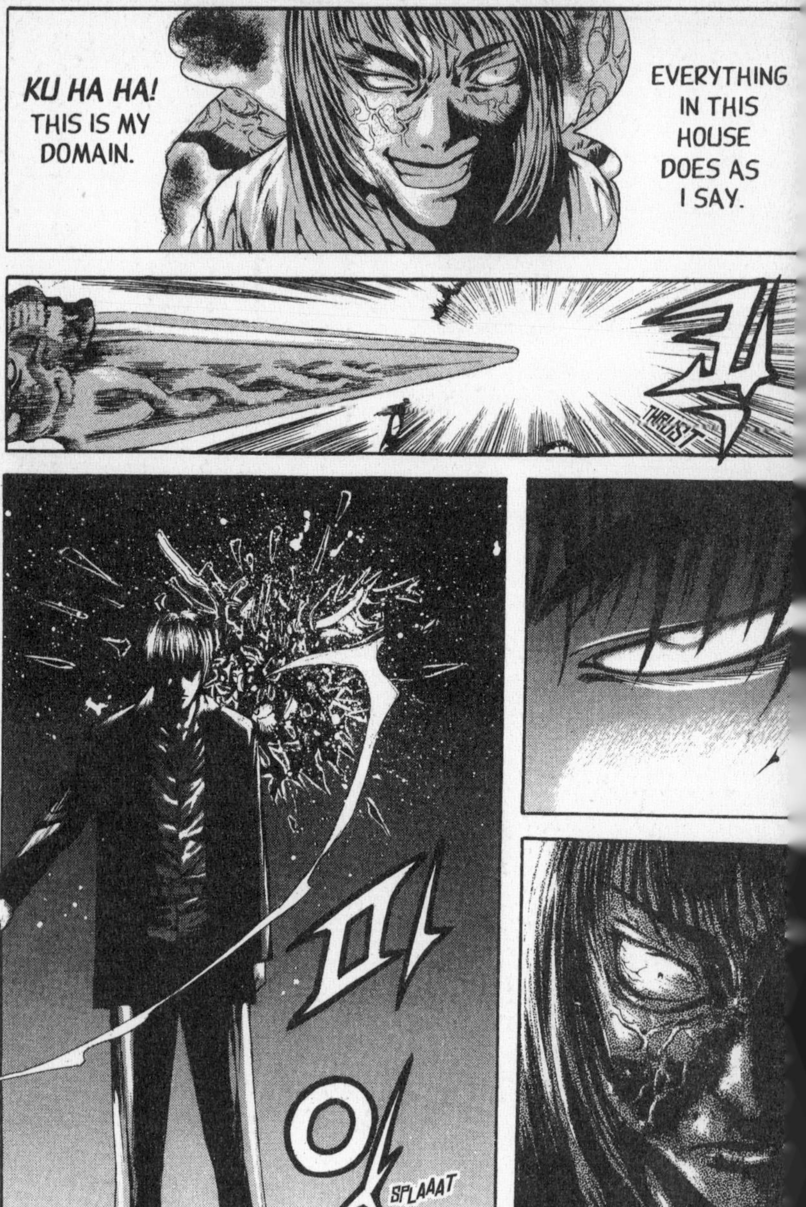
KU HA HA! THIS IS MY DOMAIN.
EVERYTHING IN THIS HOUSE DOES AS I SAY.
THRUST
SPLAAAT

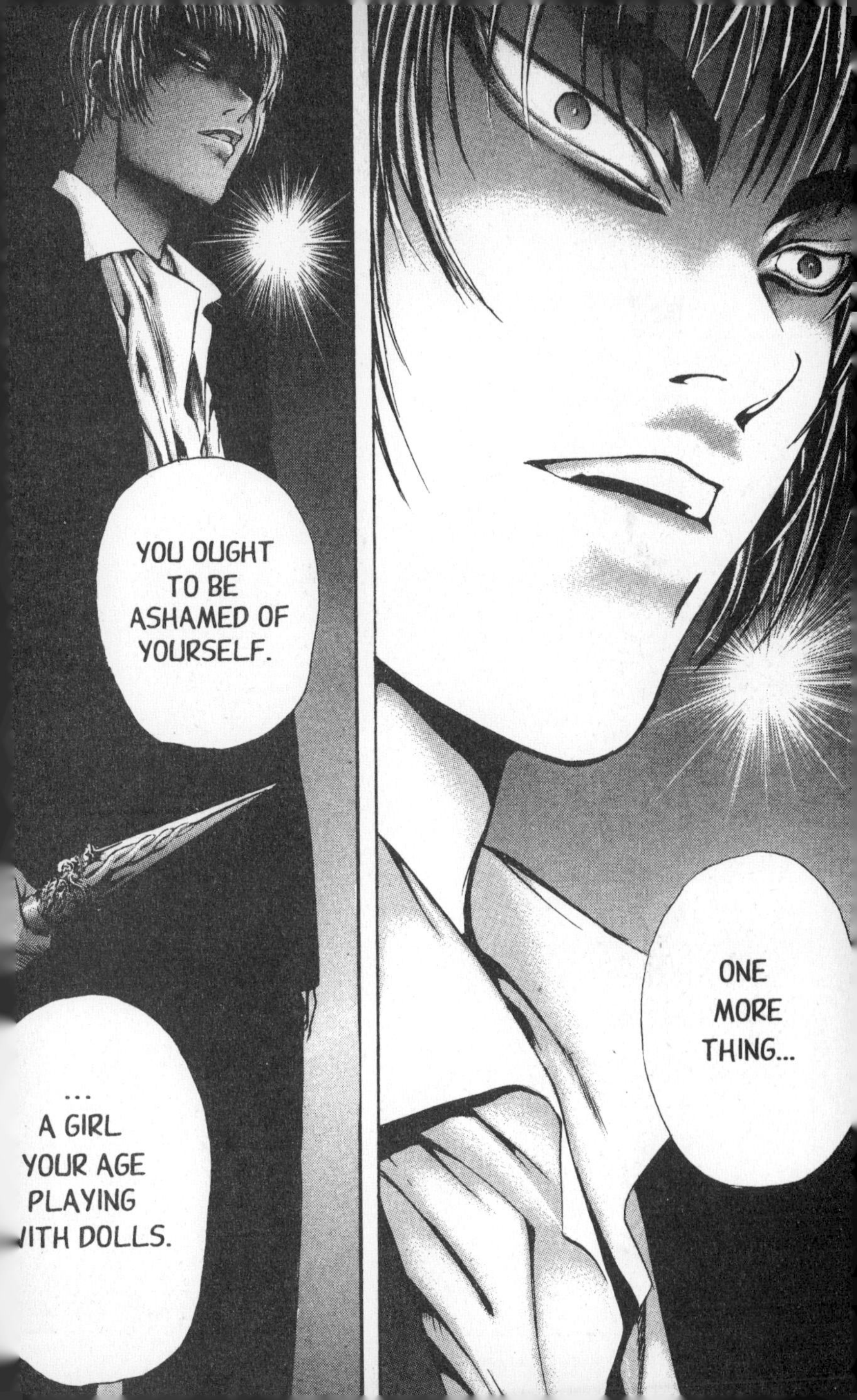
YOU OUGHT TO BE ASHAMED OF YOURSELF.
... A GIRL YOUR AGE PLAYING WITH DOLLS.
ONE MORE THING...

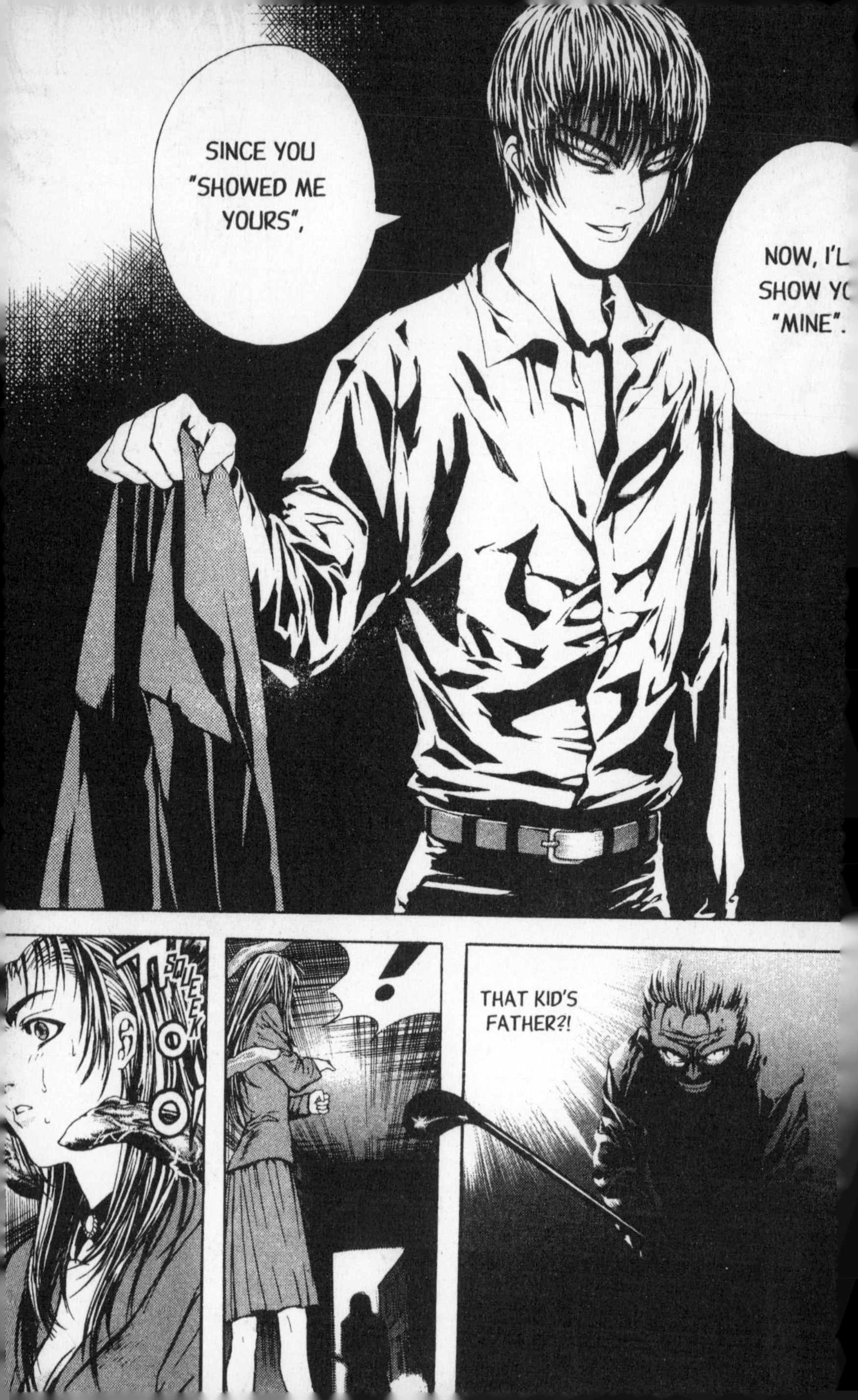
SINCE YOU "SHOWED ME YOURS",
NOW, I'L SHOW YO "MINE".
!
THAT KID'S FATHER?!

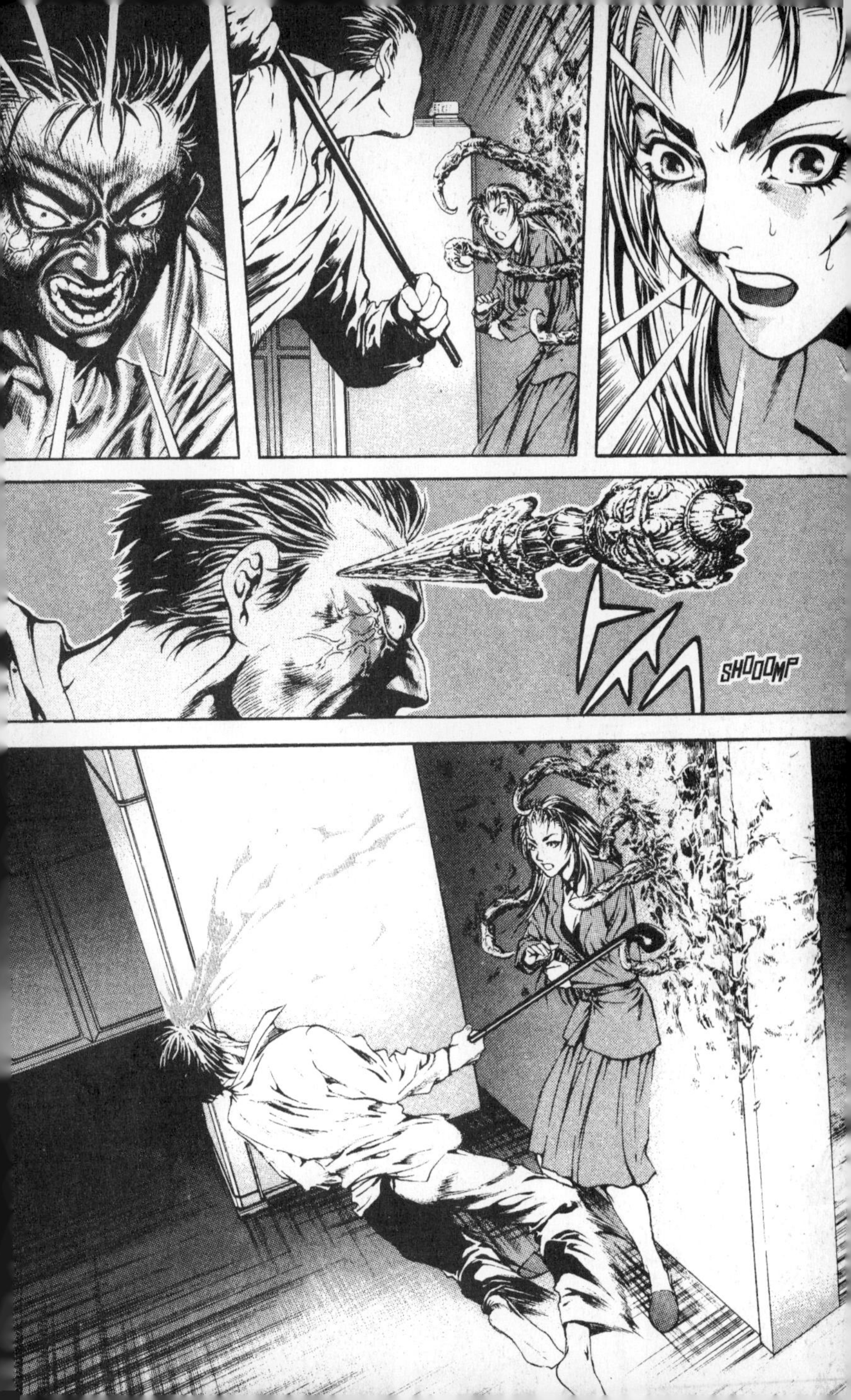
SHOOOMP

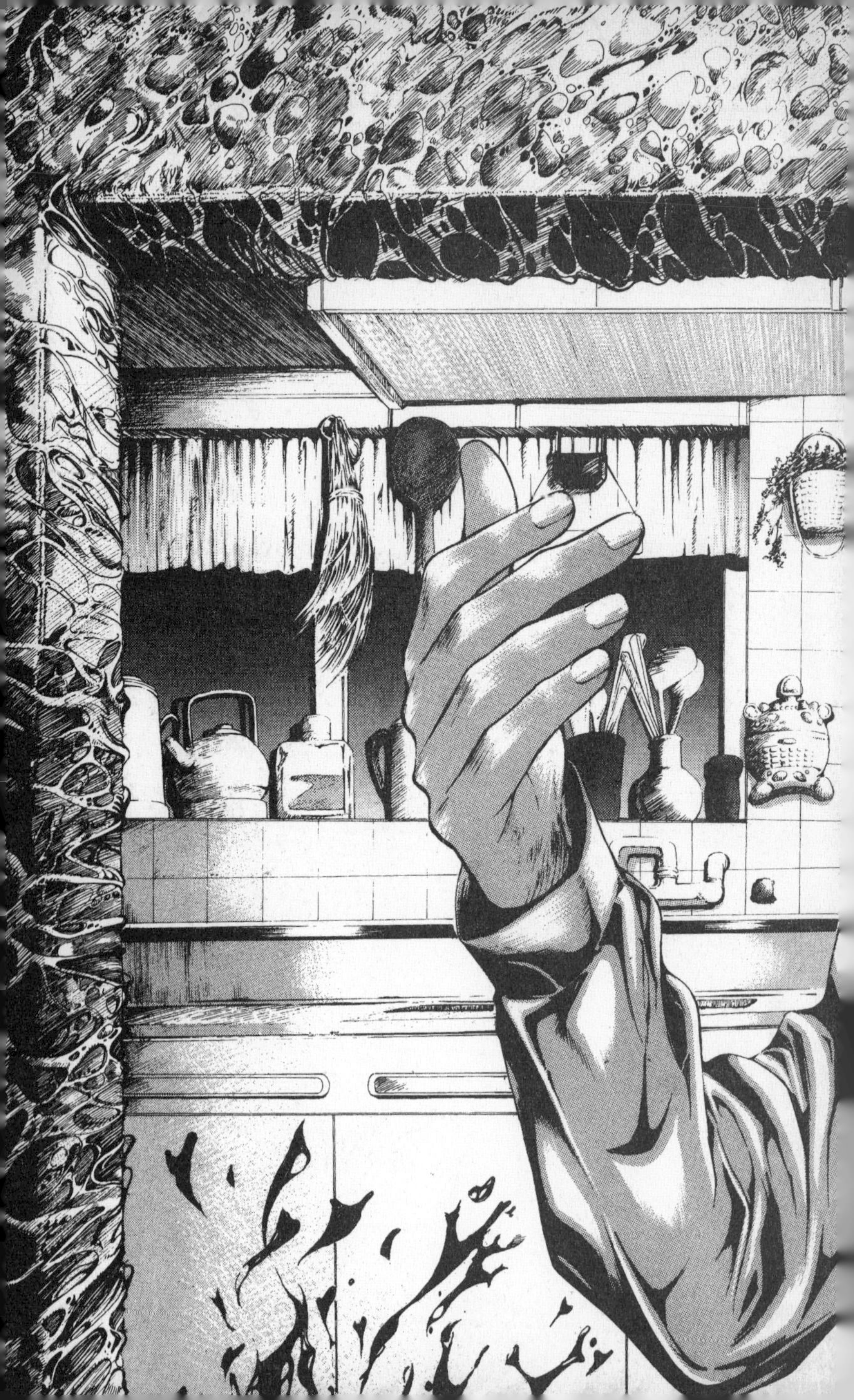

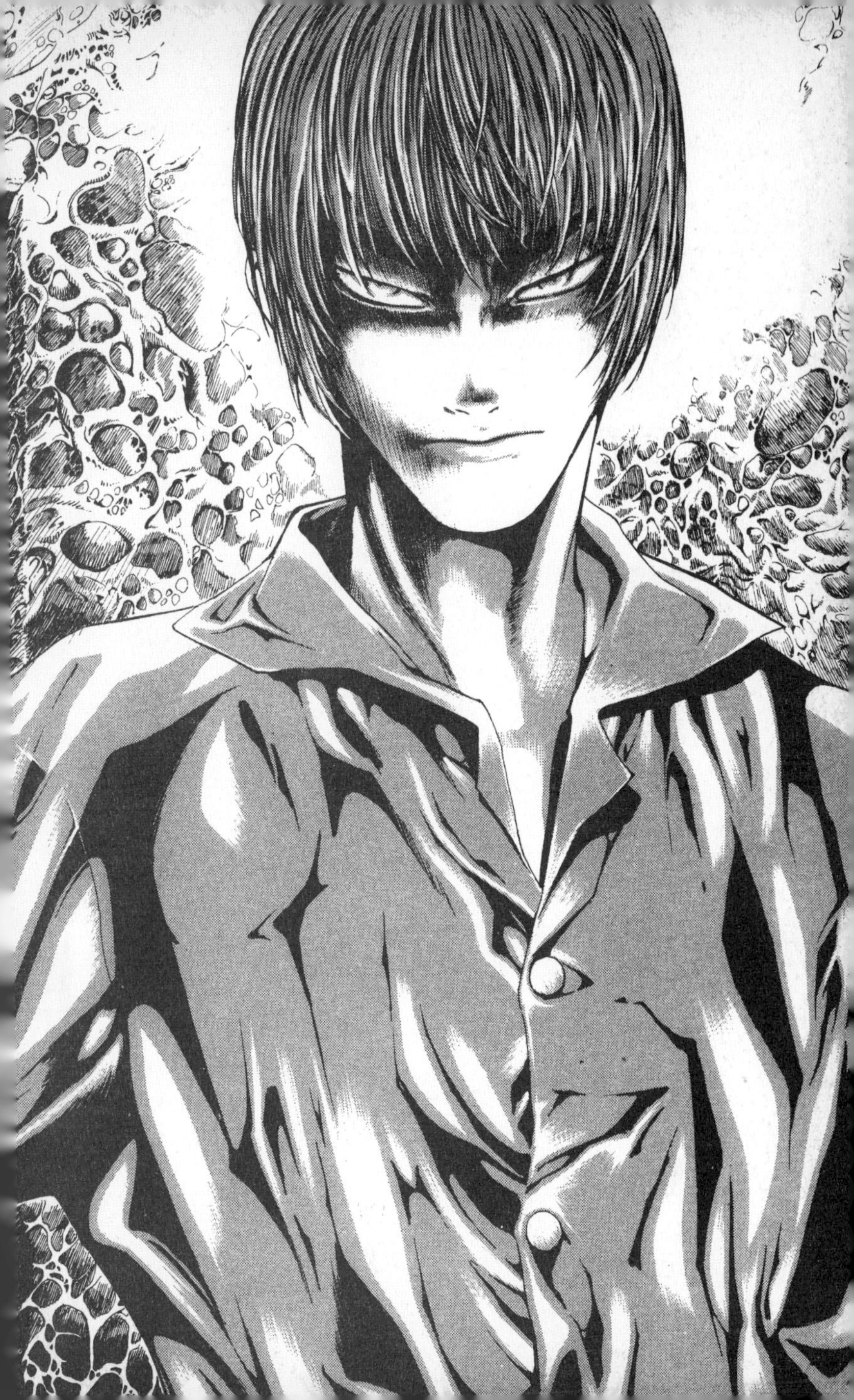

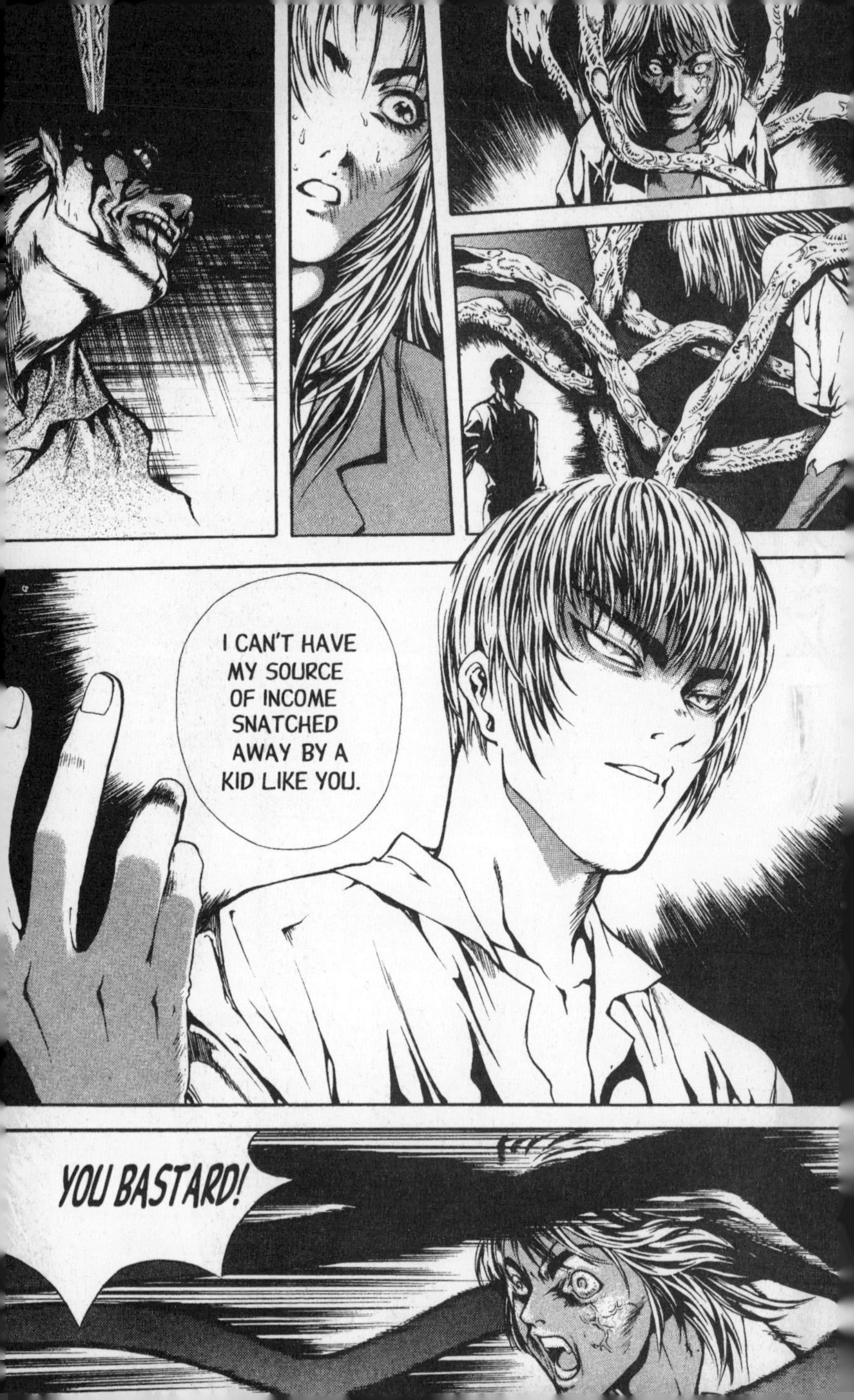
I CAN'T HAVE MY SOURCE OF INCOME SNATCHED AWAY BY A KID LIKE YOU.
YOU BASTARD!

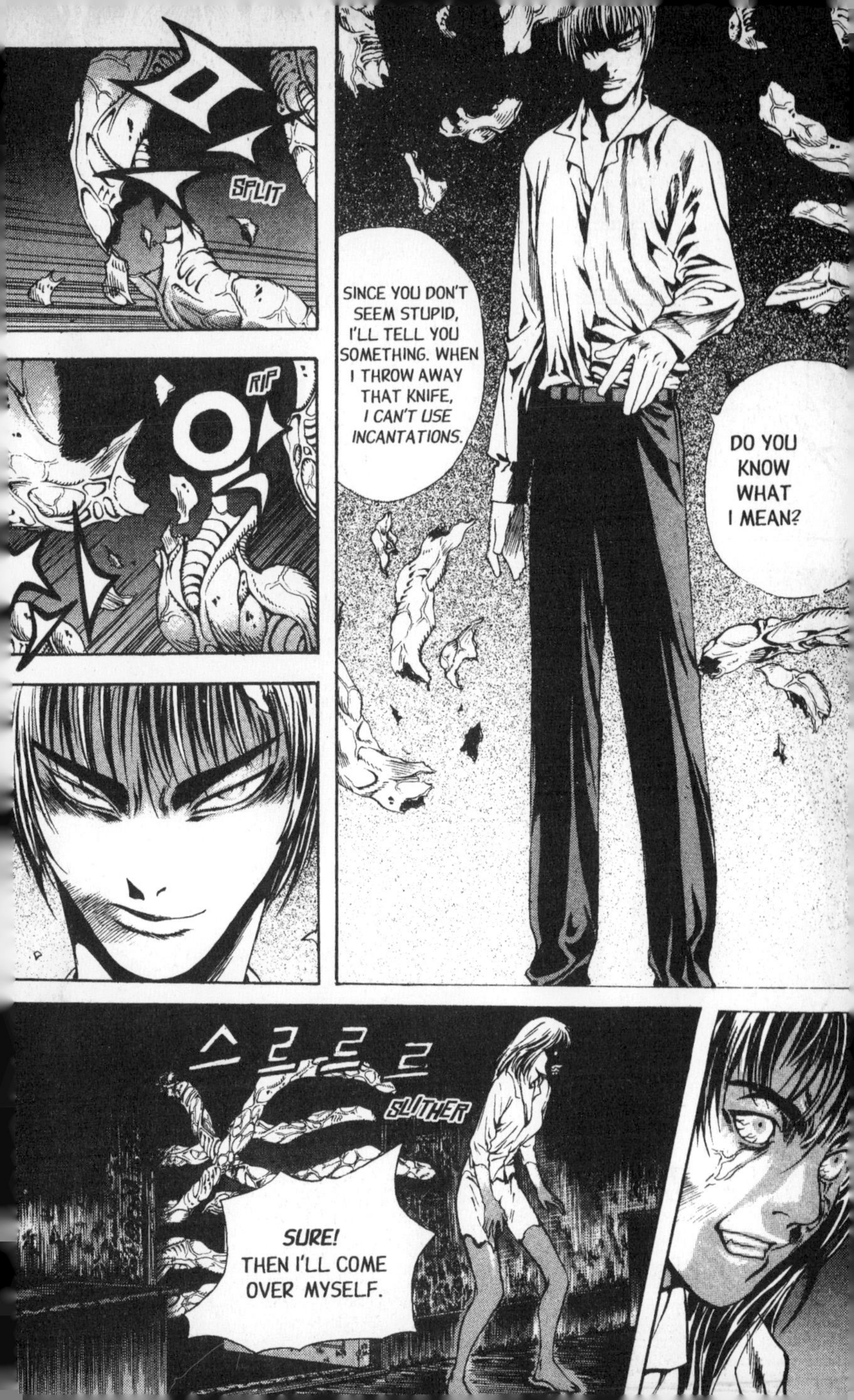
SPLIT
RIP
SINCE YOU DON'T SEEM STUPID, I'LL TELL YOU SOMETHING. WHEN I THROW AWAY THAT KNIFE, I CAN'T USE INCANTATIONS.
DO YOU KNOW WHAT I MEAN?
SLITHER
SURE! THEN I'LL COME OVER MYSELF.

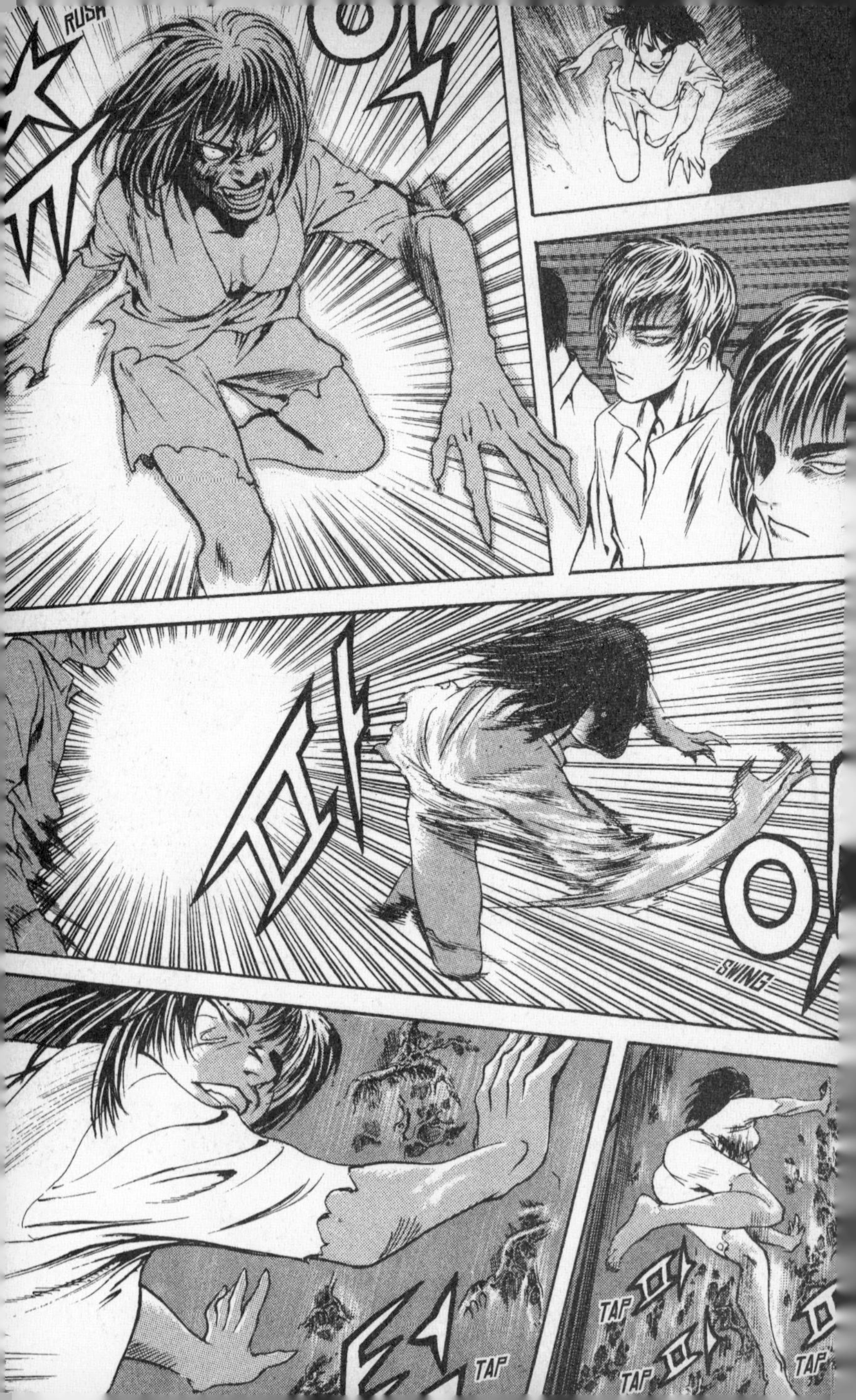
RUSH
SWING
TAP
TAP
TAP
TAP

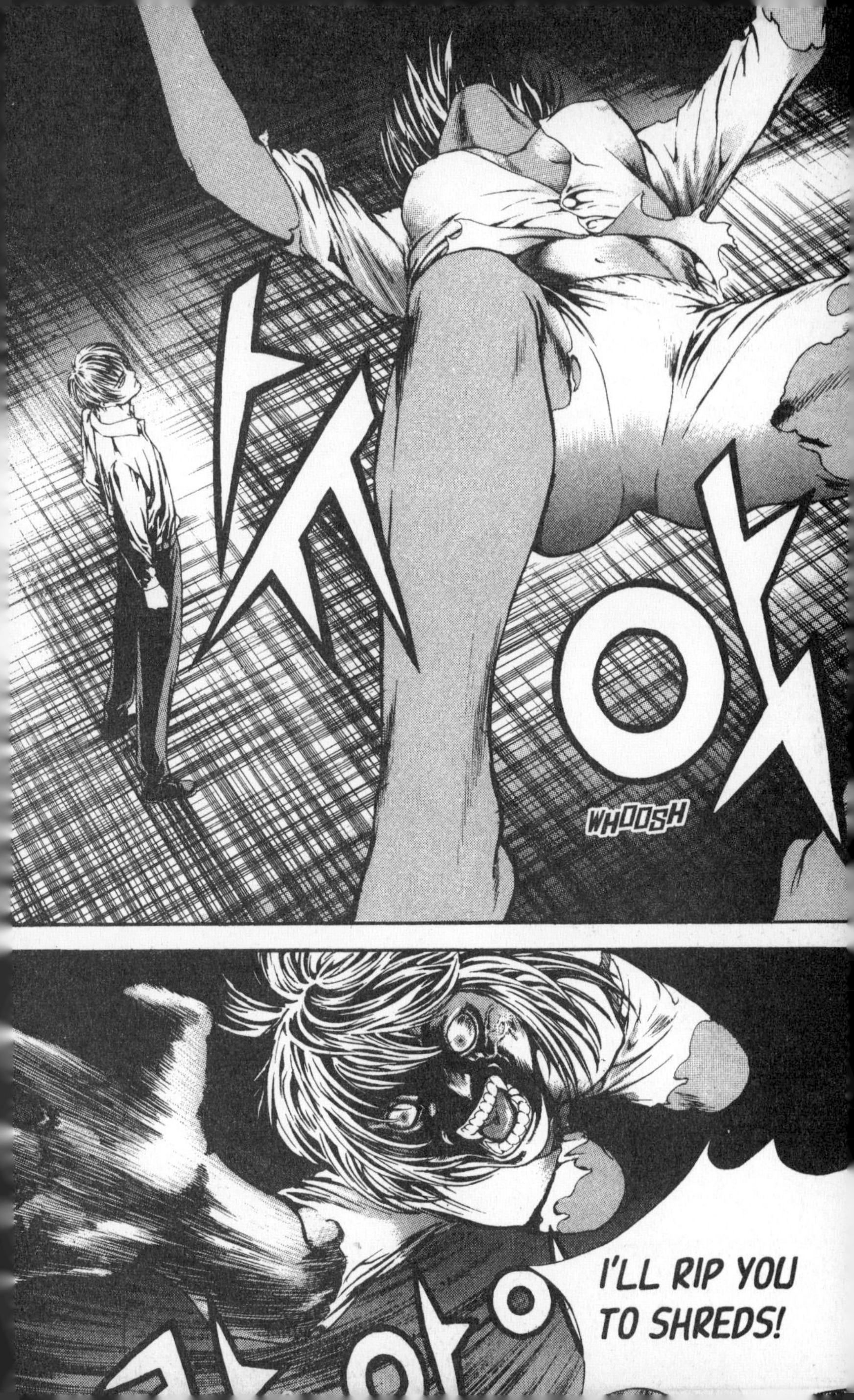
WHOOSH
I'LL RIP YOU TO SHREDS!

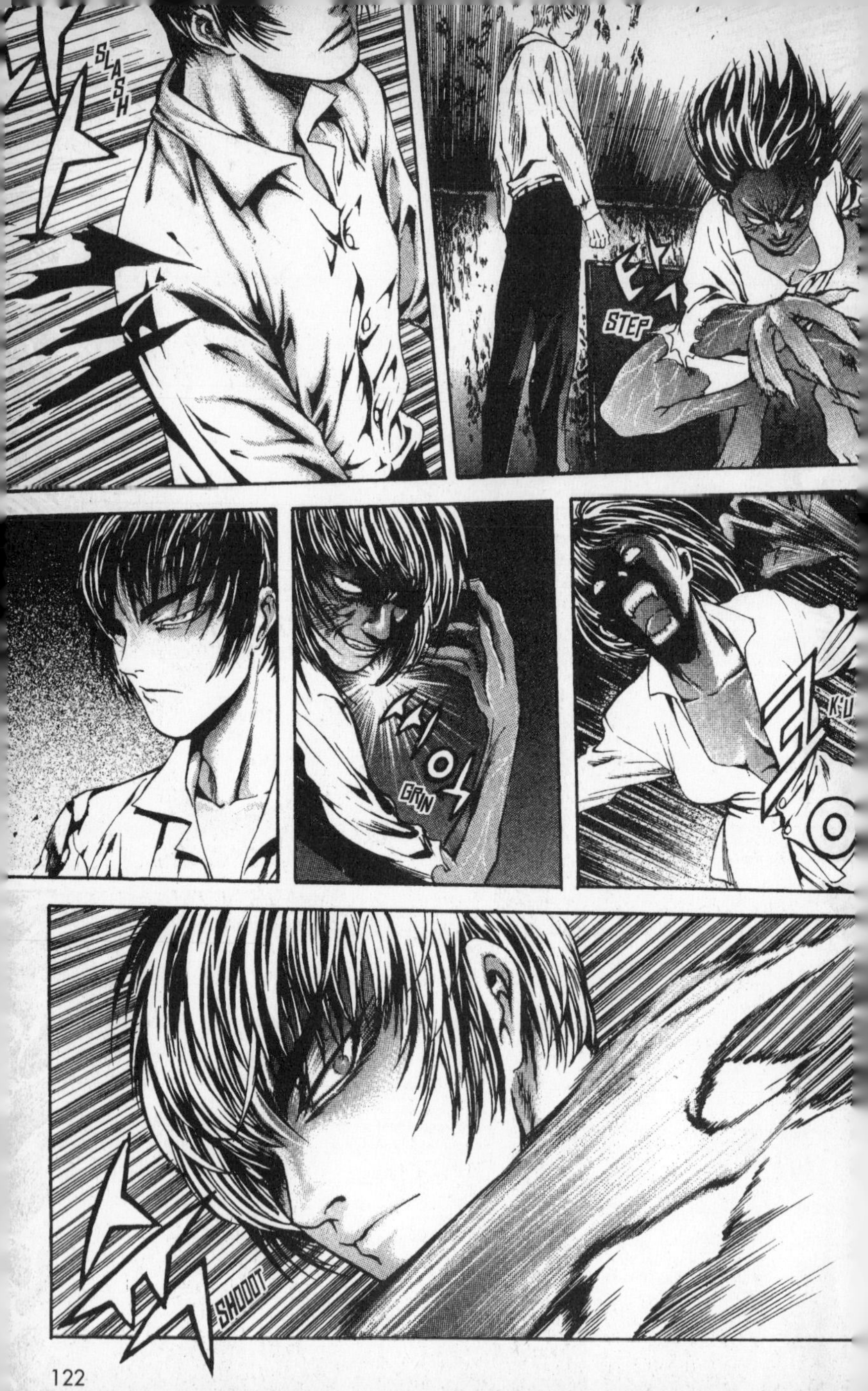
SLASH
STEP
GRIN
KU
SHOOOT

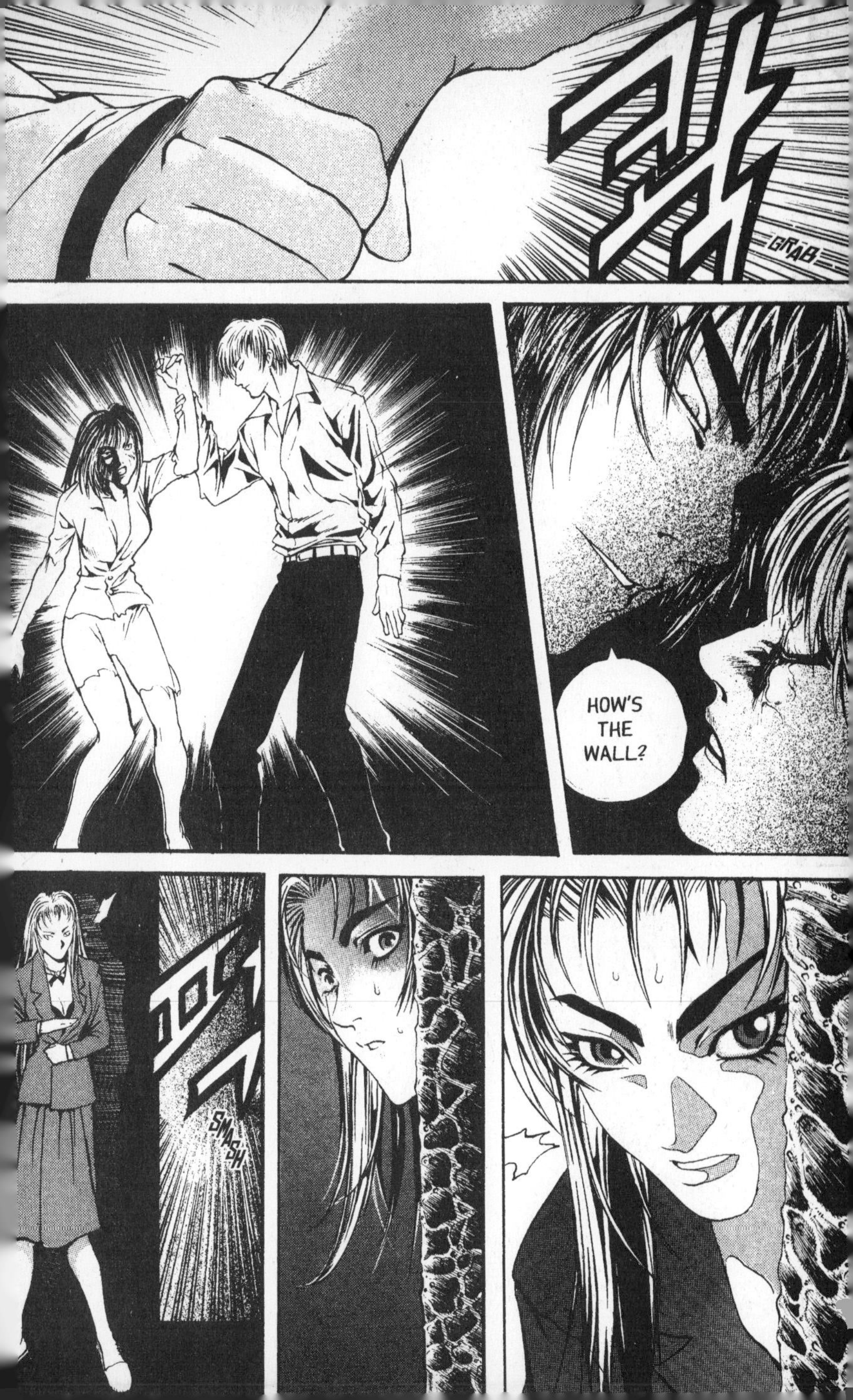
GRAB
HOW'S THE WALL?
SMASH

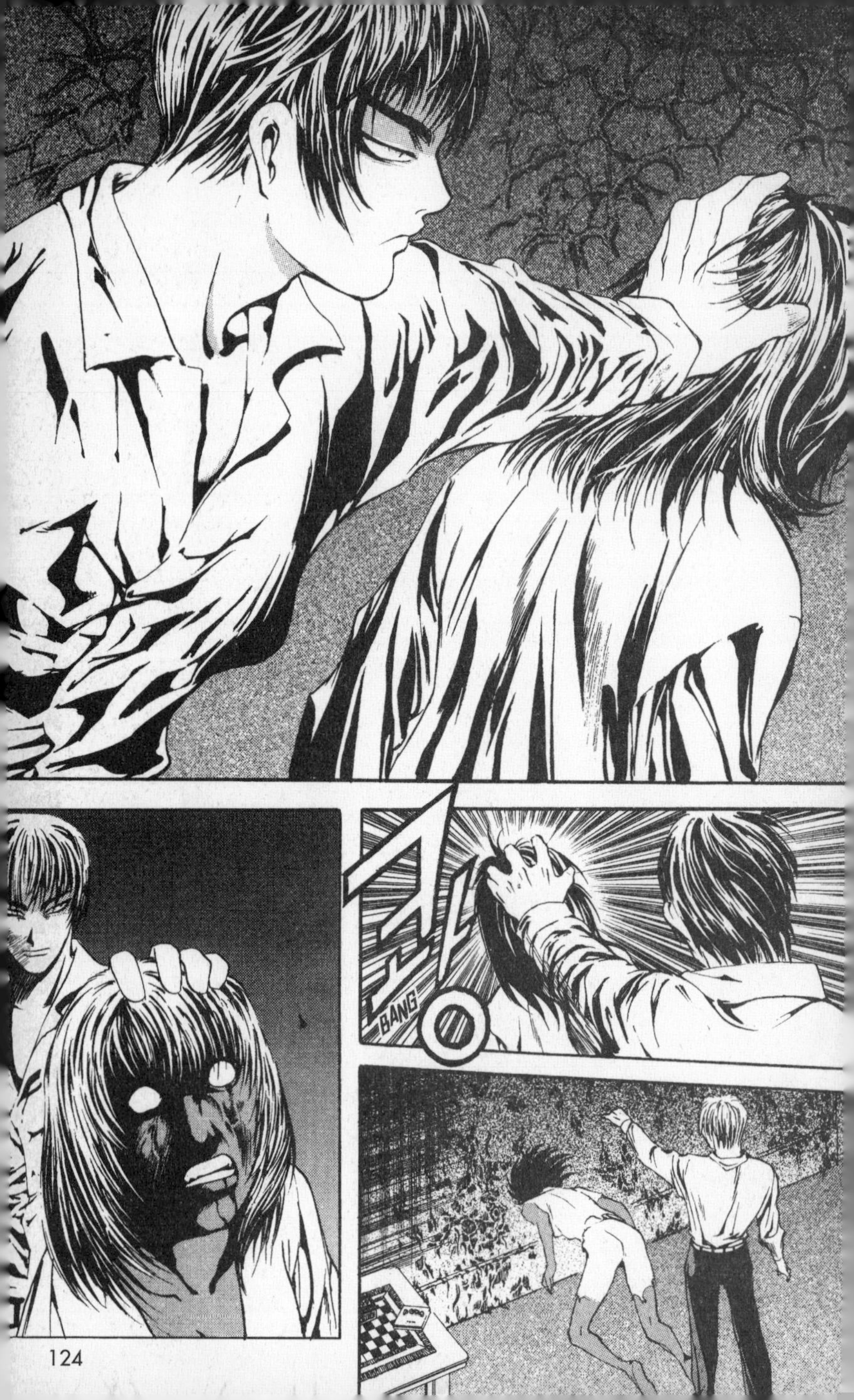
BANG

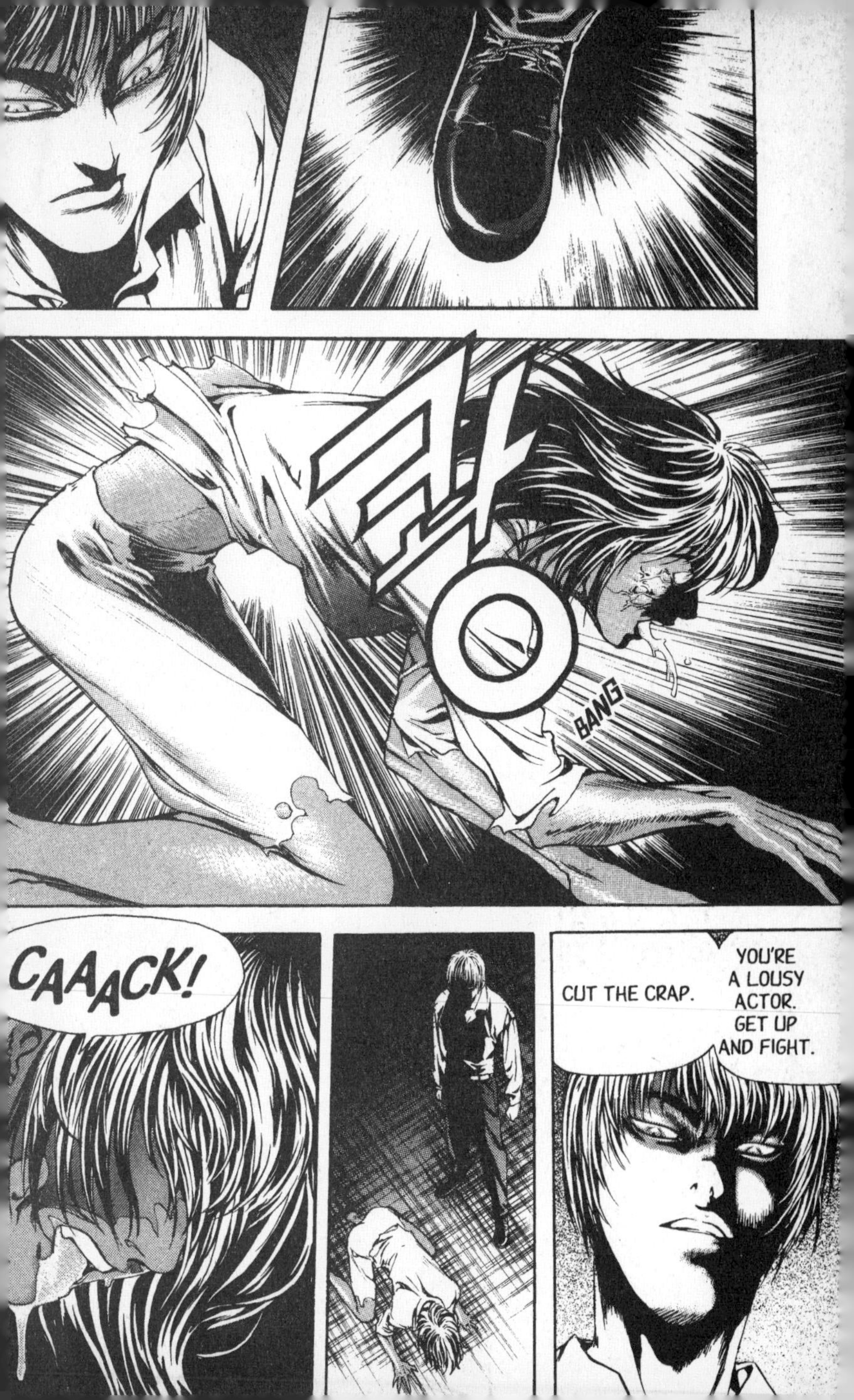
BANG
CAAACK!
CUT THE CRAP.
YOU'RE A LOUSY ACTOR. GET UP AND FIGHT.

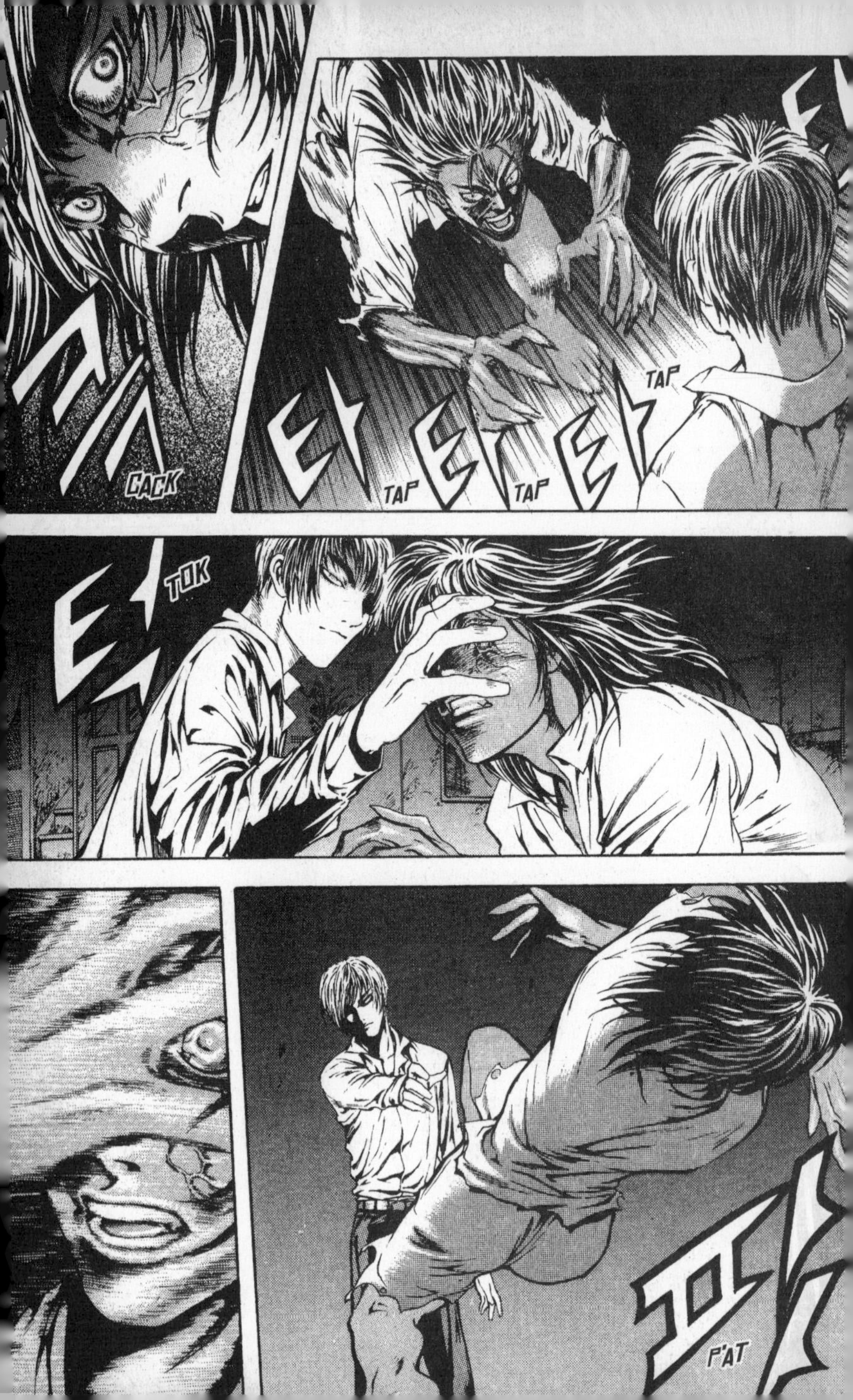
CACK
TAP
TAP
TAP
TOK
P'AT

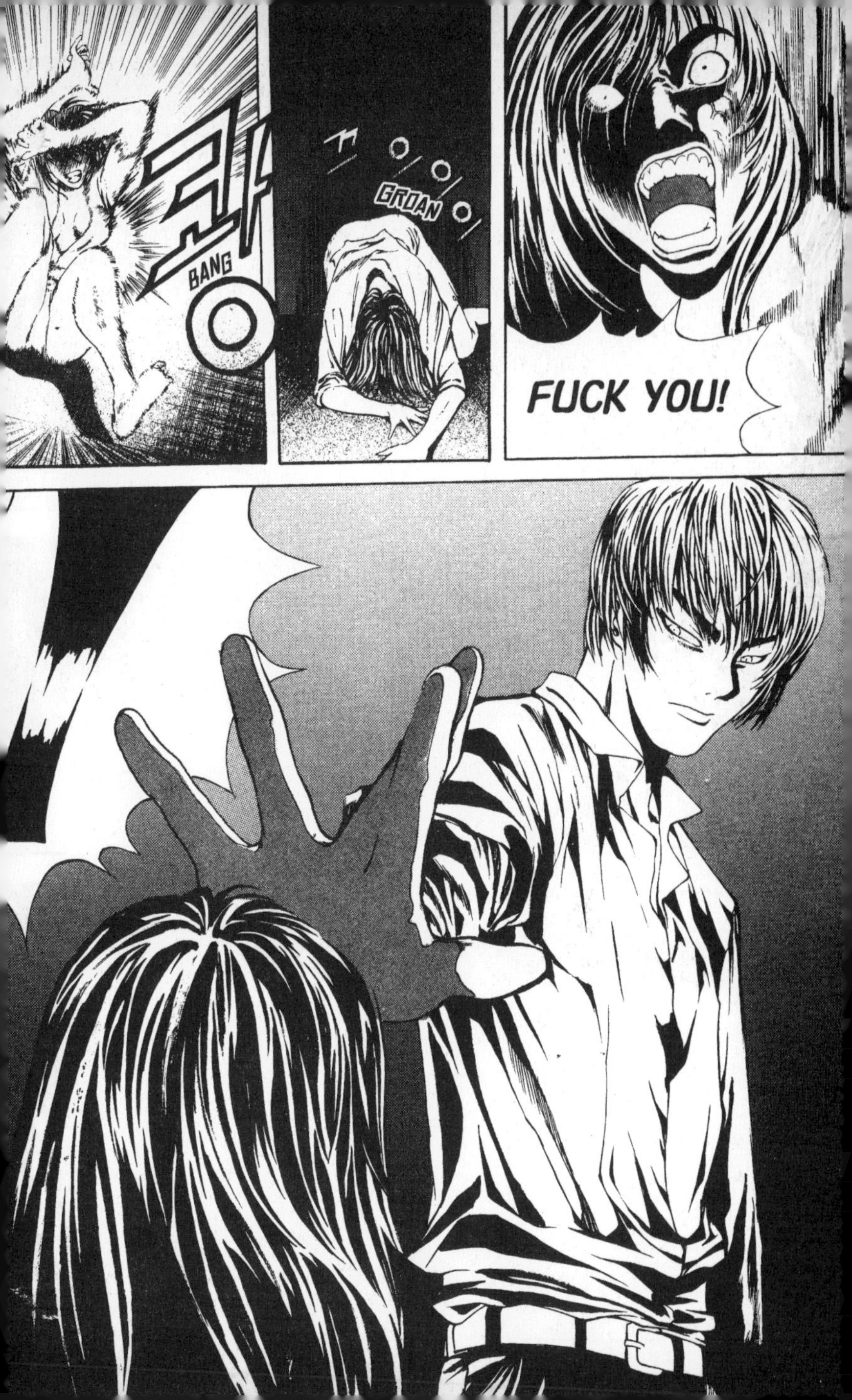
BANG
GROAN
FUCK YOU!

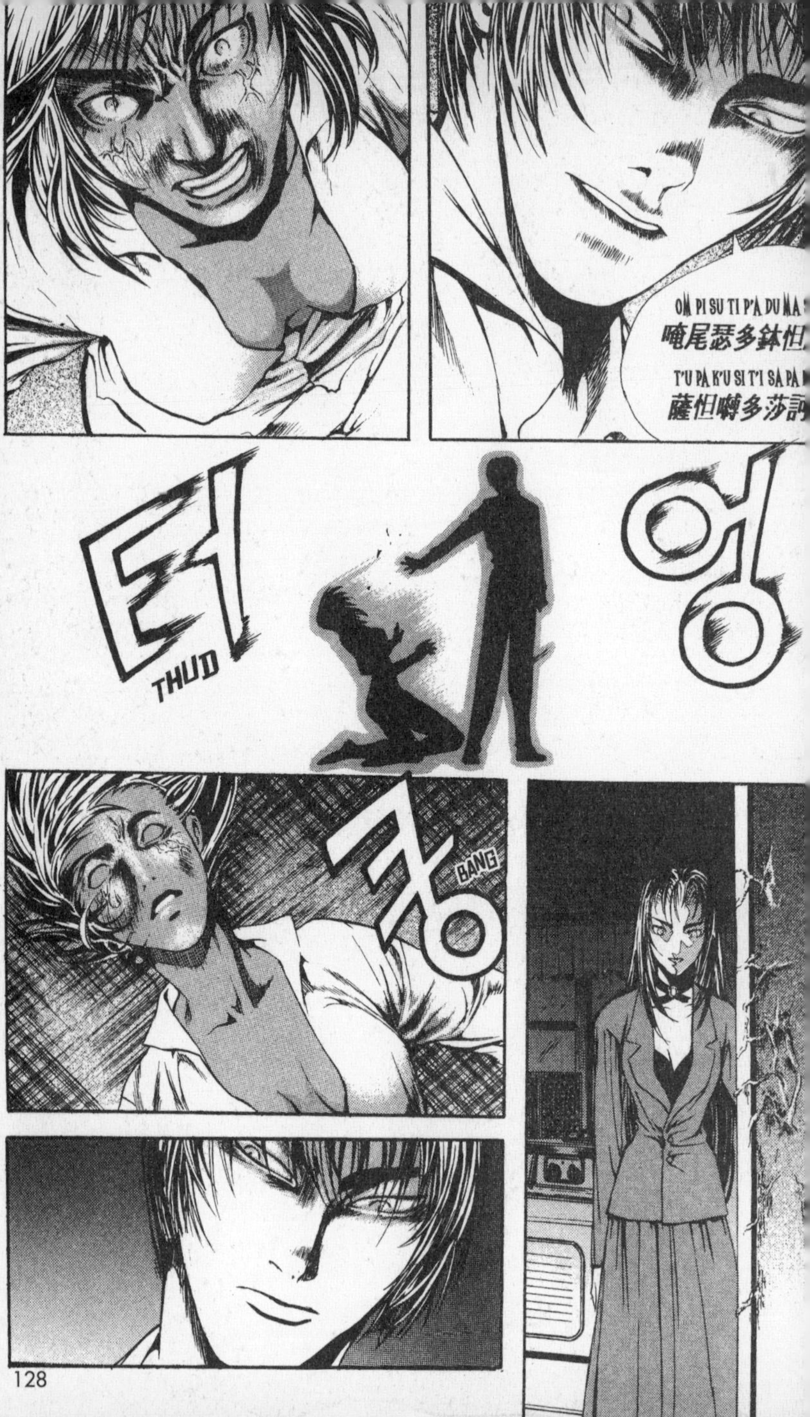
OM PI SU TI P'A DU MA
唵尾瑟多鉢怛
T'U PA K'U SI T'I SA PA
薩怛囀多莎訶
THUD
BANG

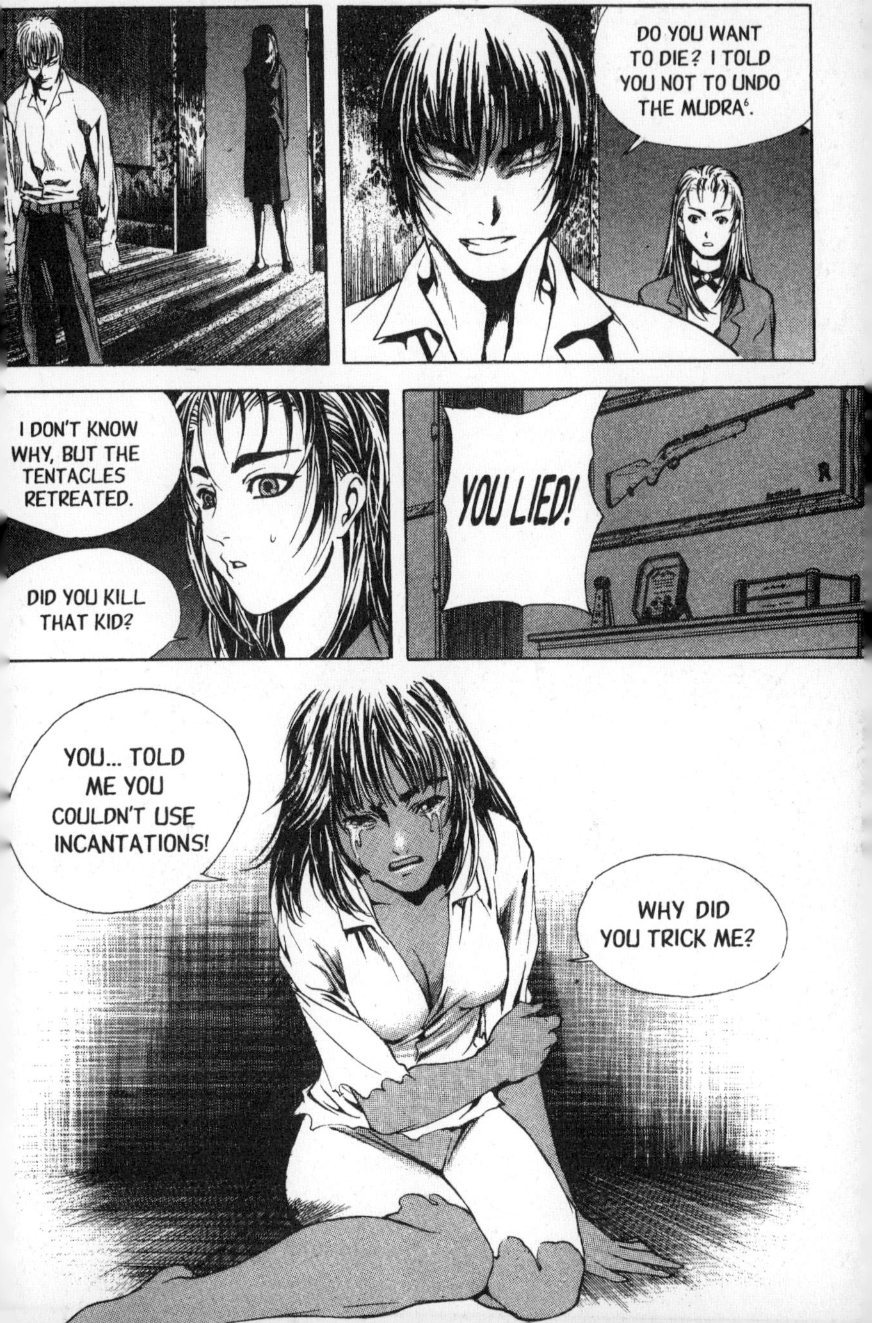
DO YOU WANT TO DIE? I TOLD YOU NOT TO UNDO THE MUDRA6.
I DON'T KNOW WHY, BUT THE TENTACLES RETREATED.
DID YOU KILL THAT KID?
YOU LIED!
YOU... TOLD ME YOU COULDN'T USE INCANTATIONS!
WHY DID YOU TRICK ME?

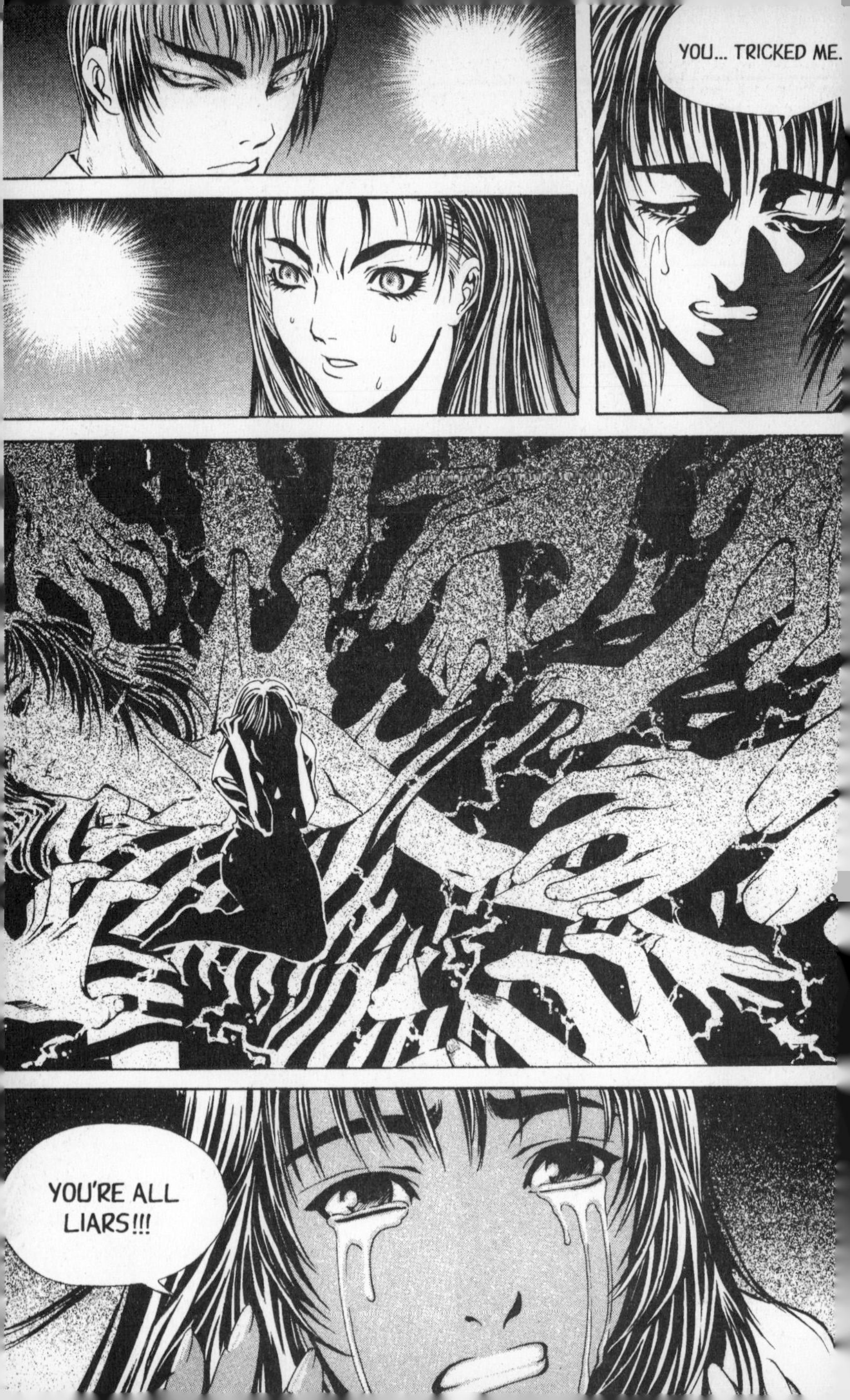
YOU... TRICKED ME.
YOU'RE ALL LIARS!!!

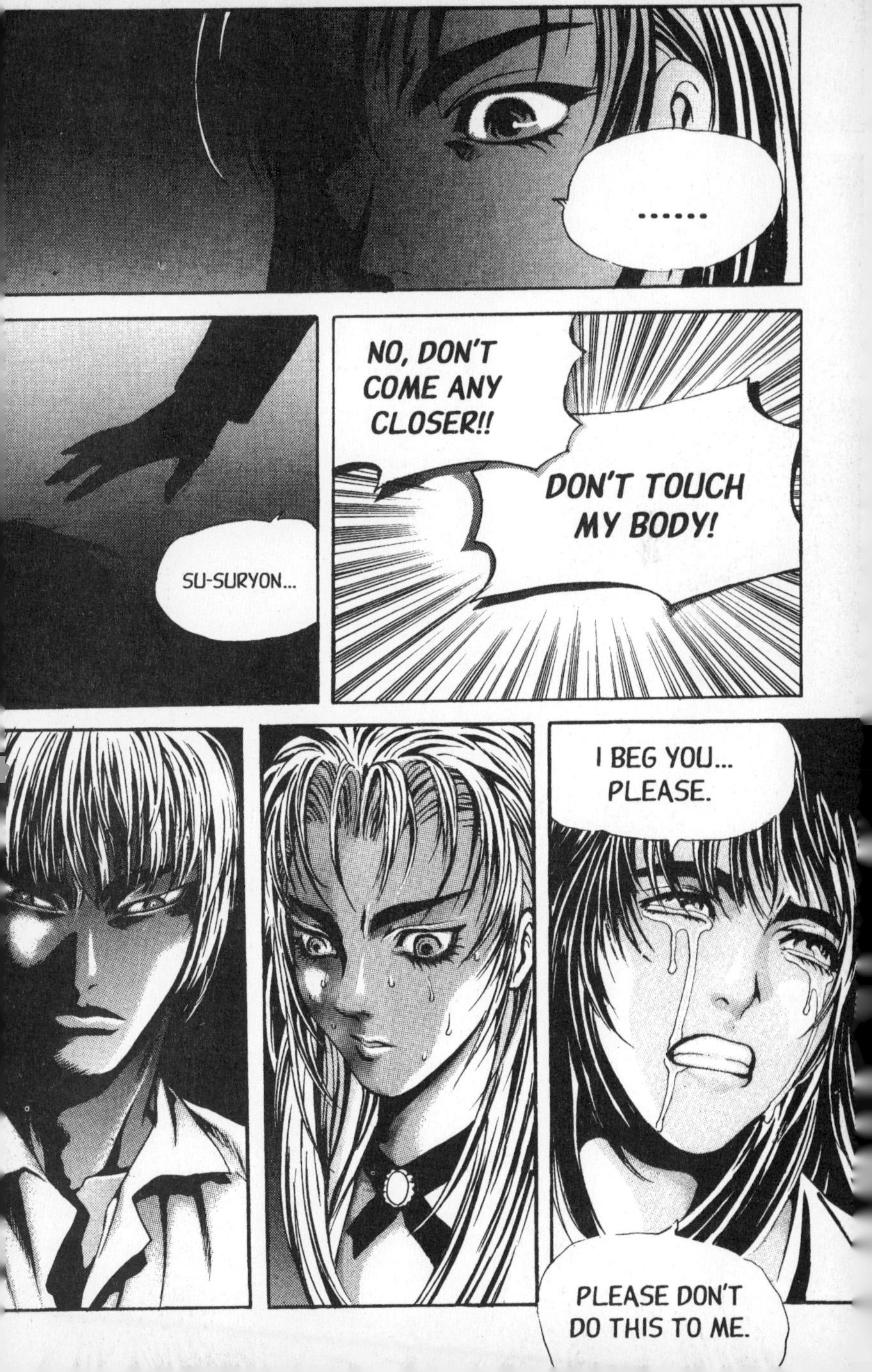
......
SU-SURYON...
NO, DON'T COME ANY CLOSER!!
DON'T TOUCH MY BODY!
I BEG YOU... PLEASE.
PLEASE DON'T DO THIS TO ME.

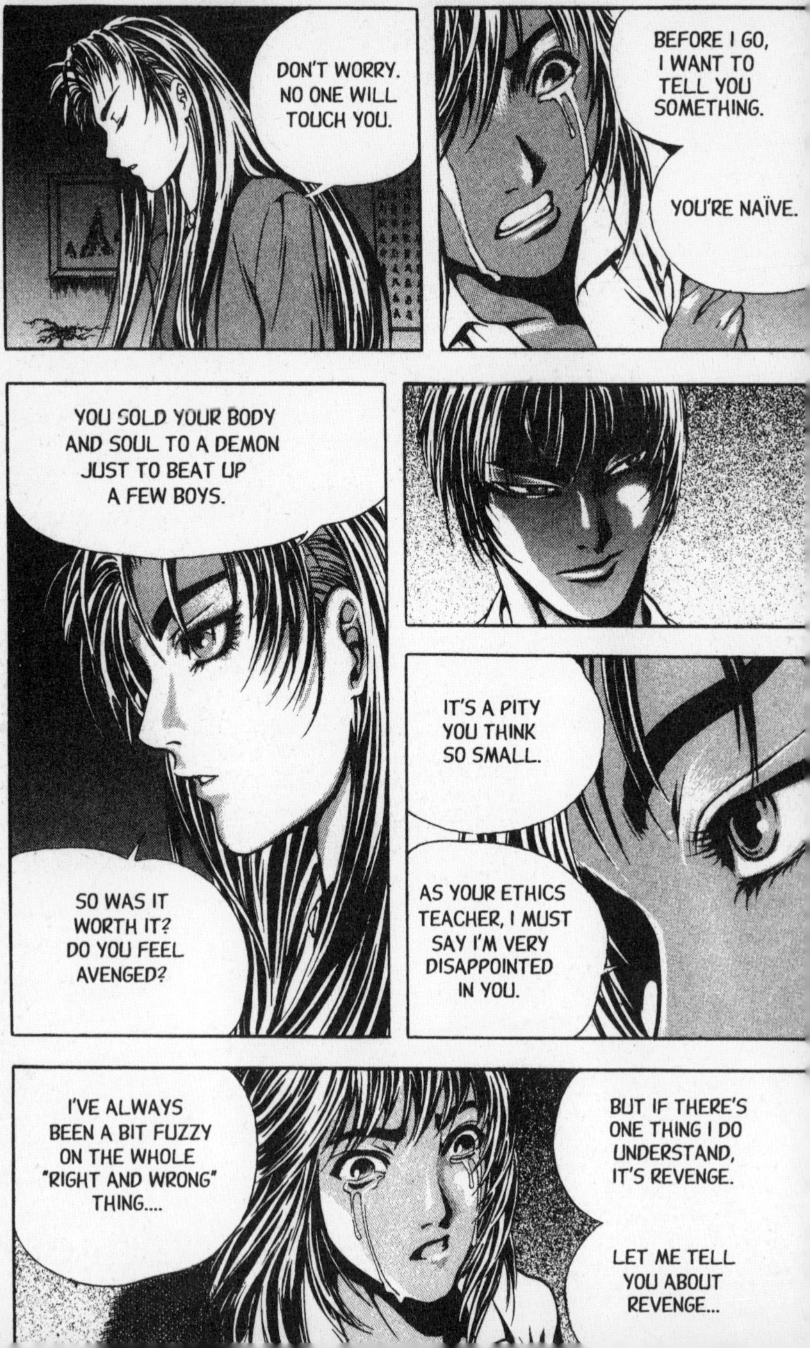
DON'T WORRY. NO ONE WILL TOUCH YOU.
BEFORE I GO, I WANT TO TELL YOU SOMETHING.
YOU'RE NAÏVE.
YOU SOLD YOUR BODY AND SOUL TO A DEMON JUST TO BEAT UP A FEW BOYS.
SO WAS IT WORTH IT? DO YOU FEEL AVENGED?
IT'S A PITY YOU THINK SO SMALL.
AS YOUR ETHICS TEACHER, I MUST SAY I'M VERY DISAPPOINTED IN YOU.
I'VE ALWAYS BEEN A BIT FUZZY ON THE WHOLE "RIGHT AND WRONG" THING....
BUT IF THERE'S ONE THING I DO UNDERSTAND, IT'S REVENGE.
LET ME TELL YOU ABOUT REVENGE...

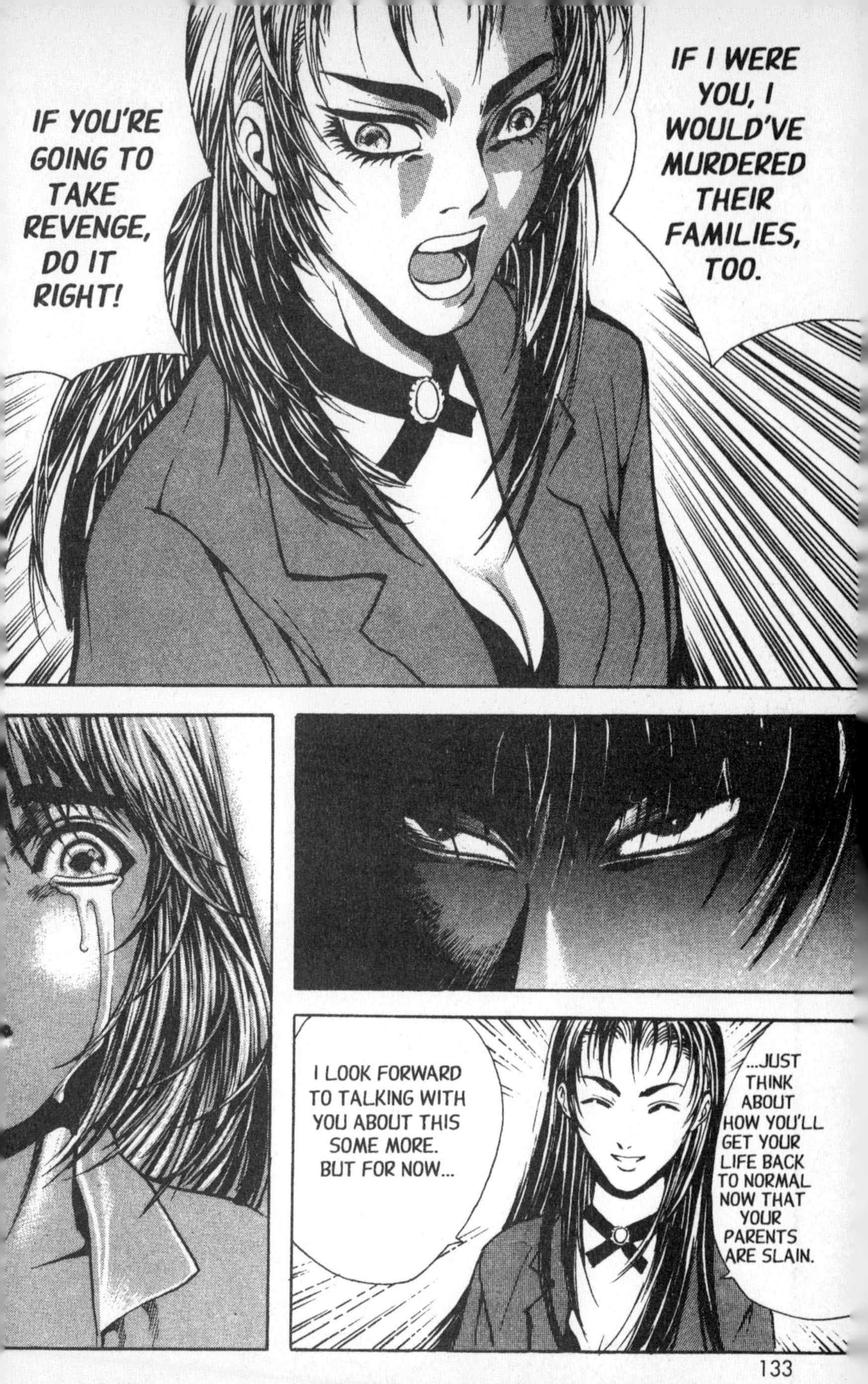
IF YOU'RE GOING TO TAKE REVENGE, DO IT RIGHT!
IF I WERE YOU, I WOULD'VE MURDERED THEIR FAMILIES, TOO.
I LOOK FORWARD TO TALKING WITH YOU ABOUT THIS SOME MORE. BUT FOR NOW...
...JUST THINK ABOUT HOW YOU'LL GET YOUR LIFE BACK TO NORMAL NOW THAT YOUR PARENTS ARE SLAIN.

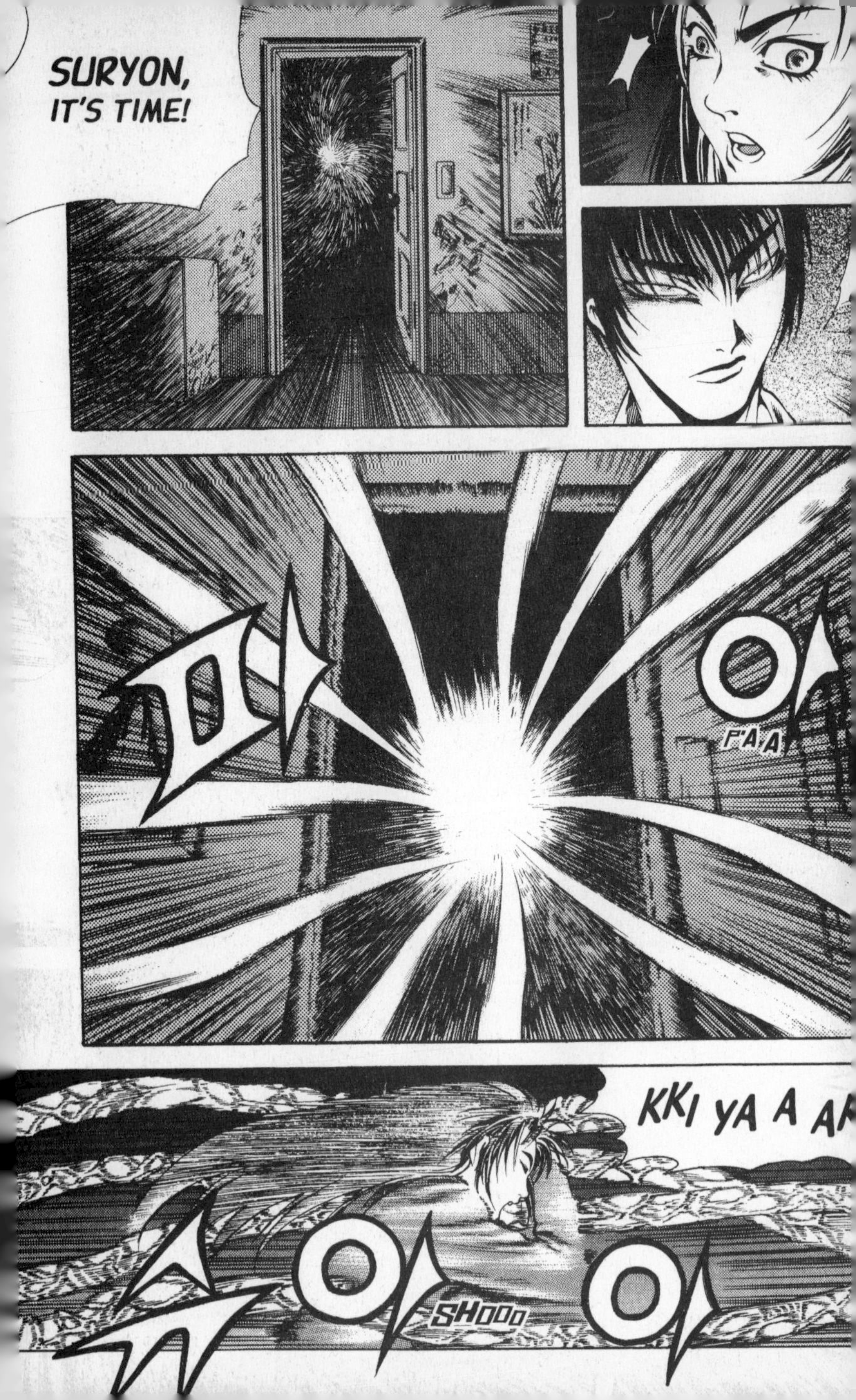
SURYON, IT'S TIME!
D
O
P'A A
KKI YA A AA
O
SHOOO
O

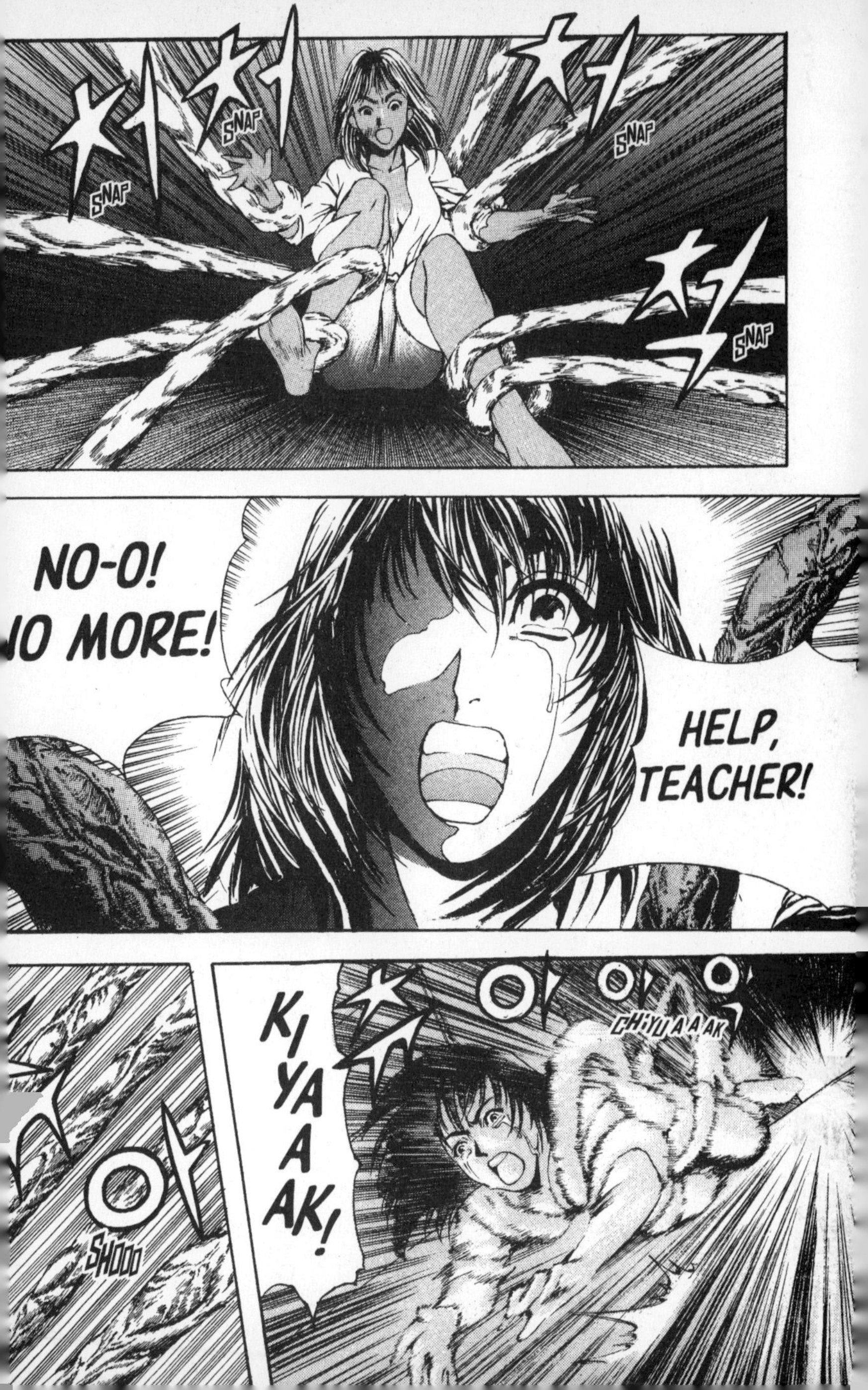
SNAP
SNAP
SNAP
SNAP
NO-O!
NO MORE!
HELP, TEACHER!
SHOOO
KIYAAAAK!
CHIYUAAAK

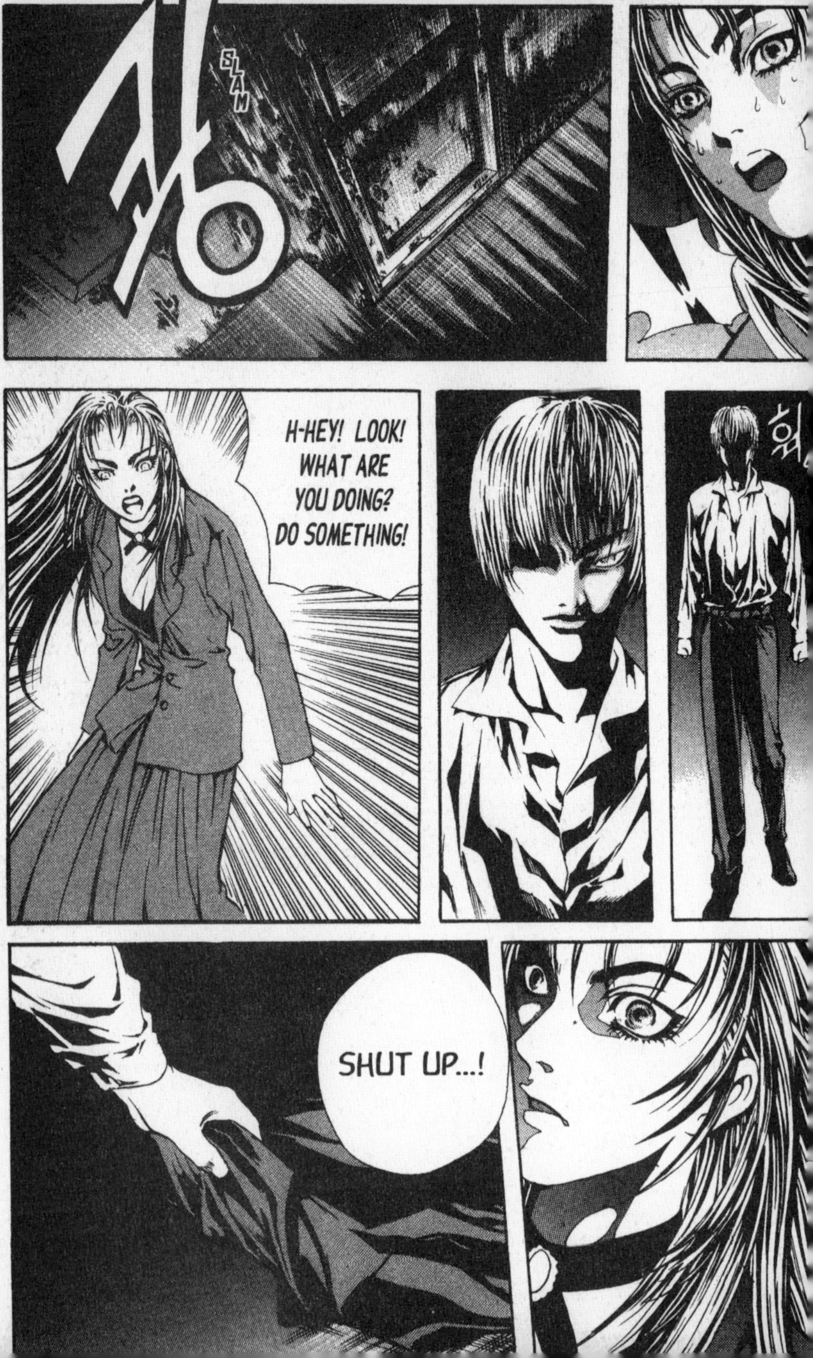
쾅
SLAM
H-HEY! LOOK! WHAT ARE YOU DOING? DO SOMETHING!
SHUT UP...!

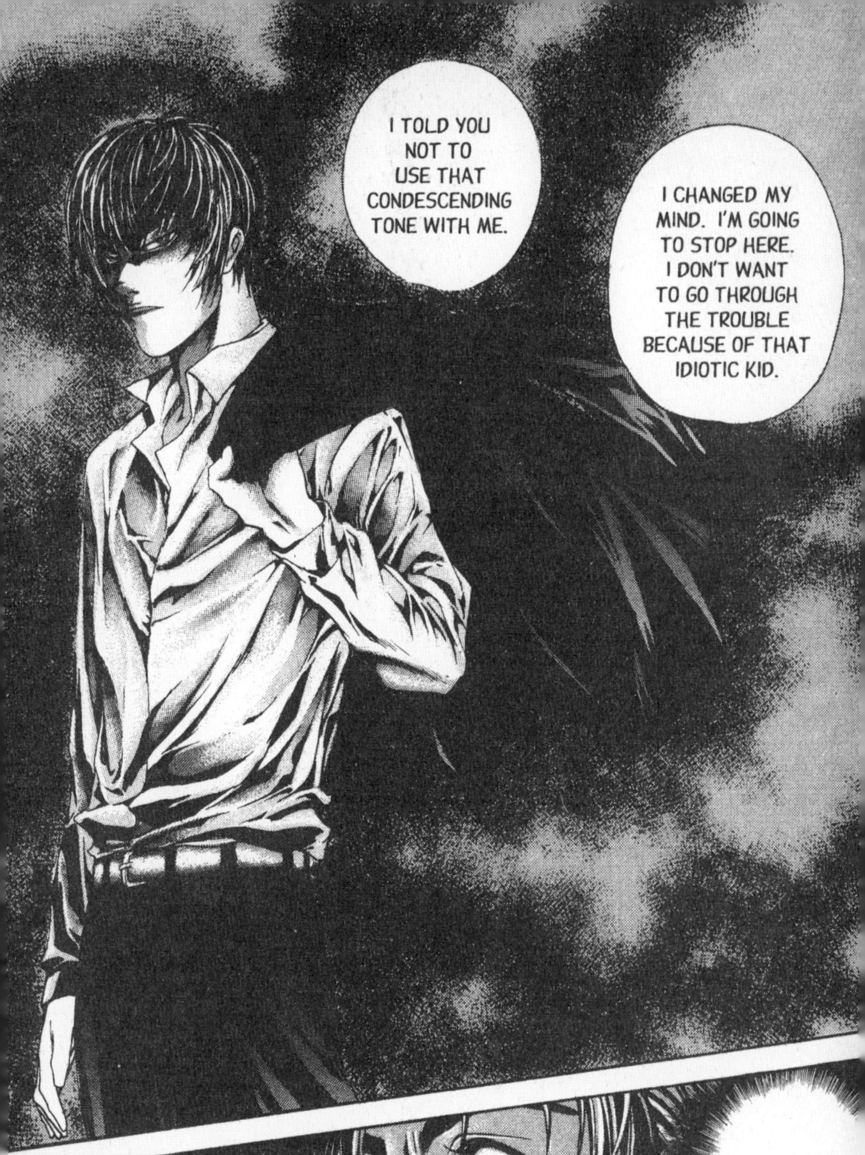
I TOLD YOU NOT TO USE THAT CONDESCENDING TONE WITH ME.
I CHANGED MY MIND. I'M GOING TO STOP HERE. I DON'T WANT TO GO THROUGH THE TROUBLE BECAUSE OF THAT IDIOTIC KID.
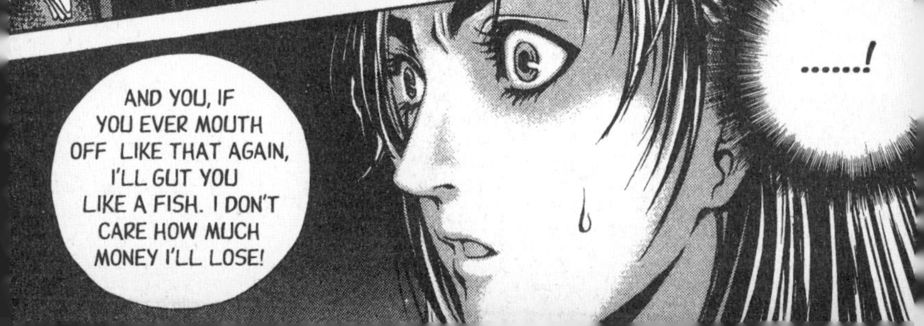
AND YOU, IF YOU EVER MOUTH OFF LIKE THAT AGAIN, I'LL GUT YOU LIKE A FISH. I DON'T CARE HOW MUCH MONEY I'LL LOSE!
......!

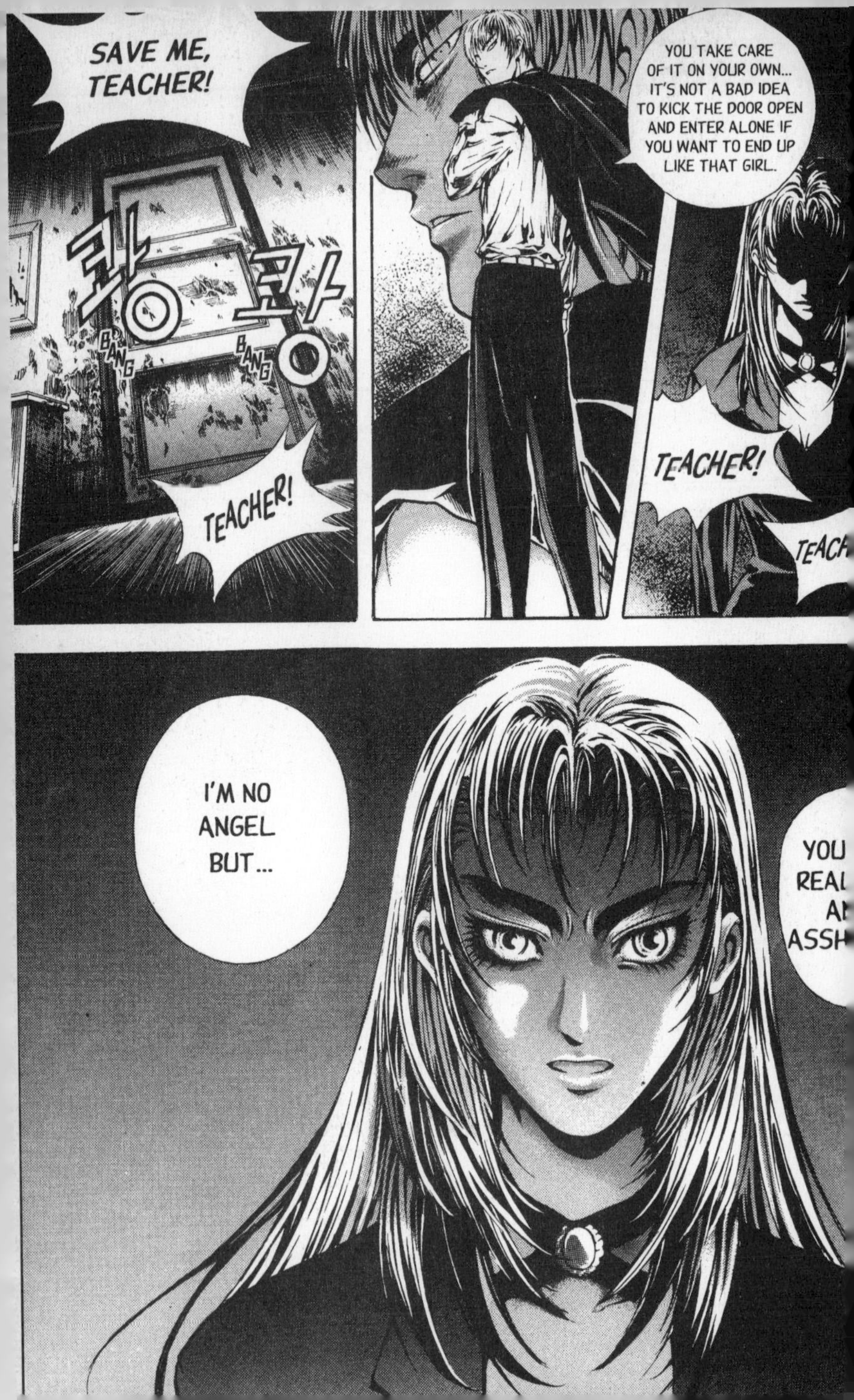
SAVE ME, TEACHER!
쾅
BANG
쾅
BANG
TEACHER!
YOU TAKE CARE OF IT ON YOUR OWN... IT'S NOT A BAD IDEA TO KICK THE DOOR OPEN AND ENTER ALONE IF YOU WANT TO END UP LIKE THAT GIRL..
TEACHER!
TEACH
I'M NO ANGEL BUT...
YOU

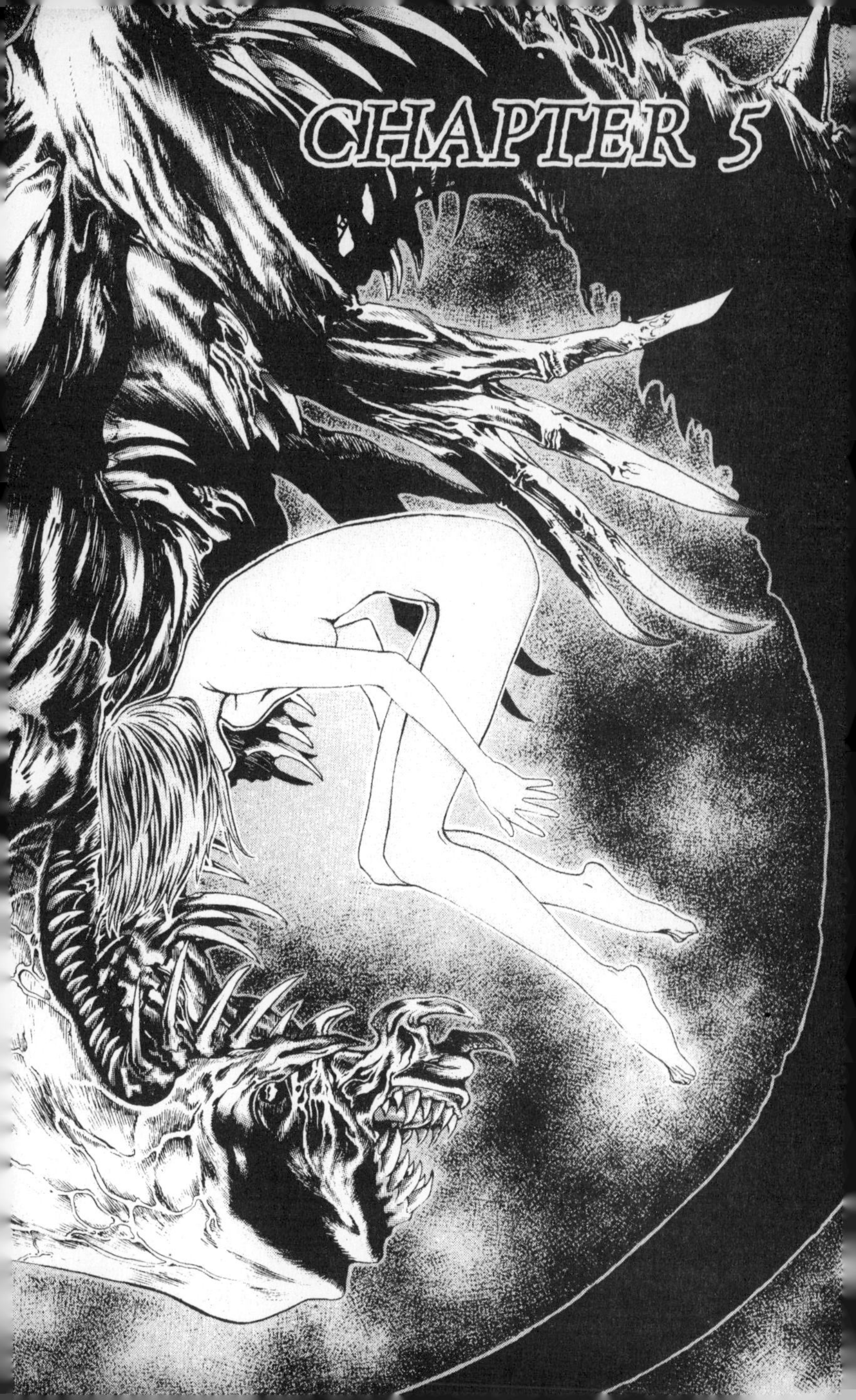
CHAPTER 5

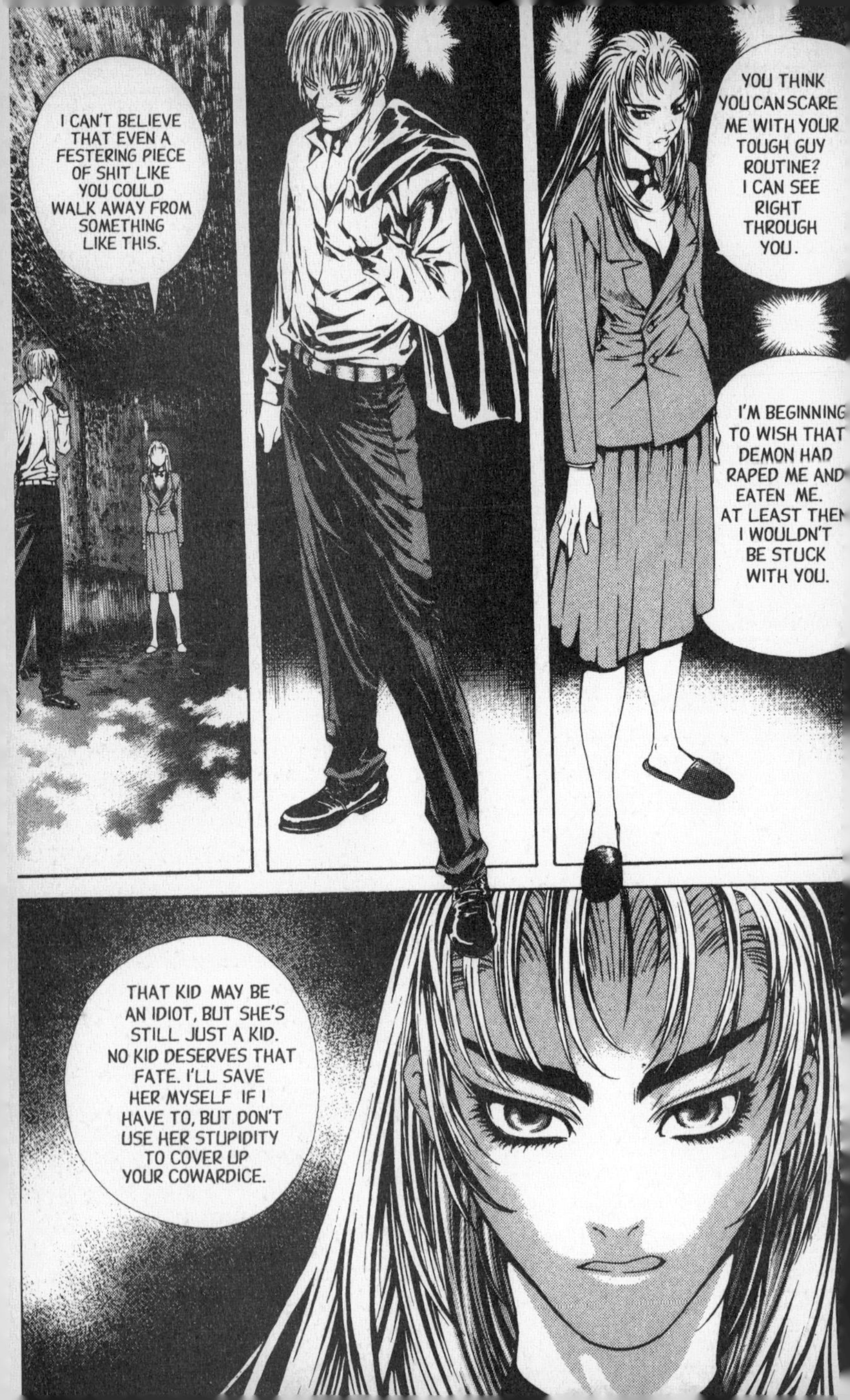
I CAN'T BELIEVE THAT EVEN A FESTERING PIECE OF SHIT LIKE YOU COULD WALK AWAY FROM SOMETHING LIKE THIS.
YOU THINK YOU CAN SCARE ME WITH YOUR TOUGH GUY ROUTINE? I CAN SEE RIGHT THROUGH YOU.
I'M BEGINNING TO WISH THAT DEMON HAD RAPED ME AND EATEN ME. AT LEAST THEN I WOULDN'T BE STUCK WITH YOU.
THAT KID MAY BE AN IDIOT, BUT SHE'S STILL JUST A KID. NO KID DESERVES THAT FATE. I'LL SAVE HER MYSELF IF I HAVE TO, BUT DON'T USE HER STUPIDITY TO COVER UP YOUR COWARDICE.

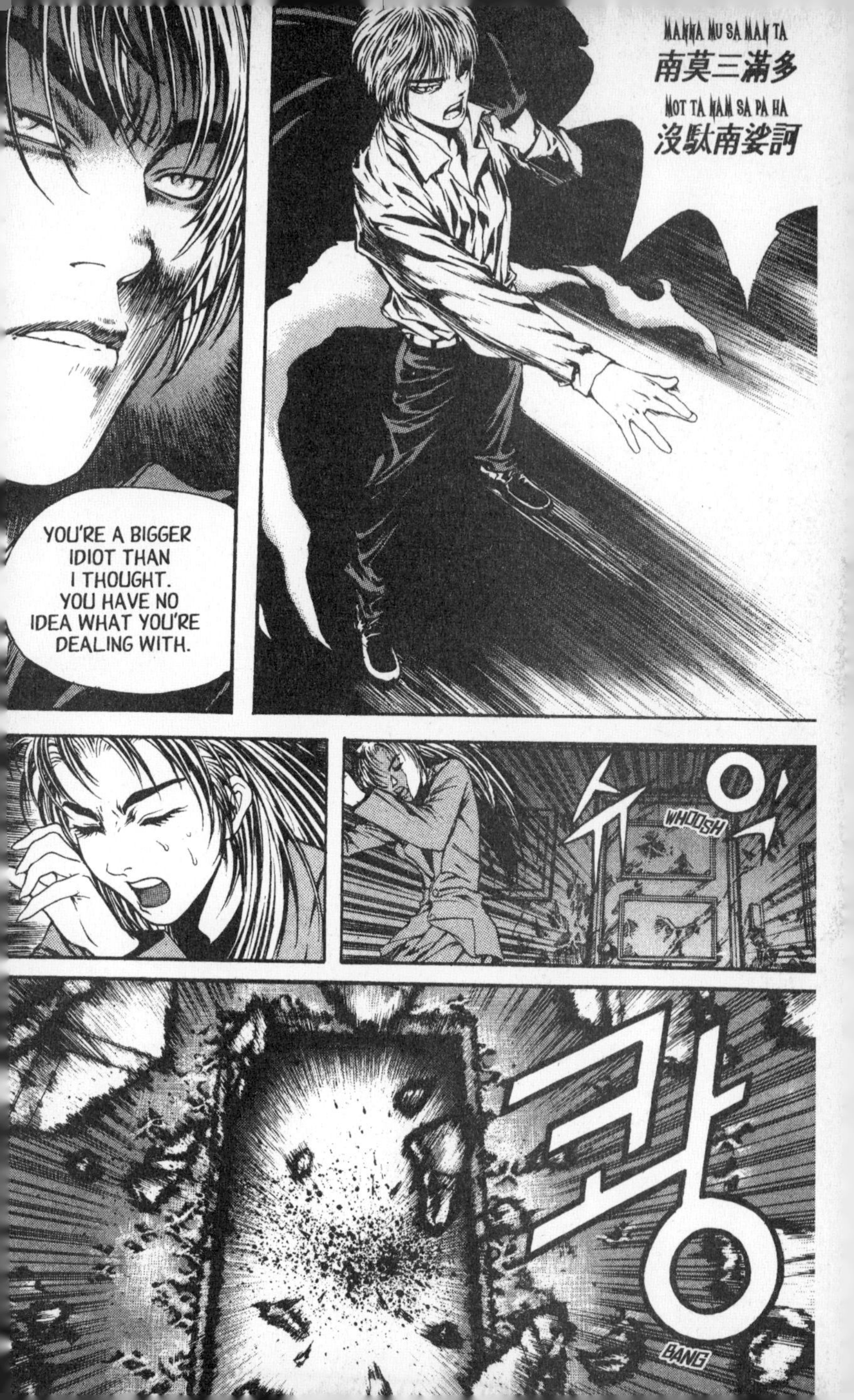
YOU'RE A BIGGER IDIOT THAN I THOUGHT. YOU HAVE NO IDEA WHAT YOU'RE DEALING WITH.
MANNA MU SA MAN TA
南莫三滿多
MOT TA NAM SA PA HA
沒馱南婆訶
WHOOSH
BANG

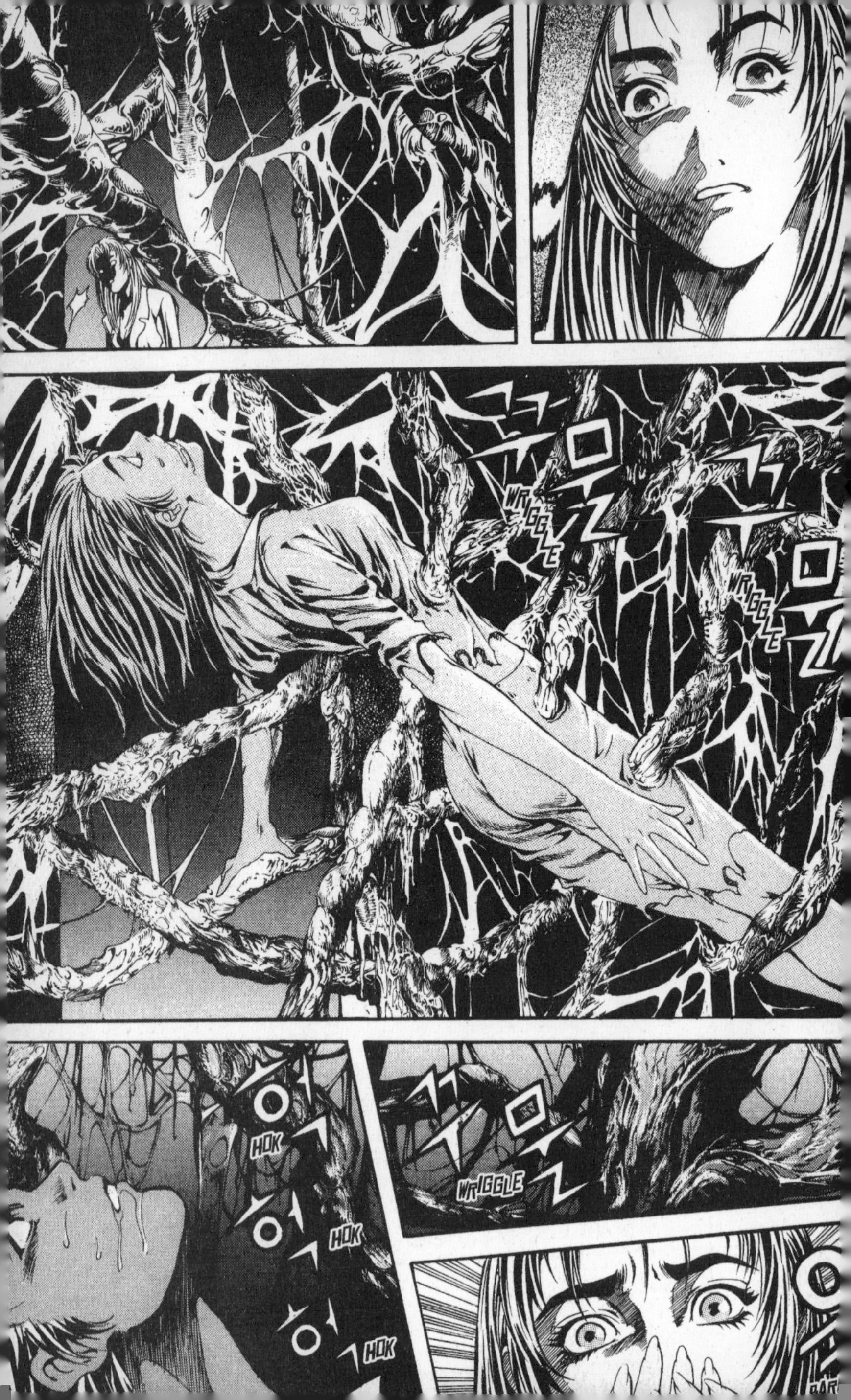
WRIGGLE
WRIGGLE
HOK
HOK
HOK
WRIGGLE

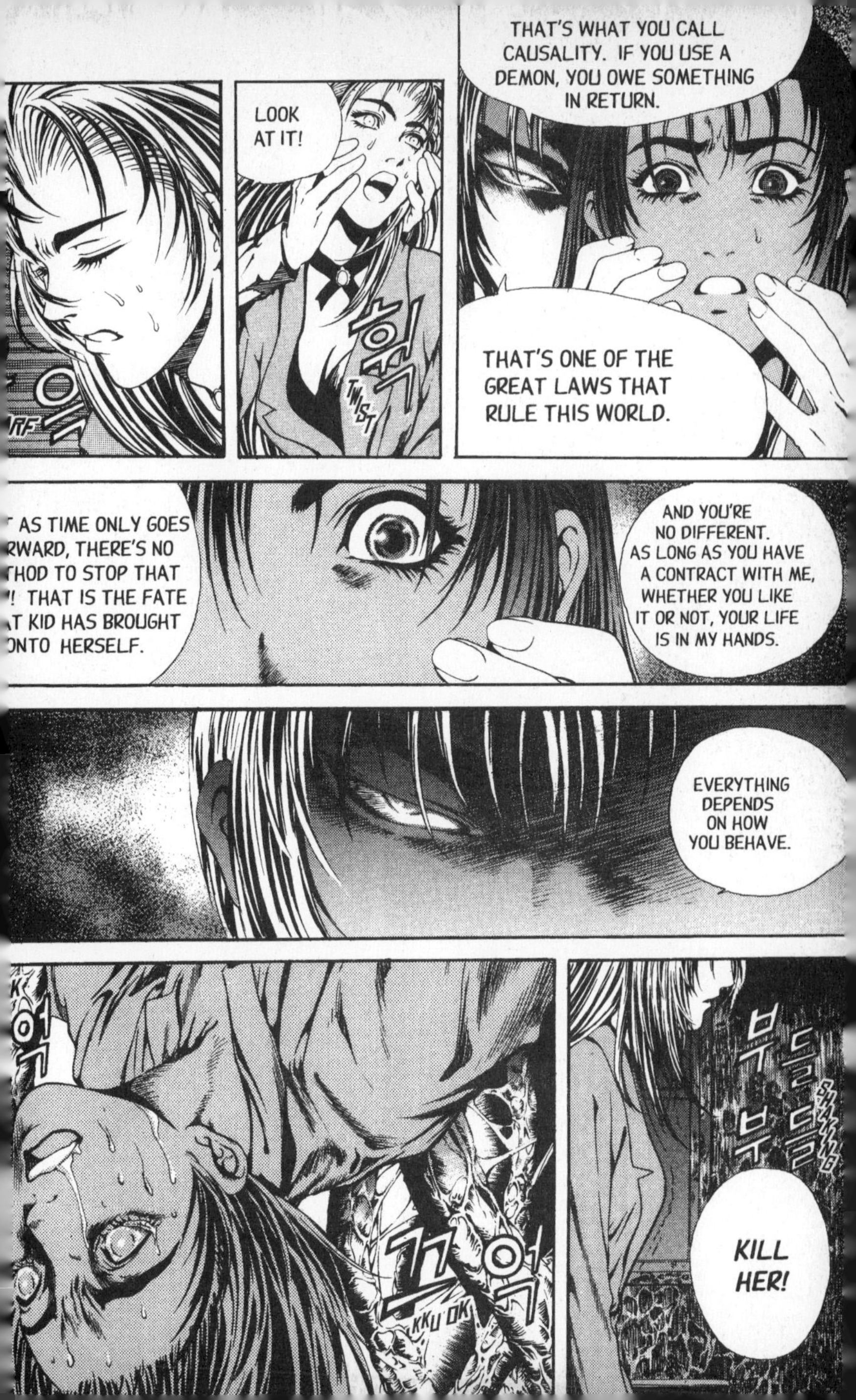
LOOK AT IT!
TWIST
THAT'S WHAT YOU CALL CAUSALITY. IF YOU USE A DEMON, YOU OWE SOMETHING IN RETURN.
THAT'S ONE OF THE GREAT LAWS THAT RULE THIS WORLD.
AS TIME ONLY GOES RWARD, THERE'S NO THOD TO STOP THAT THAT IS THE FATE T KID HAS BROUGHT ONTO HERSELF.
AND YOU'RE NO DIFFERENT. AS LONG AS YOU HAVE A CONTRACT WITH ME, WHETHER YOU LIKE IT OR NOT, YOUR LIFE IS IN MY HANDS.
EVERYTHING DEPENDS ON HOW YOU BEHAVE.
KKU'OK
SHAKING
KILL HER!

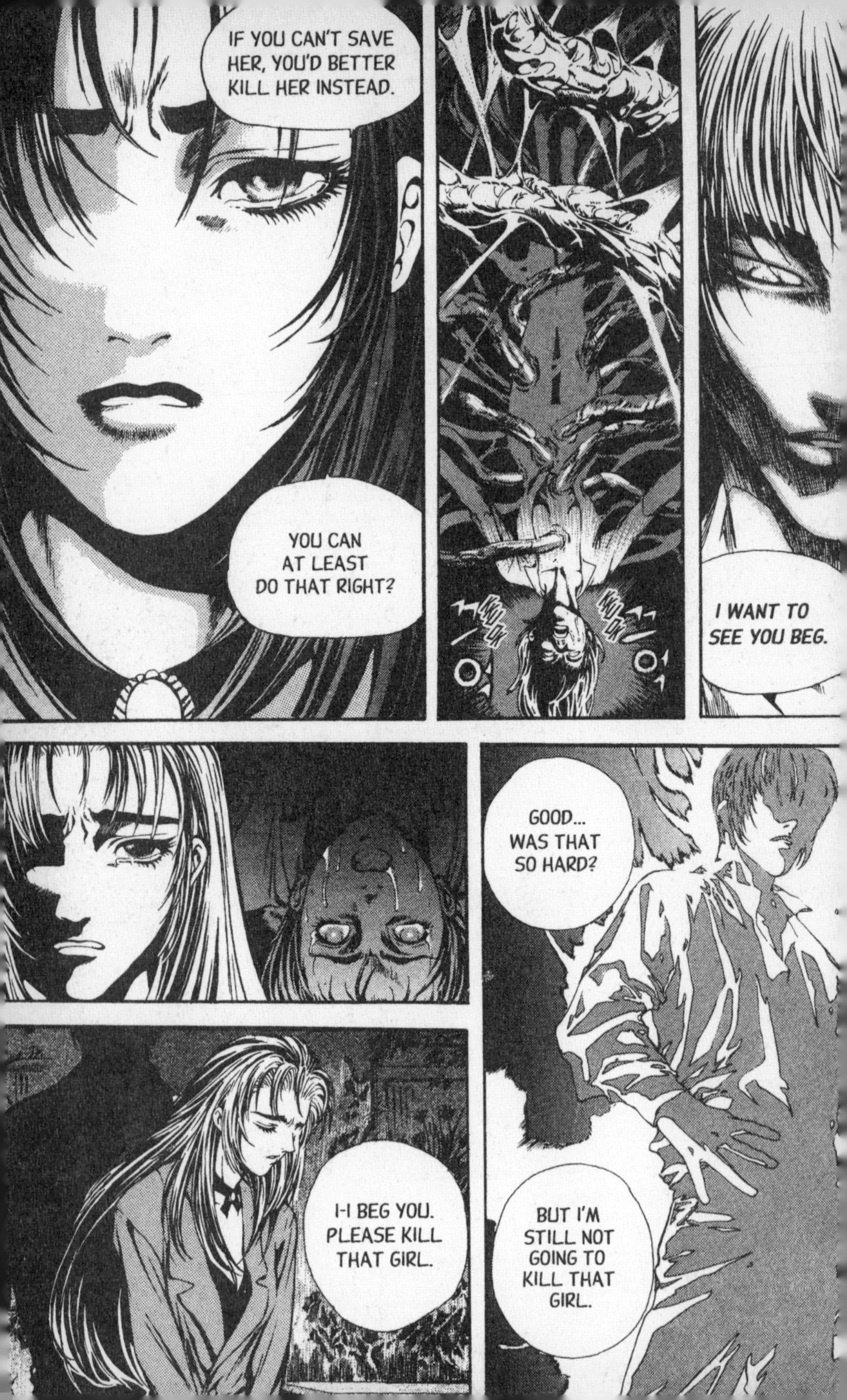
IF YOU CAN'T SAVE HER, YOU'D BETTER KILL HER INSTEAD.
YOU CAN AT LEAST DO THAT RIGHT?
I WANT TO SEE YOU BEG.
I-I BEG YOU. PLEASE KILL THAT GIRL.
GOOD... WAS THAT SO HARD?
BUT I'M STILL NOT GOING TO KILL THAT GIRL.

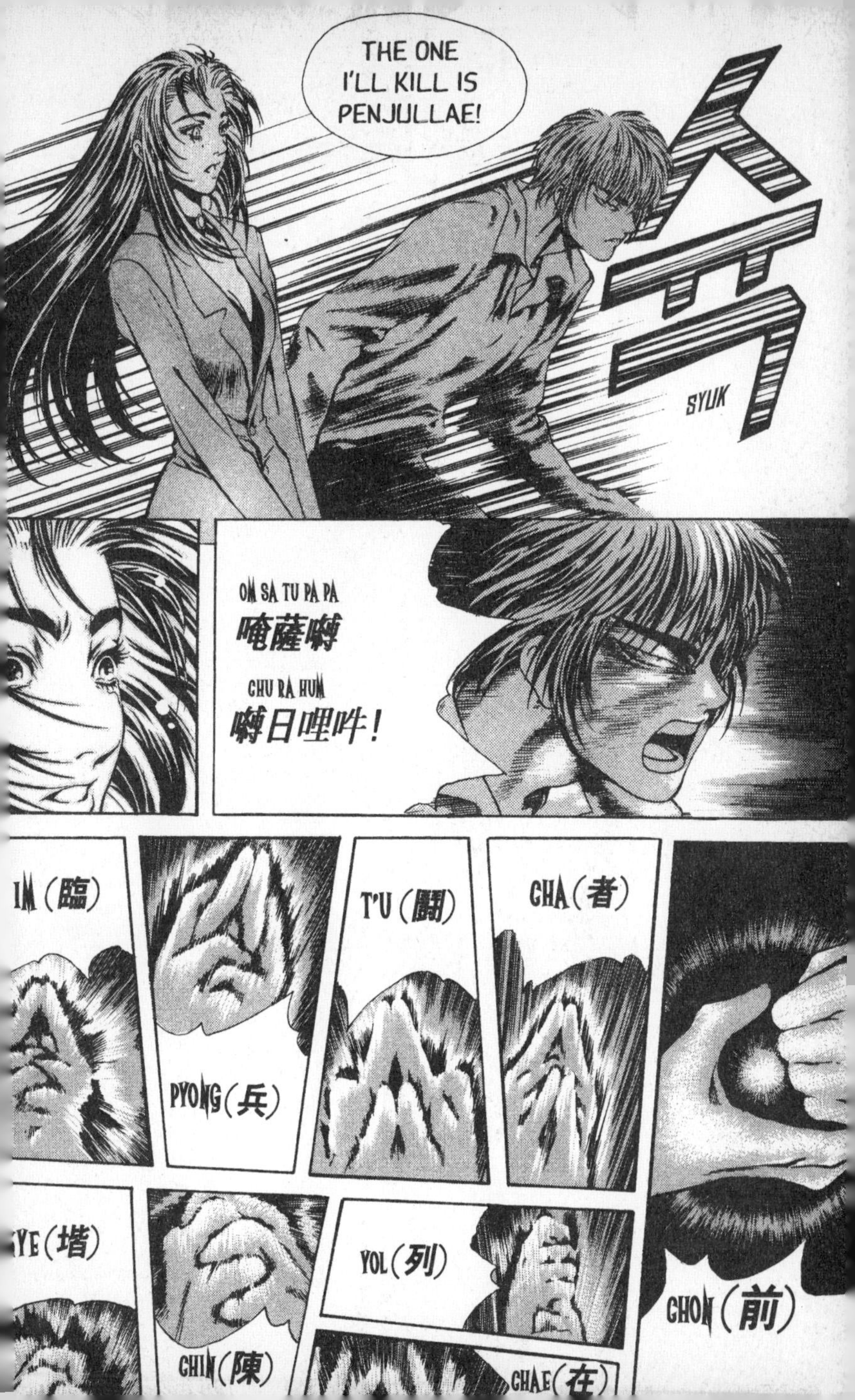
THE ONE I'LL KILL IS PENJULLAE!
SYUK
OM SA TU PA PA
唵薩嚩
CHU RA HUM
嚩日哩吽!
IM (臨)
PYONG (兵)
T'U (鬪)
CHA (者)
YE (堦)
CHIN (陳)
YOL (列)
CHAE (在)
CHON (前)

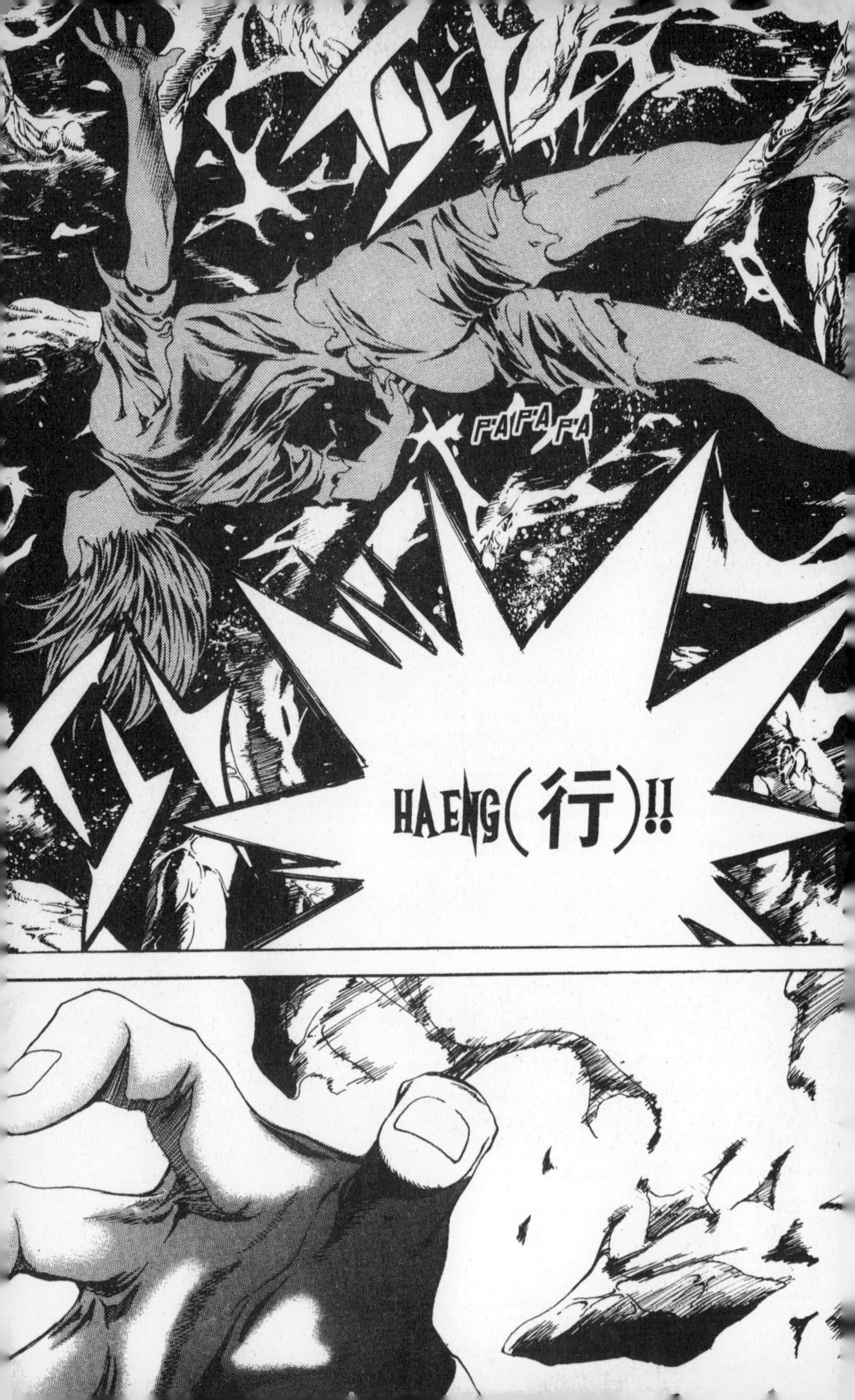
PA PA PA
HAENG(行)!!

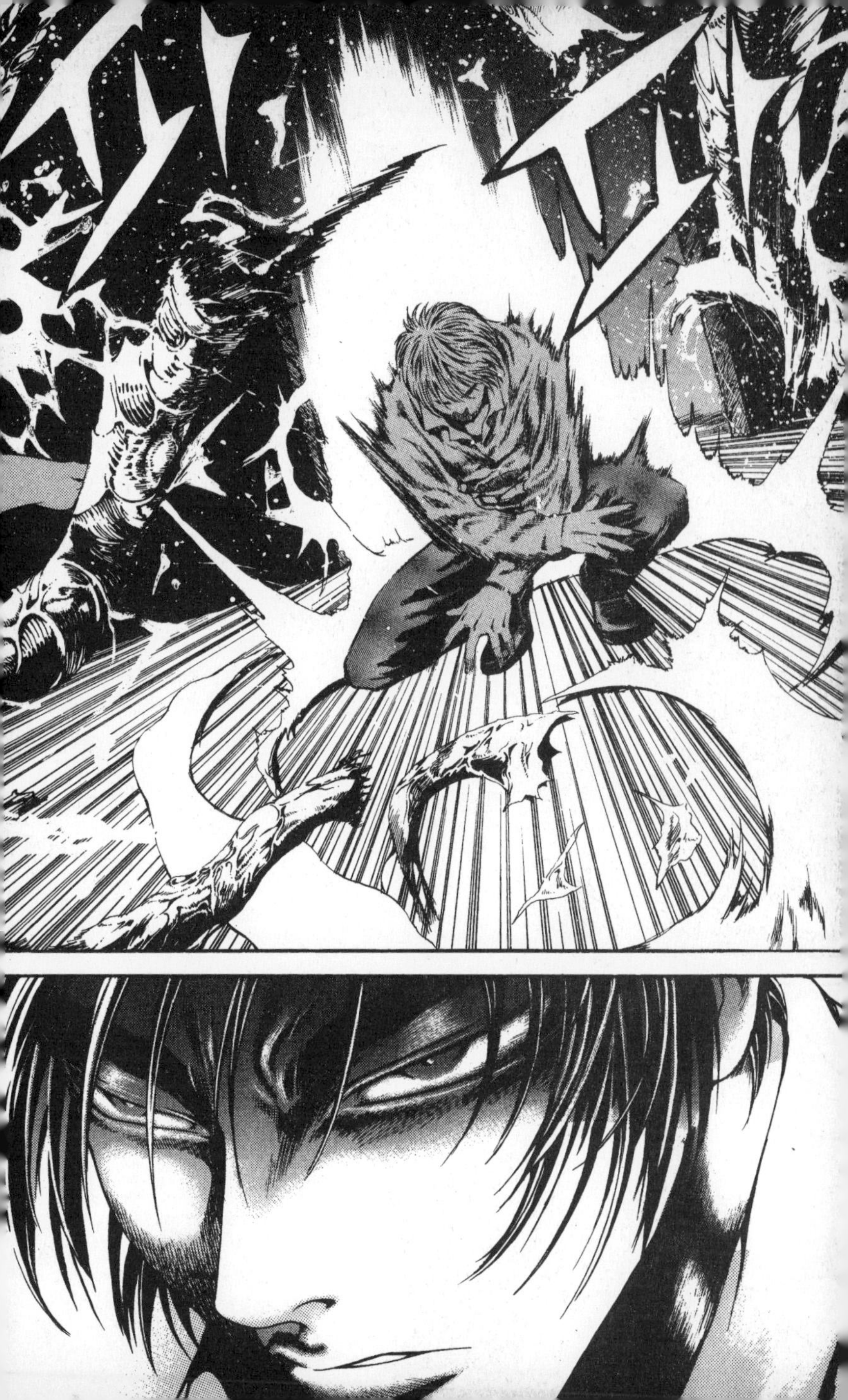

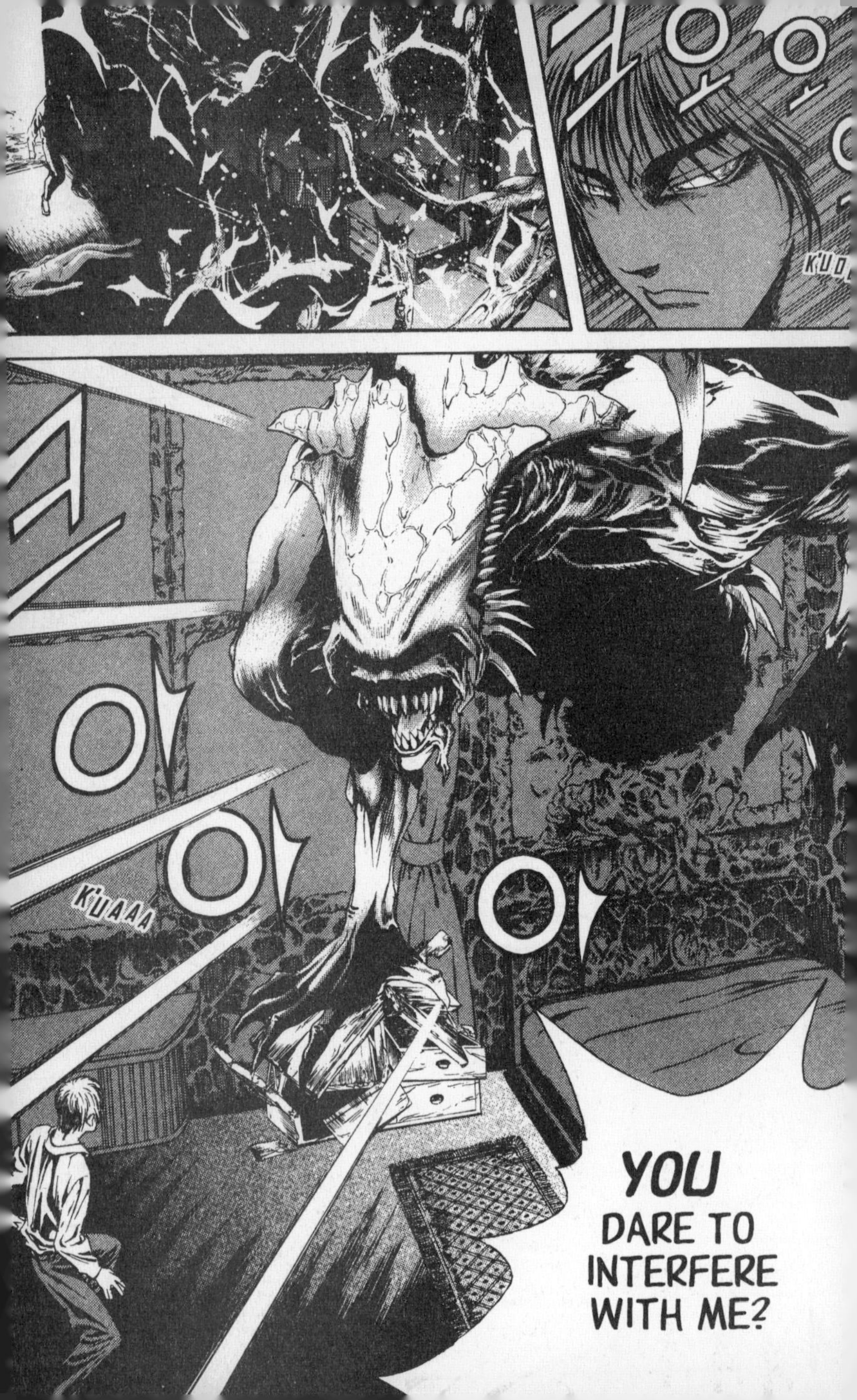
KUO
K'UAAA
YOU DARE TO INTERFERE WITH ME?

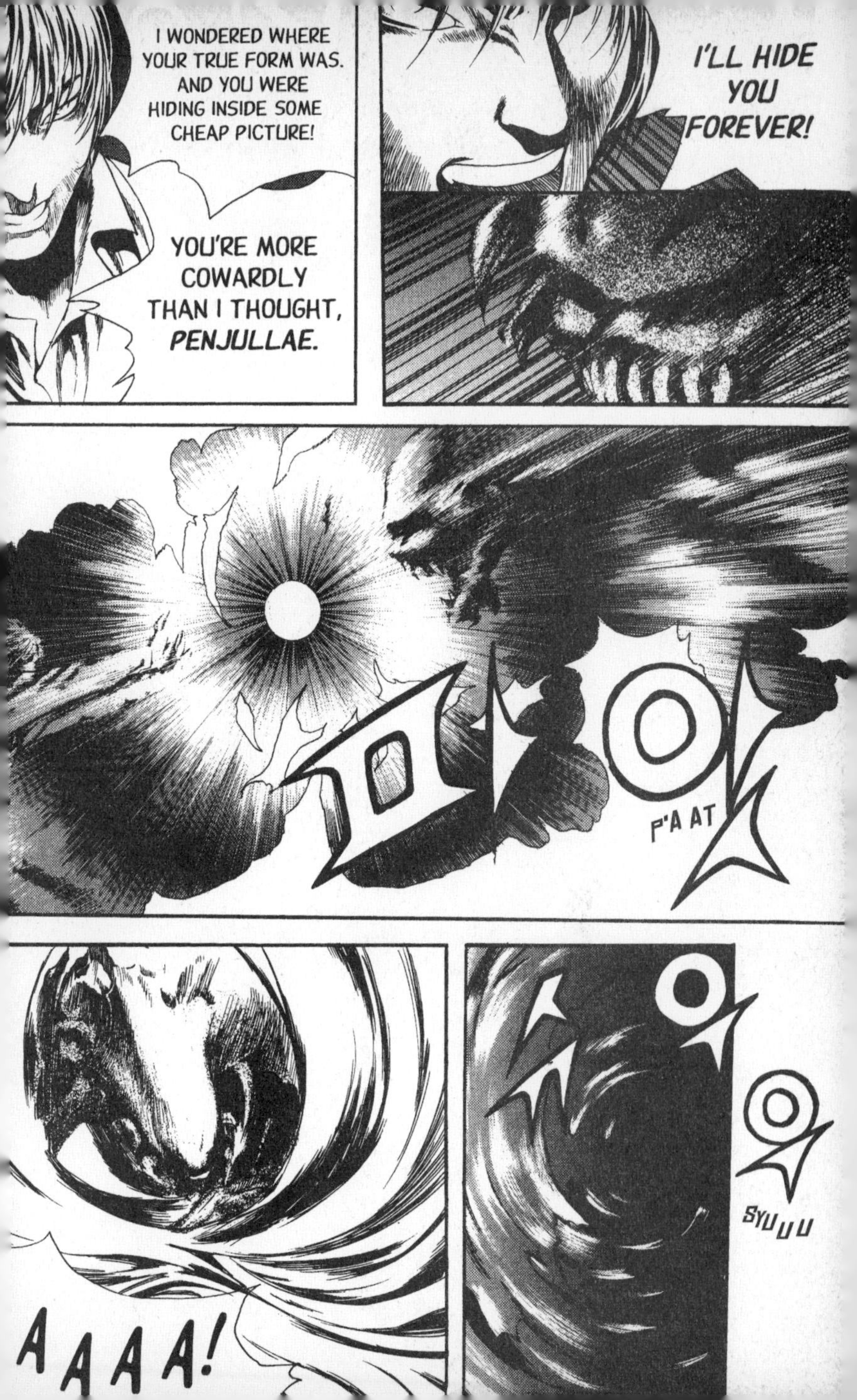
I WONDERED WHERE YOUR TRUE FORM WAS. AND YOU WERE HIDING INSIDE SOME CHEAP PICTURE!
YOU'RE MORE COWARDLY THAN I THOUGHT, *PENJULLAE.*
I'LL HIDE YOU FOREVER!
P'A AT
AAAA!
SYUUU

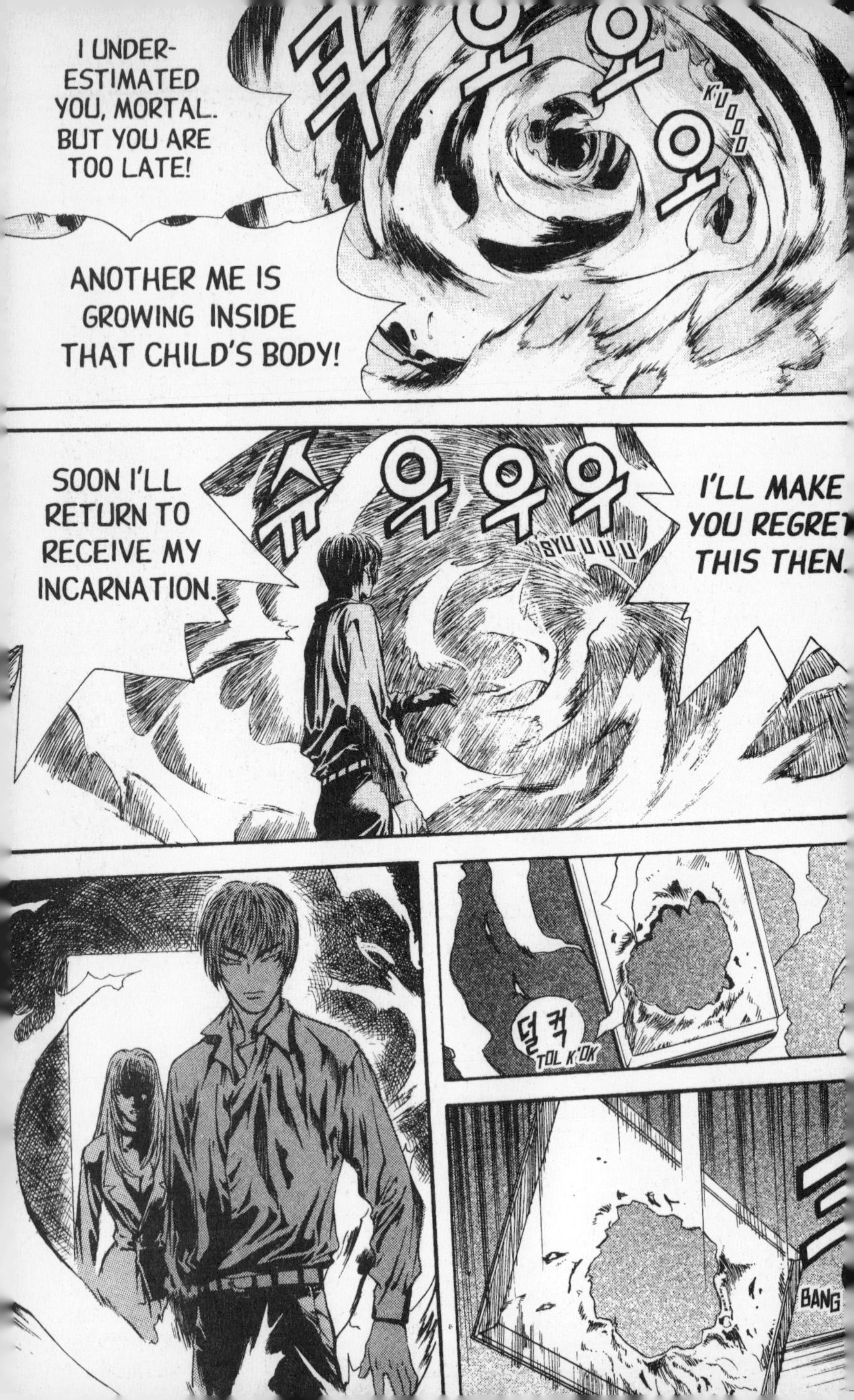
I UNDER-ESTIMATED YOU, MORTAL. BUT YOU ARE TOO LATE!
쿠우우우
K'UUUU
ANOTHER ME IS GROWING INSIDE THAT CHILD'S BODY!
SOON I'LL RETURN TO RECEIVE MY INCARNATION.
슈우우우
SYUUUU
I'LL MAKE YOU REGRET THIS THEN.
덜컥
TOL K'OK
BANG

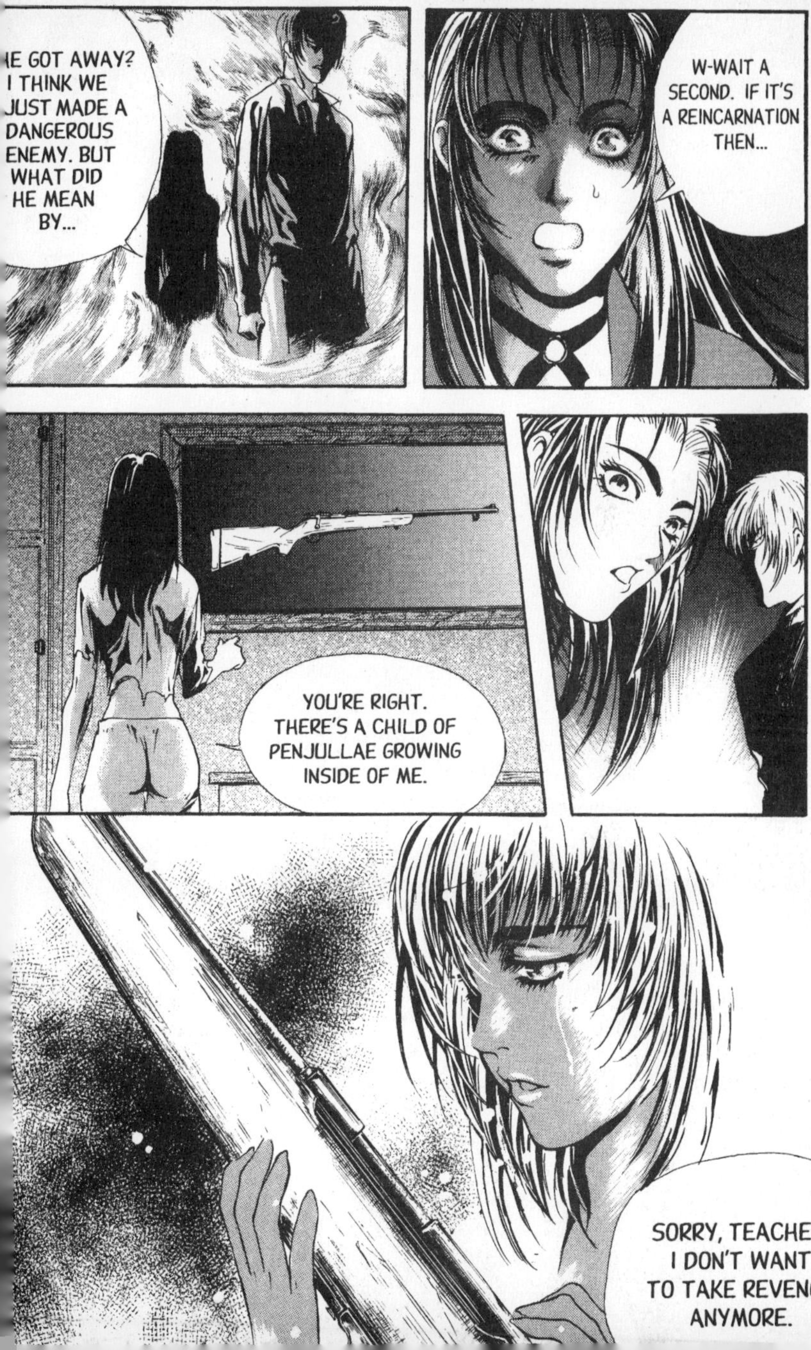
HE GOT AWAY? I THINK WE JUST MADE A DANGEROUS ENEMY. BUT WHAT DID HE MEAN BY...
W-WAIT A SECOND. IF IT'S A REINCARNATION THEN...
YOU'RE RIGHT. THERE'S A CHILD OF PENJULLAE GROWING INSIDE OF ME.
SORRY, TEACHER. I DON'T WANT TO TAKE REVENGE ANYMORE.

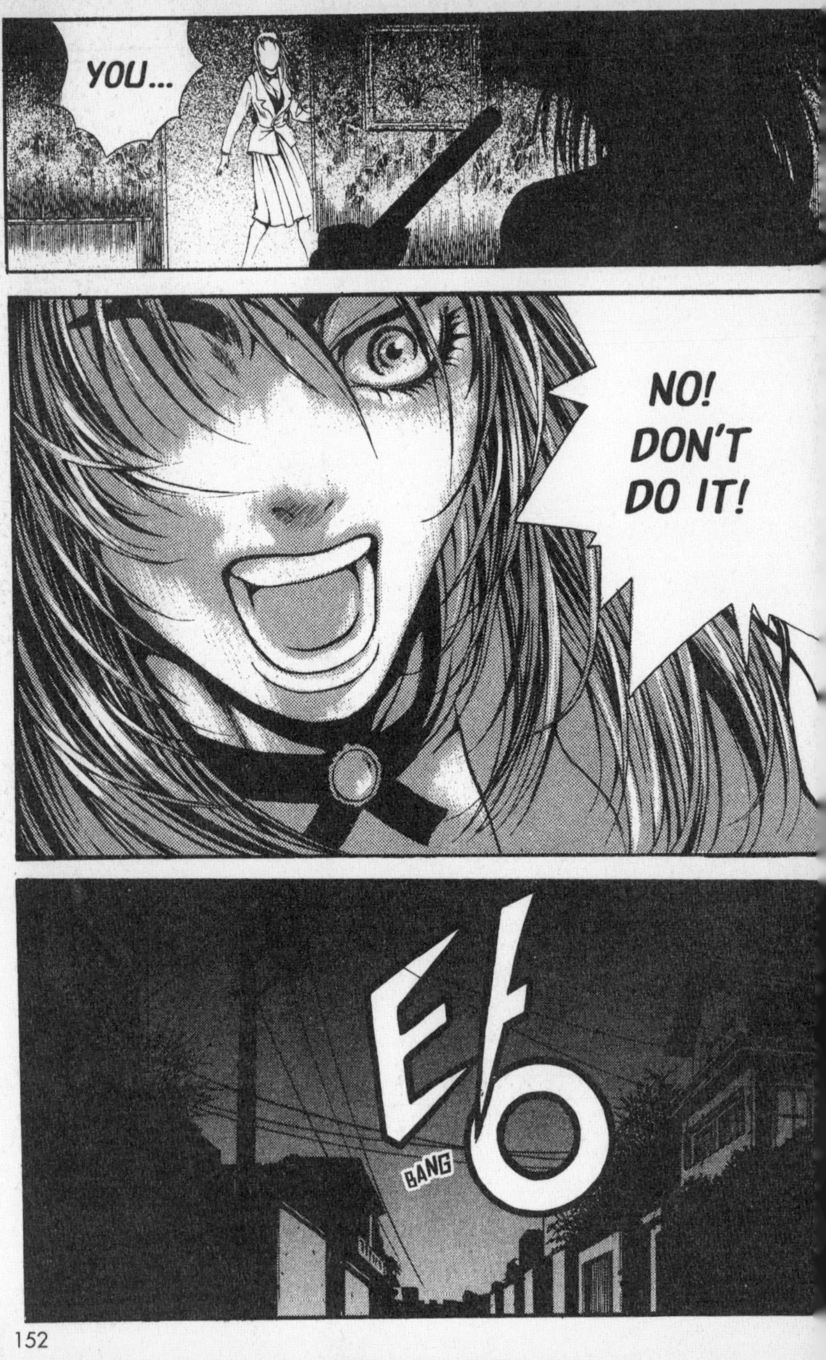
YOU...
NO! DON'T DO IT!
BANG

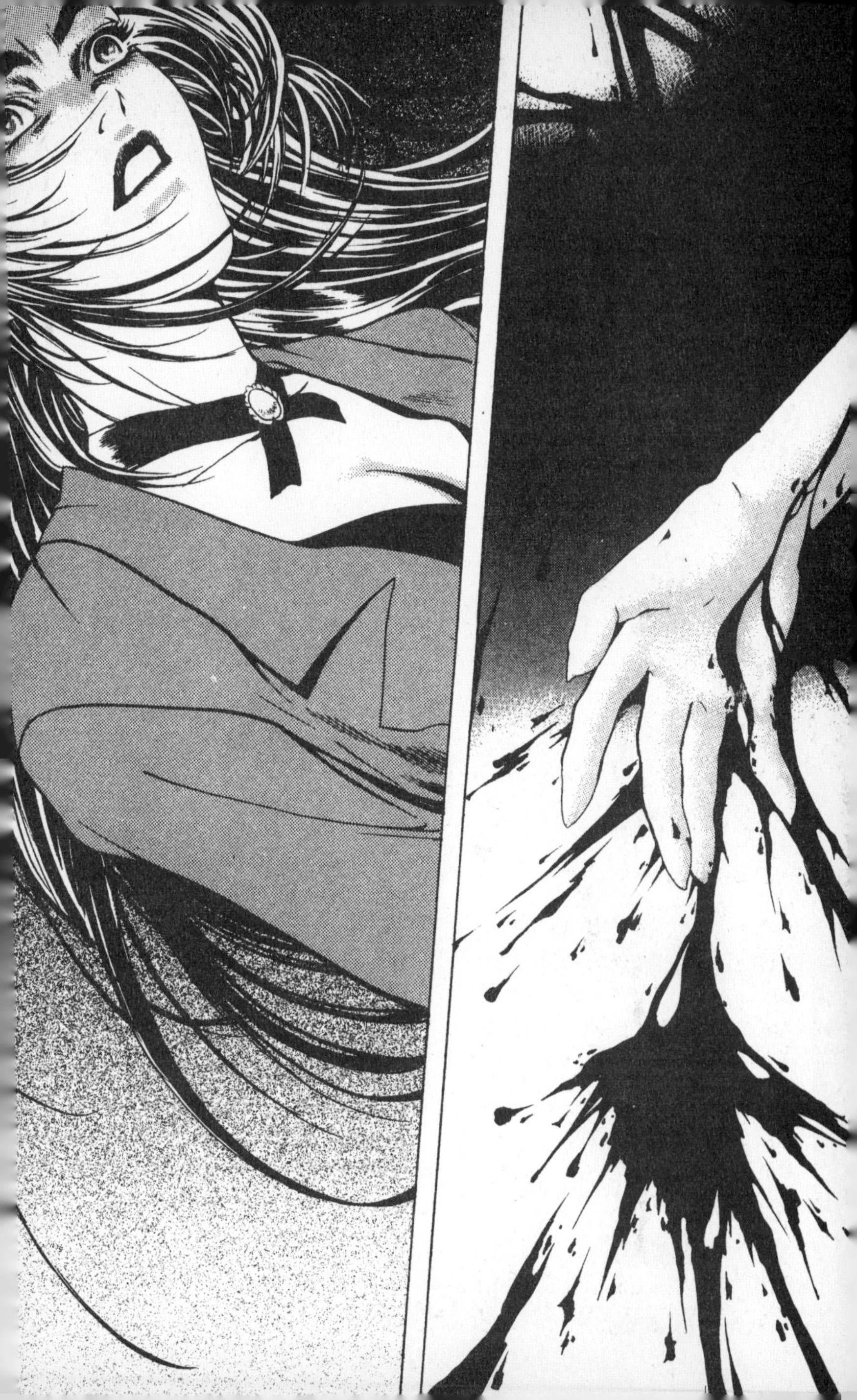

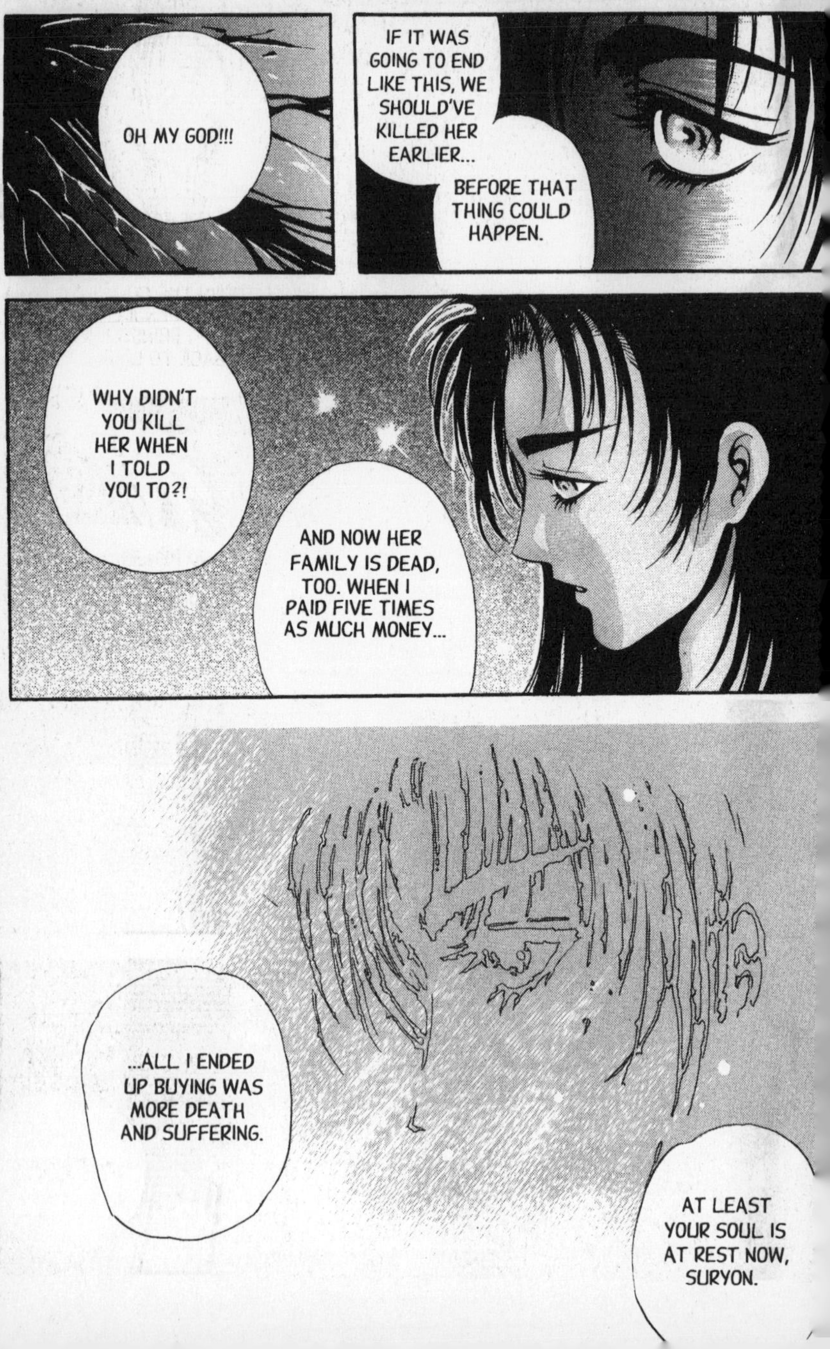
OH MY GOD!!!
IF IT WAS GOING TO END LIKE THIS, WE SHOULD'VE KILLED HER EARLIER...
BEFORE THAT THING COULD HAPPEN.
WHY DIDN'T YOU KILL HER WHEN I TOLD YOU TO?!
AND NOW HER FAMILY IS DEAD, TOO. WHEN I PAID FIVE TIMES AS MUCH MONEY...
...ALL I ENDED UP BUYING WAS MORE DEATH AND SUFFERING.
AT LEAST YOUR SOUL IS AT REST NOW, SURYON.

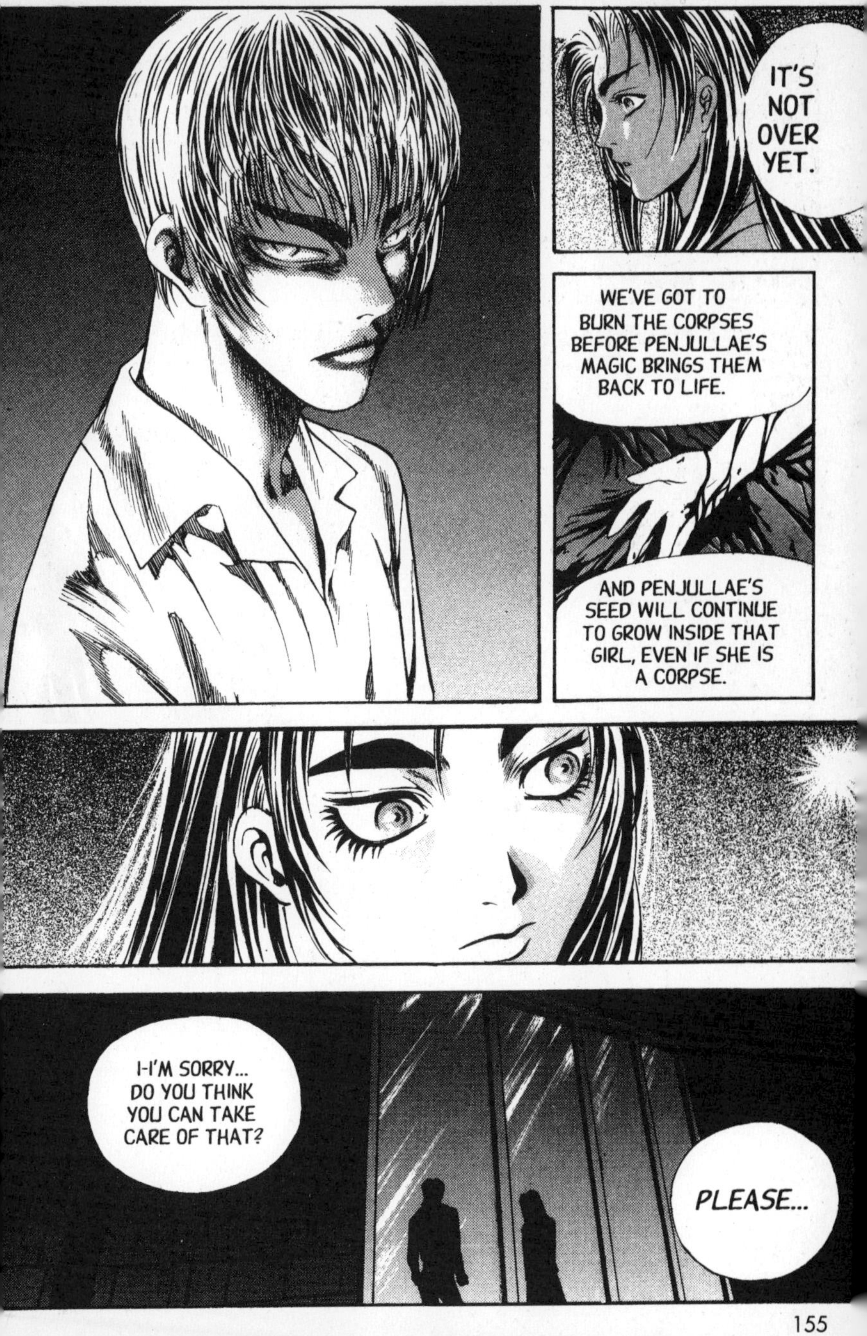
IT'S NOT OVER YET.
WE'VE GOT TO BURN THE CORPSES BEFORE PENJULLAE'S MAGIC BRINGS THEM BACK TO LIFE.
AND PENJULLAE'S SEED WILL CONTINUE TO GROW INSIDE THAT GIRL, EVEN IF SHE IS A CORPSE.
I-I'M SORRY... DO YOU THINK YOU CAN TAKE CARE OF THAT?
PLEASE...

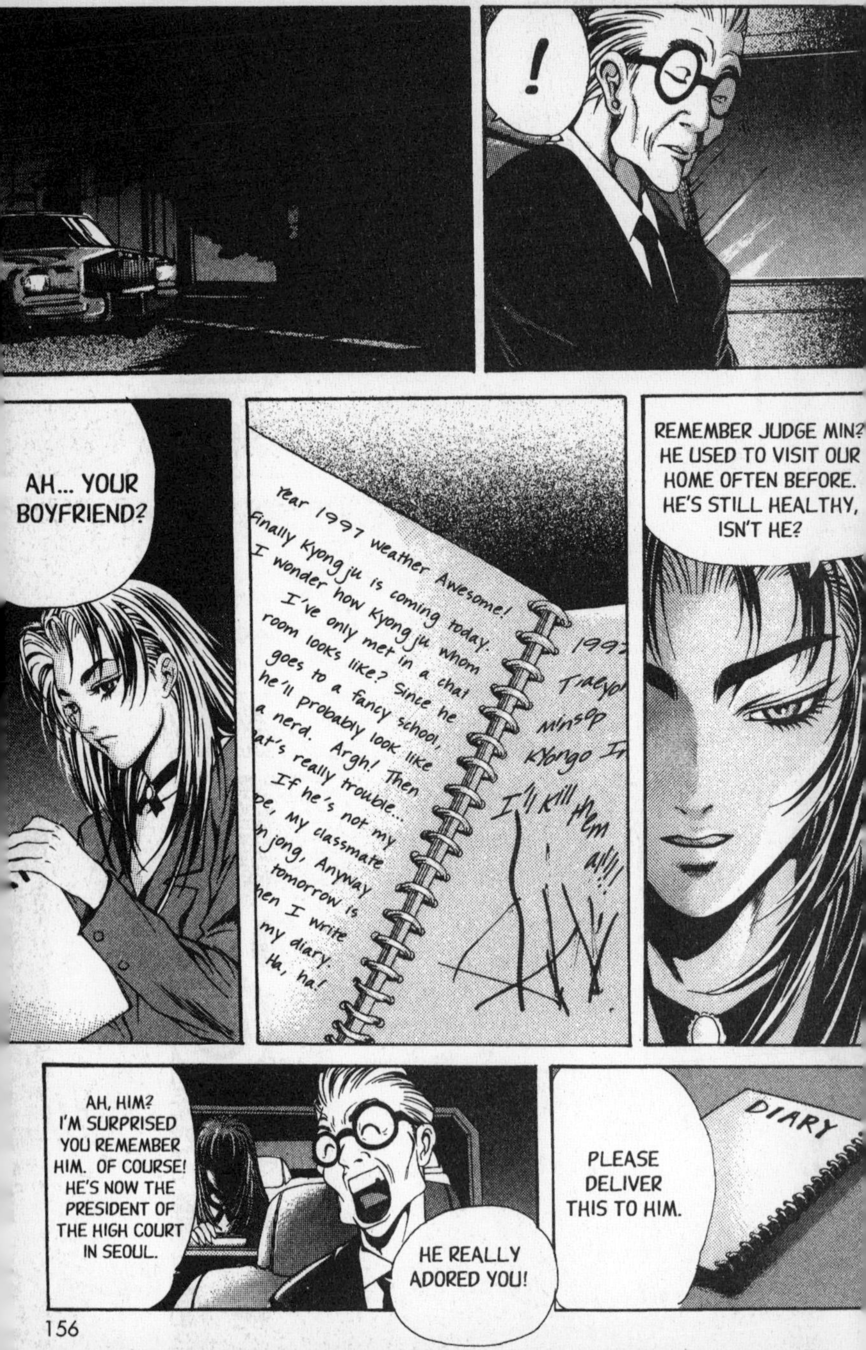
!
AH... YOUR BOYFRIEND?
Year 1997 weather Awesome!
Finally Kyong ju is coming today.
I wonder how Kyong ju whom
I've only met in a chat
room looks like? Since he
goes to a fancy school,
he'll probably look like
a nerd. Argh! Then
at's really trouble...
If he's not my
pe, my classmate
n jong, Anyway
tomorrow is
hen I write
my diary.
Ha, ha!
1997
Taeyo
Minsop
Kyongo In
I'll kill them all!!!
REMEMBER JUDGE MIN? HE USED TO VISIT OUR HOME OFTEN BEFORE. HE'S STILL HEALTHY, ISN'T HE?
AH, HIM? I'M SURPRISED YOU REMEMBER HIM. OF COURSE! HE'S NOW THE PRESIDENT OF THE HIGH COURT IN SEOUL.
HE REALLY ADORED YOU!
DIARY
PLEASE DELIVER THIS TO HIM.

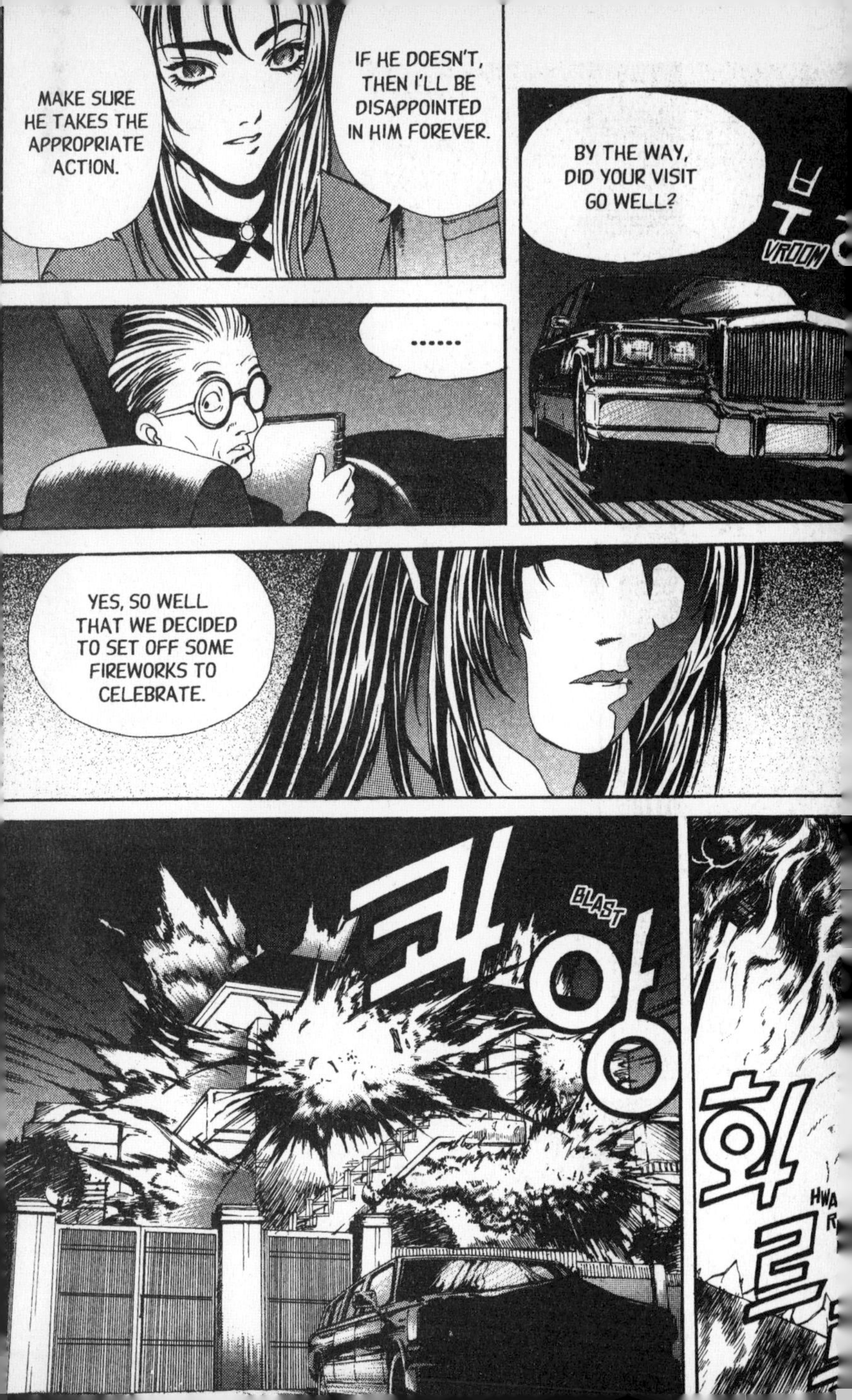

MAKE SURE HE TAKES THE APPROPRIATE ACTION.
IF HE DOESN'T, THEN I'LL BE DISAPPOINTED IN HIM FOREVER.
BY THE WAY, DID YOUR VISIT GO WELL?
부웅
VROOM
......
YES, SO WELL THAT WE DECIDED TO SET OFF SOME FIREWORKS TO CELEBRATE.
콰앙
BLAST
화르
HWAR

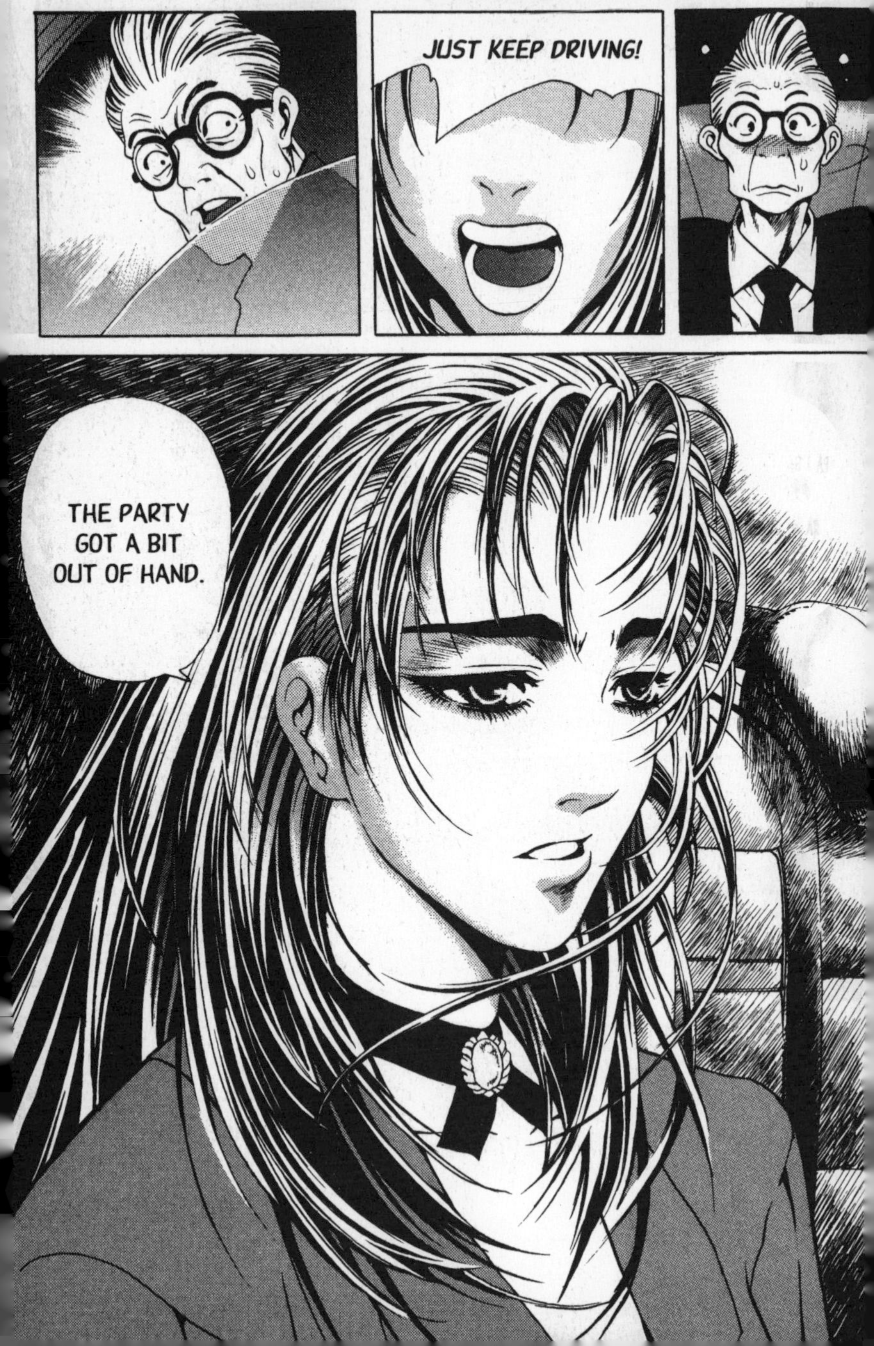
JUST KEEP DRIVING!
THE PARTY GOT A BIT OUT OF HAND.

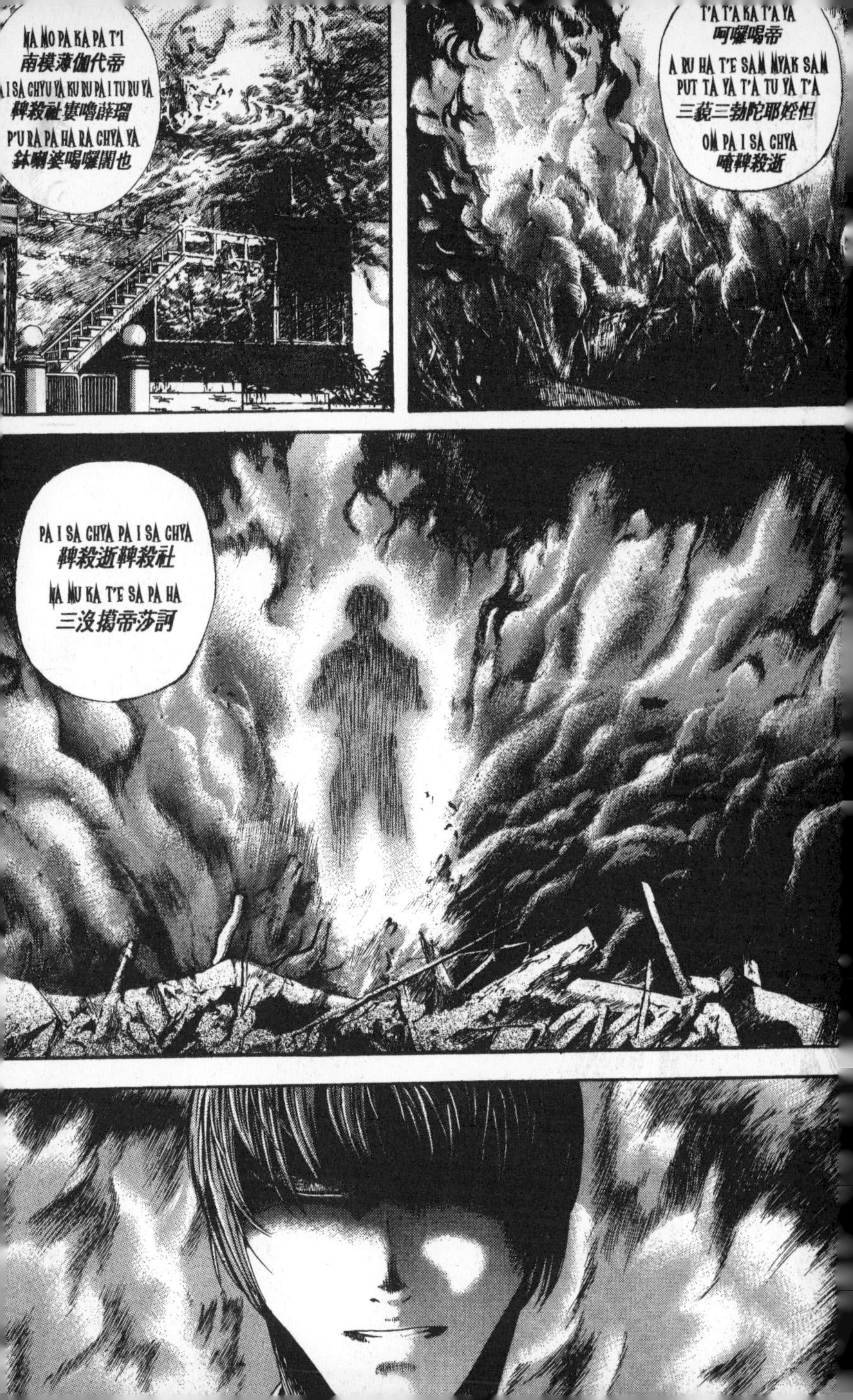
NA MO PA KA PA T'I 南模薄伽代帝 I SA CHYU YA KU RU PA I TU RU YA 鞞殺社窶嚕薜瑠 P'U RA PA HA RA CHYA YA 鉢喇婆喝囉闍也
T'A T'A KA T'A YA 呵囉喝帝 A RU HA T'E SAM MYAK SAM PUT TA YA T'A TU YA T'A 三藐三勃陀耶姪怛 OM PA I SA CHYA 唵鞞殺逝
PA I SA CHYA PA I SA CHYA 鞞殺逝鞞殺社 NA MU KA T'E SA PA HA 三沒揭帝莎訶

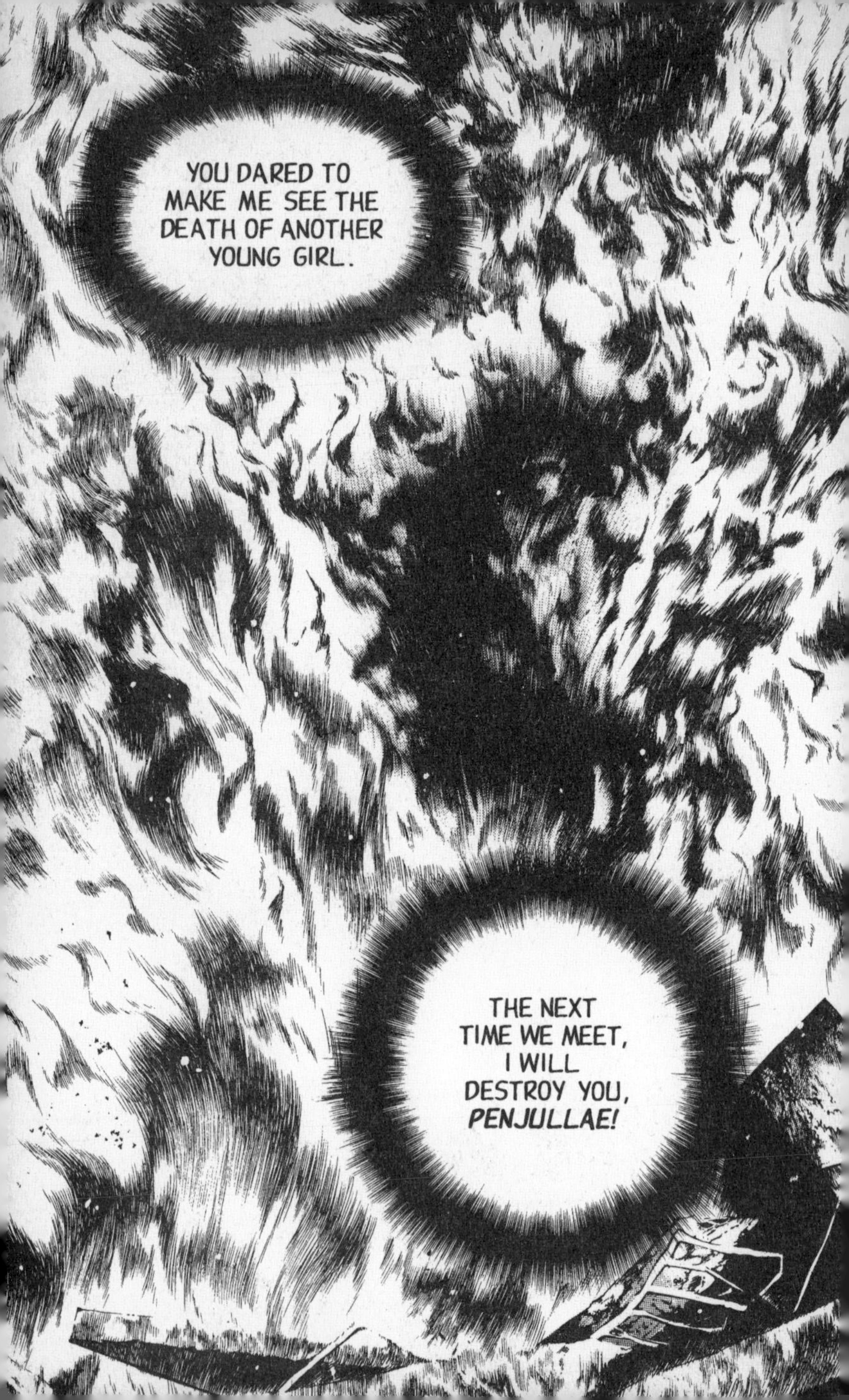
YOU DARED TO MAKE ME SEE THE DEATH OF ANOTHER YOUNG GIRL.
THE NEXT TIME WE MEET, I WILL DESTROY YOU, *PENJULLAE!*

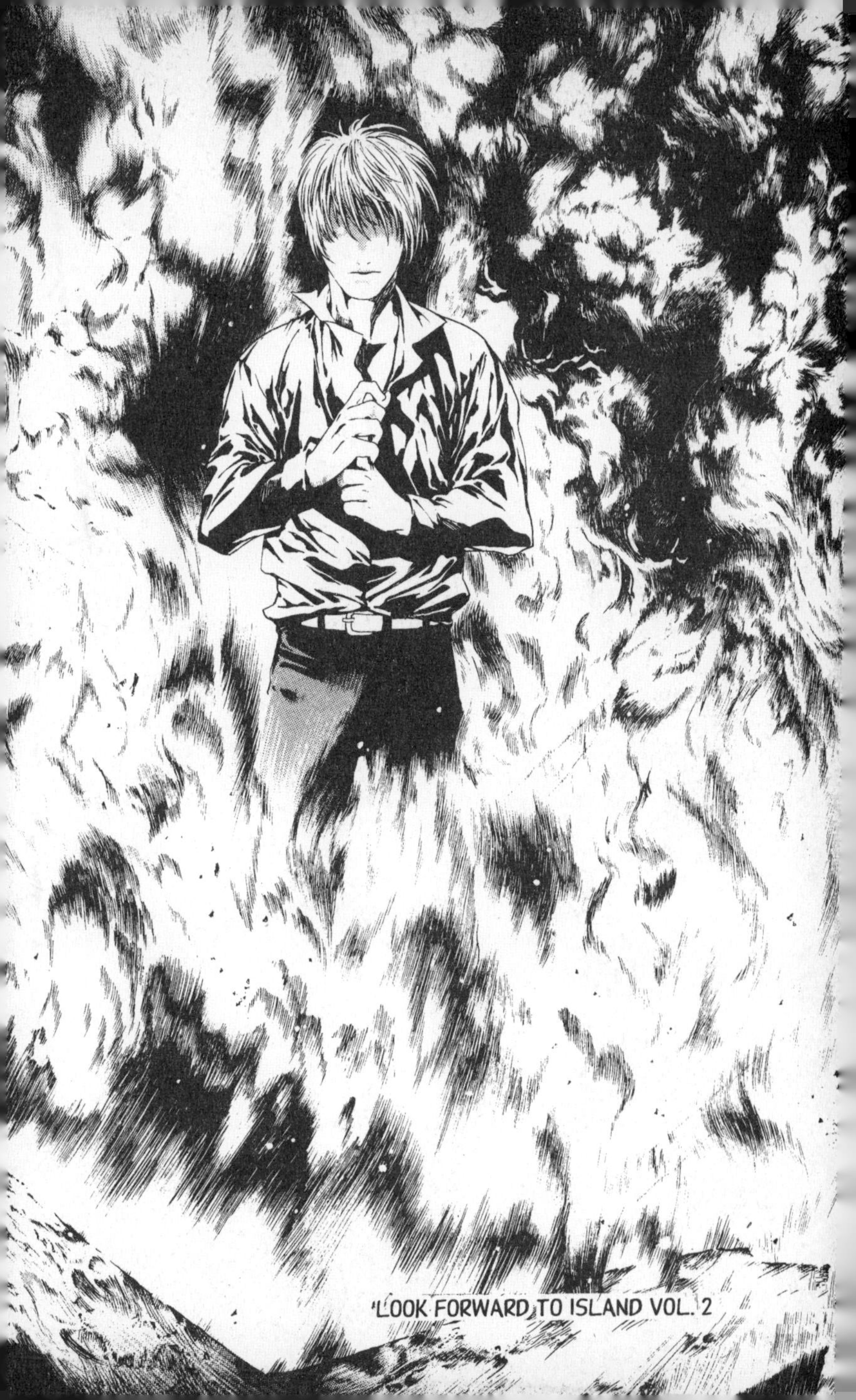
LOOK FORWARD TO ISLAND VOL. 2

The Explanation of Annotations

1) Chongyom （情炎鬼）: Gives humans sexual powers and it's widely classified as a demon. It often appears in representative oral literature such as *Miscellany of Songhyon* and *Historical Record of the Three Kingdoms.* It is the vicious demon that appears on the first wedding night to rape the new bride or impregnate a widow to banish her from her village. It may be added that Pak Yonggu, the author of *Bizarre Tales of Korea* (1996, Somunmungo), writes in the introduction "Chongyom's lust is hotter than the pillar of fire in hell and if there is a beautiful woman, he will follow her to the summit of Paektu Mountain to destroy her purity."

2) Penjullae: It means "Ttabi" (a farming tool that is a kind of sickle) in Cheju dialect. The legend of Penjullae, a contract god in the sketch "Purity of 18" was reconstructed to respect, as much as possible, the oral account of Chong Sunghyon (Cheju, Yongdamgu), who provided the material. But for the sake of the development of the story, its appearance and temperament was created as a kind of Burning Desire Demon.

3) Haute Couture: It means "high-class fashion" and in a wider sense, it also refers to a high-quality dress by a top designer. It is the height of French fashion in which it is distinguished from *pret-a-porter* that attaches greater importance on practicality and mass appeal; and it is a collection of artistic, aristocratic characteristics in which the designer's originality is highlighted as much as possible.

4) Causality （因果性）: The nature of cause and effect, the relationship in which evil is met with evil, and goodness is met with a good result. It also coincides with causality that says that what goes around, comes around.

5) Kwigangsul （鬼更術）: It is a secret magic trick in *Miscellany of O Sukkwon*, an oral tradition from Choson period. It says that if you write on the forehead of the dead person the logograph "kwi" (鬼) with the blood of his fourth finger, you can control the corpse. This method is used on the story of Suryon's parents (in "Purity of 18") but it was not given that much weight.

6) Mudra （手印）: This hand gesture incorporates magic. It is a method used by a specific religion that we cannot yet reveal due to the development of the story.

7) IM （臨）(to face ; front on), **PYONG**（兵）(soldier), **T'U** （鬪） (fight ; to fight), **CHA** （者）(person), **KYE**（皆）(all; whole), **CHIN**（陳）(formation; position), **YOL**（列）(column; row; line), **CHAE**（在）(existence; to exist), **CHON** （前）(front; in front of ; before)**:** This is called "Diamond World and Nine Assemblies Mandala." （金剛界九會曼荼羅）This is a religious art and in magic, it's called incantation of nine characters.（九字印）It is the foundation of all of the magic that the main character uses.

8) The incantation that the main character uses is widely called **mantra**, the language of the 3rd universe. They imply dozens of meanings and each syllable contains a spirit. All the incantations actually exist but we want to make clear that their effects are fictionally exaggerated.

Reference Literature of "Purity of 18"

Legend of Cheju Island, Hyon Yongjun, 1996 Somunmungo
Orthodoxy of Esoteric Buddhism, Chong T'aehyok, 1984, Kyongsowon
Fashion Show of Paris, Q Channel, 1996
Explanation to The Soul Guardians, Yi Uhyok, 1995, Tullyok
Bizarre Tales of Korea, Pak Yonggu, 1996 Somunmungo

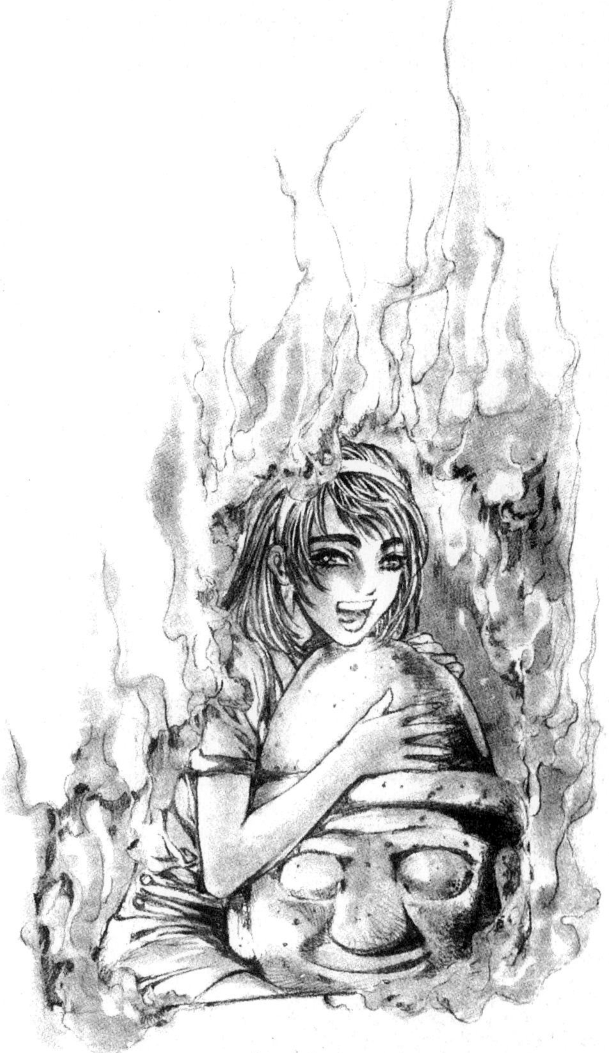

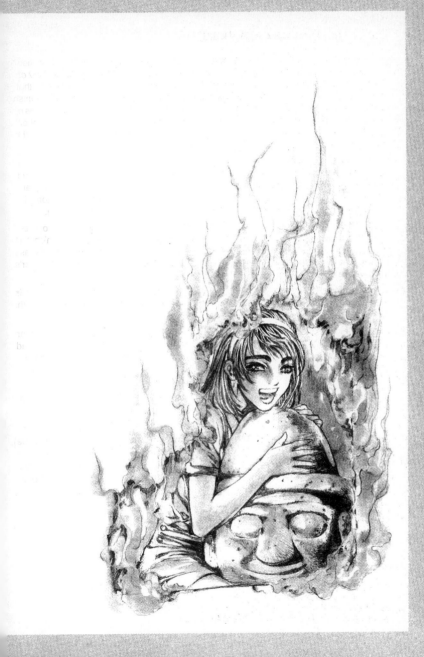

New Series Publication
Commemorative Flash Interview

10 Things we want to know about

What are your motivations for making Island?
IN-WAN YOUN: I have had a lot of interest in legends and old stories in which ghosts and demons come out. It's material that appears often in novels, dramas, and Japanese comics but it's a theme that is not dealt I word our comics. I thought that it would be fun to make a Korean demon story into a comic.

What kind of story is Island?
IN-WAN YOUN: There are many stories about ghosts and demons that are handed down on Cheju Island which is our country's greatest tourist attraction. It is a work that reconstructed them contemporarily. But if I tell you all the details beforehand, it won't be fun, so read the work and enjoy...

How long was the preparation?
KYUNG-IL YANG: We first started working on the story in the spring of 1996. When we polished the story and entered the work of establishing characters, it was early 1997. Before two months of serialization, we almost completed the portion for Vol.1 but we abandoned it because we didn't like it. The fundamental manuscript work started when the serialization of *Soma's Legendary Record* ended in June.

Have you been to Cheju Island which is the background of the work?
KYUNG-IL YANG: I was going to go there in late June, but a monsoon forced me to cancel. Then I immediately went into full-time pre-production on the series. For the time being, I'm using the photos and materials gathered here and there by fans who live in Cheju Island. I'm thinking about going to Cheju Island soon to collect more materials and get a sense of the physical space.

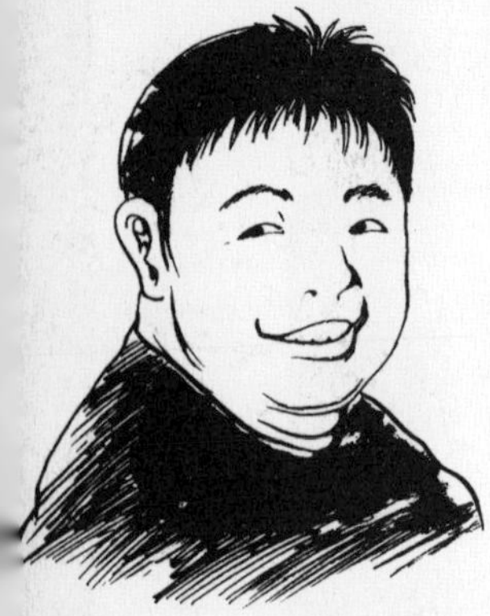

Introduce the main characters.
KYUNG-IL YANG: The mystery fellow named Pan and the woman named Won Miho are the main characters. The relationship of the two is like water and oil, and they don't have much in common but they become a team. Unlike conventional characters you have seen, I'm going to make them into characters who will continue to surprise you. Anticipate!

ISLAND

With
KYUNG-IL YANG
and IN-WAN YOUN

There are a lot of people who are curious about the story writer.
IN-WAN YOUN: My third year in high school, I began as a student at Yi T'ahaeng and Yang Kyongi Studios. Actually, my dream is to be a comic artist. Now, I concentrate on writing *Island*, but if there's an opportunity, I'll become a comic artist.

This is much different from your previous work, "Soma's Legendary Record."
KYUNG-IL YANG: *Soma* was a fantasy comic so the events continue in a freely created space, but *Island* is set in the real world. I'm very mindful of the contemporary setting, so I made every effort to see that the world of Cheju Island was depicted accurately.

What's the reason for not making your face public?
KYUNG-IL YANG: There's no particular reason. It's from the thought that a comic artist should meet his readers through his work. I have not once made a photo for this interview. (The members of the studio hinted that it is because he does not want to reveal to the public how fat he is, but KYUNG-IL YANG vehemently denied this).

What will happen with "Soma's Legendary Record"?
KYUNG-IL YANG: Soma is finished in three parts for now. It was scheduled to go on to part four but it didn't. In the future, with story writer Hwang Yongsu, I plan to start work again on part four. This is the concluding volume. But when that will be hasn't been decided yet.

What is the future of Island?
IN-WAN YOUN & KYUNG-IL YANG: We are hoping to make a new work that has never been seen before. With each volume, we will do our best to make a work that will satisfy the readers.

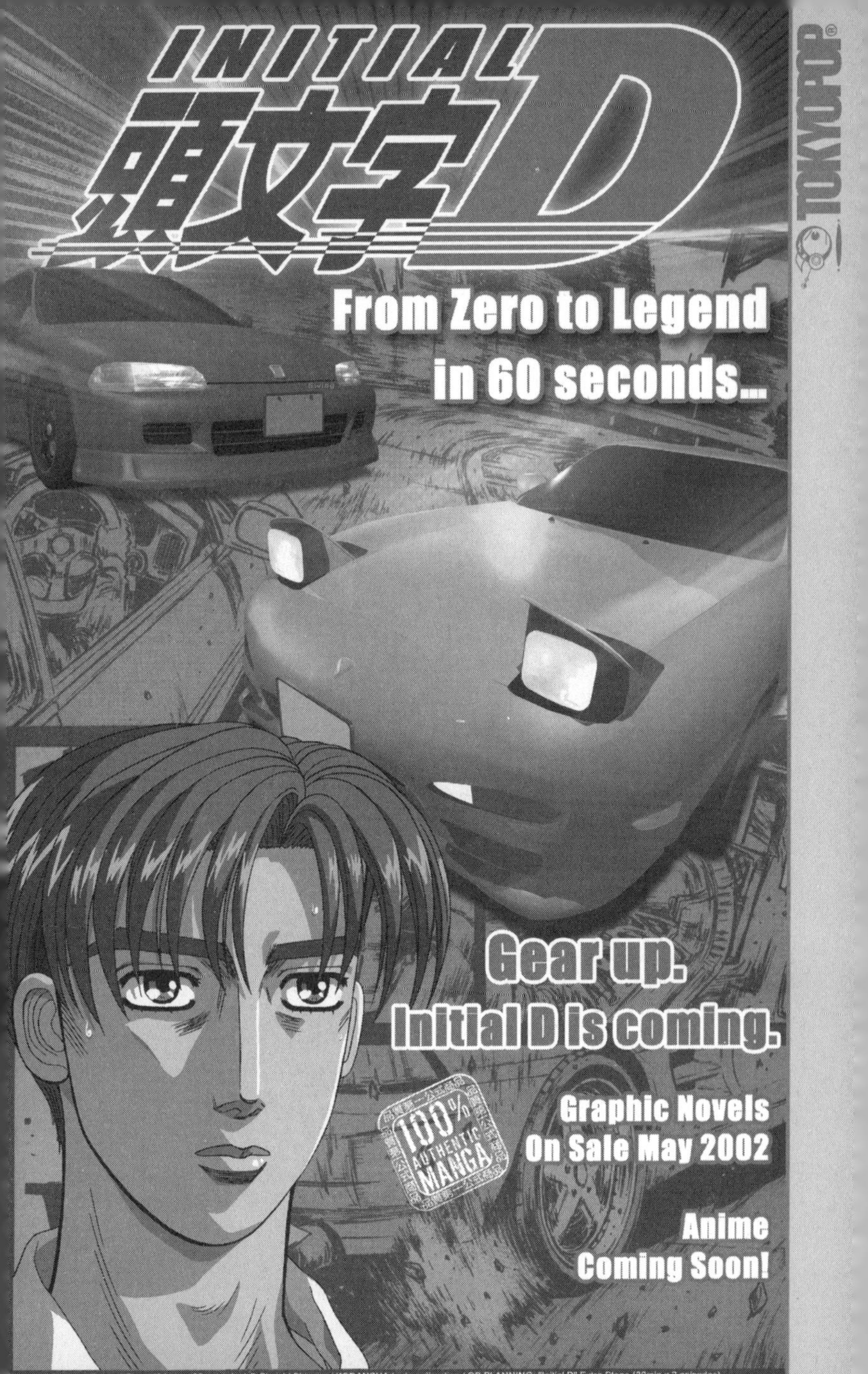
INITIAL
頭文字D
From Zero to Legend
in 60 seconds...
Gear up.
Initial D is coming.
100% AUTHENTIC MANGA
Graphic Novels
On Sale May 2002
Anime
Coming Soon!
TOKYOPOP®